Mastering React Native

Mastering React Native helps the reader master the React Native framework for faster and more robust mobile app development.

React Native is an open-source JavaScript framework that allows you to create applications for many platforms, including iOS, Android, and the web, all with the same code base. It is built on the React framework, and it provides all of React's power to mobile app development.

React Native was a natural continuation of React. It is a mobile framework that includes JavaScript to create near-native apps. JSX, a hybrid of JavaScript and XML-like markup, is used to make React Native applications. The React Native "bridge" then calls the native rendering APIs in Objective-C (for iOS) or Java (for Android) behind the scenes (for Android). As a result, your app will appear and feel like any other mobile app, as it will be rendered using genuine mobile UI components instead of web views. React Native also offers JavaScript interfaces for platform APIs, allowing your React Native apps to use features such as user location and the phone camera.

If your app is UI focused, React Native is an excellent choice because it comes with an extensive UI library. Becoming a React Native developer gives you access to exciting, cutting-edge projects which frequently incorporate innovative technology like Augmented Reality. Job opportunities for React Native devs are aplenty, and it is undoubtedly a skill worthy of consideration owing to its popularity with startups and corporates alike.

With *Mastering React Native*, learning React Native becomes easy and will help readers undoubtedly advance their careers.

The *Mastering Computer Science* series is edited by Sufyan bin Uzayr, a writer and educator with more than a decade of experience in the computing field.

Mastering Computer Science
Series Editor: Sufyan bin Uzayr

Mastering React Native: A Beginner's Guide
Lokesh Pancha, Jaskiran Kaur, and Divya Sachdeva

Mastering Visual Studio Code: A Beginner's Guide
Jaskiran Kaur, D Nikitenko, and Mathew Rooney

Mastering Rust: A Beginner's Guide
Divya Sachdeva, Faruq KC, and Aruqqa Khateib

Mastering Bootstrap: A Beginner's Guide
Lokesh Pancha, Divya Sachdeva, and Rubina Salafey

Mastering Django: A Beginner's Guide
Jaskiran Kaur, NT Ozman, and Reza Nafim

Mastering React: A Beginner's Guide
Mohammad Ammar, Divya Sachdeva, and Rubina Salafey

For more information about this series, please visit: https://www.routledge.com/Mastering-Computer-Science/book-series/MCS

The "Mastering Computer Science" series of books are authored by the Zeba Academy team members, led by Sufyan bin Uzayr.

Zeba Academy is an EdTech venture that develops courses and content for learners primarily in STEM fields, and offers education consulting to Universities and Institutions worldwide. For more info, please visit https://zeba.academy

Mastering React Native

A Beginner's Guide

Edited by Sufyan bin Uzayr

CRC Press
Taylor & Francis Group
Boca Raton London New York

CRC Press is an imprint of the
Taylor & Francis Group, an **informa** business

First Edition published 2023
by CRC Press
6000 Broken Sound Parkway NW, Suite 300, Boca Raton, FL 33487-2742

and by CRC Press
2 Park Square, Milton Park, Abingdon, Oxon, OX14 4RN

CRC Press is an imprint of Taylor & Francis Group, LLC

© 2023 Sufyan bin Uzayr

Library of Congress Cataloging-in-Publication Data

Names: Bin Uzayr, Sufyan, editor.
Title: Mastering React Native : a beginner's guide / edited by Sufyan bin Uzayr.
Description: First edition. | Boca Raton : CRC Press, 2022. | Includes bibliographical references and index.
Identifiers: LCCN 2022021427 (print) | LCCN 2022021428 (ebook) | ISBN 9781032315898 (hbk) | ISBN 9781032314723 (pbk) | ISBN 9781003310440 (ebk)
Subjects: LCSH: JavaScript (Computer program language) | React Native. | Application software--Development. | Mobile apps--Development. | Cross-platform software development. | Cellphones--Programming.
Classification: LCC QA76.73.J39 M38 2022 (print) | LCC QA76.73.J39 (ebook) | DDC 005.2/762--dc23/eng/20220729
LC record available at https://lccn.loc.gov/2022021427
LC ebook record available at https://lccn.loc.gov/2022021428

ISBN: 9781032315898 (hbk)
ISBN: 9781032314723 (pbk)
ISBN: 9781003310440 (ebk)

DOI: 10.1201/ 9781003310440

Typeset in Minion
by Deanta Global Publishing Services, Chennai, India

Contents

Mastering Computer Science Series Preface

THE *MASTERING COMPUTER SCIENCE* covers a wide range of topics, spanning programming languages as well as modern-day technologies and frameworks. The series has a special focus on beginner-level content, and is presented in an easy to understand manner, comprising:

- Crystal-clear text spanning various topics sorted by relevance

- Special focus on practical exercises, with numerous code samples and programs

- A guided approach to programming, with step-by-step tutorials for absolute beginners

- Keen emphasis on the real-world utility of skills, thereby cutting the redundant and seldom-used concepts and focusing instead on industry-prevalent coding paradigm

- A wide range of references and resources to help both beginner and intermediate-level developers gain the most out of the books

The *Mastering Computer Science* series of books start from the core concepts and then quickly moves on to industry-standard coding practices to help learners gain efficient and crucial skills in as little time as possible. The books assume no prior knowledge of coding, so even the absolute newbie coders can benefit from this series.

The *Mastering Computer Science* series is edited by Sufyan bin Uzayr, a writer and educator with more than a decade of experience in the computing field.

About the Editor

Sufyan bin Uzayr is a writer, coder, and entrepreneur with more than a decade of experience in the industry. He has authored several books in the past, pertaining to a diverse range of topics, ranging from History to Computers/IT.

Sufyan is the Director of Parakozm, a multinational IT company specializing in EdTech solutions. He also runs Zeba Academy, an online learning and teaching vertical with a focus on STEM fields.

Sufyan specializes in a wide variety of technologies, such as JavaScript, Dart, WordPress, Drupal, Linux, and Python. He holds multiple degrees, including ones in Management, IT, Literature, and Political Science.

Sufyan is a digital nomad, dividing his time between four countries. He has lived and taught in universities and educational institutions around the globe. Sufyan takes a keen interest in technology, politics, literature, history, and sports, and in his spare time, he enjoys teaching coding and English to young students.

Learn more at sufyanism.com.

## CHAPTER 1

Getting Started with React Native

IN THIS CHAPTER

➤ What is React Native

➤ Advantages and disadvantages

➤ Risks and drawbacks

In this chapter, you will learn about React Native, what it is and how it can be used, and advantages and disadvantages of React Native, and risks and drawbacks of it. Now let's jump toward the first section of our chapter and learn what React Native is.

WHAT IS REACT NATIVE

React Native is an open-source framework for JavaScript Mobile from Facebook that is specifically designed to build iOS and Android mobile apps. React Native is based on the ReactJS JavaScript library, which helps build user interaction for mobile platforms.

React Native can be used directly within the existing IOS or Android app or you can create a traditional app from scratch. Currently, React Native is used in other popular apps like Facebook mobile app, Instagram, Pinterest, Skype, etc.

DOI: 10.1201/9781003310440-1

Some of the key features of React Native that make mobile development so popular today are:

- **Cross-Platform Support**: To improve mobile applications, you do not need a team specialist in iOS and Android applications, JavaScript engineers who are passionate about building applications can use React Native to build native applications without learning Kotlin or Java for Android and Swift or Objective-C for IOS apps. You can also write one common code and React Native will take care to display it on iOS and Android.

- **React Native Components**: React Native provides native components such as View, Text, and Image that can be converted to native iOS or Android UI.

Here is a simple example of using a native native that displays the text Hello World:

Example:

```
import React from 'react';
import { Text, View} from 'react-native';
const App = () => {
  return (
  <View style={{flex :1, justifyContent: 'center',
  margin: 15}}>
  <Text style={{color:'red', fontSize:30}}>Hello
  World</Text>
  </View>
  );
}
export default App;
```

JSX

Since React JS belongs to the web world, React Native is designed for the world of mobile applications. React Native uses JSX i.e., XML coding replacement for HTML and CSS. The benefits of JSX are as follows:

- It is faster because it makes improvements while compiling code in JavaScript.

- It is also safe and most errors can be caught during integration.

- It makes it easier to write templates if you are good with HTML.

Building and Testing the React Native App

It is extremely easy to build your app in a responsive traditional way and test the changes without covering the head. Changes are available and quickly displayed when you save your code.

About React Native Release

The first version of React Native was released by Facebook in 2015 and from then on, they have been reviewing and making upgrades to it. It became very popular after its release as it is one of the leading frameworks for mobile app development. As per the official React Native website, in 2018, React Native had the second-highest number of contributors as compared to other repositories on GitHub. Today, React Native is supported by donations from individuals and companies around the globe, including Callstack, Microsoft, Expo, Infinite Red, and Software Mansion. The Facebook community has been extremely active and updates projects regularly with new updates across all platforms.

If you would like to build mobile apps for Android and iOS, what should you learn? Each of the native languages of each application, namely Java for Android and Swift/Objective-C for iOS? Actually NO. The traditional upgrades for Android and iOS are quite different and expensive – firstly, the language itself is quite different, and secondly, all the basic APIs are different – how to use GPS is different, how to make photos is different, how you make network calls is different.

We are always looking for shorter upgrade cycles, faster feed time, and better app performance. And there are many interactive mobile frameworks such as NativeScript, React Native, Ionic, Xamarin, PhoneGap, etc.

React Native is a framework developed by Facebook to create traditional-style apps for iOS and Android under one common language, JavaScript. Initially, Facebook developed the React Native only to support iOS. However, with its latest support for the Android operating system, the library is now able to offer mobile UI for both platforms.

Prerequisite

- Basic knowledge of *HTML, CSS,* and *JS.*
- Basic knowledge of *ReactJS.*
- NodeJs should be installed in your system.

Building with React Native works extremely well and is very addictive but getting started can be tricky. React Native uses Node.js, a JavaScript term, to generate your JavaScript code. If you don't have Node.js installed, it is time to get it!

Installation

Here we use the Expo CLI version that will be much easier to use in your React Native applications. You should follow the steps below one by one to set up your native React location.

Step 1: Open your terminal and use the command below.

npm install -g expo-cli

Step 2: Now the Expo CLI is installed worldwide, so you can create a project folder using the command below.

expo init "projectName"

Step 3: Now create one folder and start the server by using the following command given below:

cd "projectFolder"

npm start application_name

Project structure.

HISTORY OF REACT NATIVE

Facebook developed React Native in 2013 through their in-house hackathon project. Later, it was released publicly in January 2015 as React.js, and in March 2015, Facebook announced that React Native was open and available on GitHub. React Native was originally designed for the iOS app. However, recently it also supports the Android operating system.

In 2012 Mark Zuckerberg commented that "the biggest mistake we have made as a company is to bet more on HTML than on the native." Using HTML5 in the mobile version of Facebook has resulted in an unstable application that has slowed data recovery. He promised that Facebook would soon bring better mobile information.

Inside Facebook, Walke found a way to create iOS UI elements from the JavaScript thread domain, which was to become the basis for the React web framework. They decided to set up an internal hackathon to complete this prototype so they could make constructive applications with this technology.

In 2015, after several months of development, Facebook released the first version of the React JavaScript Configuration. During a technical talk, Christopher Chedeau explained that Facebook was already using React Native in the production of their Group Program and their Ad Manager program.

VARIOUS STEPS TO OPTIMIZING THE PERFORMANCE OF THE REACT NATIVE APPLICATIONS

Facebook's React Native has become one of the most popular JavaScript library code frameworks for creating cross-platform applications. Although the first launch was five years ago, in 2013 on GitHub, it has created a lot of noise compared to Xamarin and Ionic. One feature that supports React Native is that it allows developers to improve mobile and web applications at faster speeds. Additionally, you can build both Android and iOS apps by sharing and reusing codes easily.

Another advantage offered by React Native is that there is not much difference between completed applications created using Objective-C or Java and React Native. React Native enjoys the support of a large network of experienced developers.

However, it also has some drawbacks. One of the great pitfalls of React Native is that it has its limitations and is therefore on the road to development. You will not find any other custom modules, which means you must invest extra time to create your own module. Therefore, we will easily discuss some of the most important ways you can improve the performance of your React Native applications.

Before we give you a glimpse of how you can fix problems based on React Native-related functionality, you need to fully understand that the functionality of this JavaScript library depends on a highly rated structure.

An increase in the number of navigation controls, animations, and tabs reduces the use of speed seen in the application. In addition, during the development of the app, the version is often modified and can be a key bottleneck in the performance of the app.

React Native connects to the native cable with the help of a bridge. And the architecture of React Native can be divided into two categories, namely, React Native is developed in Java, Swift, or Objective-C, and natively created in JavaScript. Therefore, we can focus on these important parameters to improve performance.

Reduce System Size

JavaScript framework applications rely heavily on native components and third-party libraries. Additional use of components improves application size.

- So, if you must reduce the app size, you should use ProGuard and upgrade apps of varied sizes with a list of device properties.

- In addition, please focus on photo features and images.

- You can also take another step to reduce the size, such as changing parts from native to traditional, reducing the size of the bridge used by JavaScript to integrate with traditional.

- You can also go through open-source libraries to check their stability before using them.

- Do not use the main thread to transfer parts that rely on heavy message lines.

Reduce Image Size

If you want to improve the performance of your React Native apps, you also need to reduce the image size without reducing the app size.

You should be aware that images often consume a substantial portion of memory. There are other various ways to achieve your goals.

- The first one uses images that are smaller in size.

- Second, you must select a PNG file format to upload an image compared to the most widely used JPG or JPEG format.

- However, it may be best to convert your image version to a WebP format.

- This is because the Web offers several benefits, such as increasing download speeds up to 28% and reducing iOS and Android binary sizes by 25%. Apart from that, it also reduced Code Push by 66% and made the sailor's transition smoother.

Photo Caching

Image cache is considered a crucial step if you plan to improve the performance of React Native applications. Helps to load photos faster. However, React Native only supports image storage in the iOS repository. For Android OS, you get the help of npm image storage libraries, but it does not offer the best performance.

Otherwise, you may face a few other problems, such as library failure by not being able to import previously uploaded images when the app page is updated. This is known as cache miss. Another problem that may support operational efficiency is when cache logic is running on the JS side of the application.

Improving Application Release Time

Improving the release time of your React Native app should also be a major goal for developers. However, it can be any task as you need to evaluate each component to improve the performance of the libraries. Therefore, if you are looking for the desired result here you should focus on Object.Finalize element, which is considered the main obstacle in reducing the performance of the application. Therefore, even if you use subtle conclusions, you will still have to deal with memory-related problems or errors, even after having enough memory space. The main reason graduates are obstacles is that they work in a single series. So, if there are a few graduates who need to be run, you can only imagine how much it costs time they would eat up in this entire process.

JSON Data Upgrade

Applications search the cargo we receive on the service or the URL of the remote control for the purpose of receiving requests to download data from the server. Data obtained from a private or public API are usually accessed via the JSON method with integrated components embedded in the nest.

Performance often decreases because editors retain the same data to gain local offline access as JavaScript renders data gradually. Therefore, it may be best to turn raw JSON data into simple items before donating.

Do Not Give if Not Needed

It is highly recommended that you do not combine different life cycles with resources. This is because, initially, it is important to decide whether you can upgrade the components or not and make sure you do not over-load the component with unnecessary work, which can reduce the FPS of the JavaScript cable.

Memory Leaks

It has always been said that memory leaks have become a major problem with the Android app as there are a few unwanted processes running in the background.

However, you can fix this problem by scrolling through different lists, including Virtual List, Section List, and Flat List etc. You do not need to use List view. There are other benefits to scrolling as well as the smoothness of the scrolling.

Animation in React Native

React Native provides an easy episode to create animation and always looks clean. This can be achieved with the help of a cartoon library that allows a React Native engineer to authorize a native driver. Animation is sent to the traditional side before it starts.

Animation also aids in the independent use of the main series of blocked JavaScript series as it provides seamless animation. And a few independent drops. You can use Indigenous Drive to configure animation.

Navigation Development

Navigation is the backbone of the application; you should focus more on bringing improvements to navigation and better functionality between JavaScript and native objects.

Thus, you can use the four main roaming components in the app. These include Navigator, iOS Navigator, Navigation Experiment, and React Navigation.

- Navigator is used sparingly for prototyping and small applications and does not provide the same native functionality.

- IOS Navigator is widely used in iOS applications.

- Navigation experiment is used to develop pending projects based on GitHub, and a few applications use it similarly.

- Lastly, React Navigation provides a smooth and seamless experience and is used by many applications.

Lack of Multithreading

We have previously shown that React Native works in a single series which makes it difficult to perform multiple tasks at once.

When the JS library offers a section, some must wait until the process is complete. For example, you cannot combine live chat and live video feeds at the same time.

Improving Screen Orientations

Developers also must solve a serious screen layout problem where users have complained about the app crashing as they change the screen layout from standalone to landscape.

React Native navigation has been thought of as a viable solution to the problem, but it really is not, especially for iOS devices where it has failed to identify stop lock.

Make Maps Better

Maps in React Native also face the challenge of slowing down during navigation. So, if you want to fix this problem, you need to remove console.log and not allow it to store any data in XCode and disable auto location updates. You need to reduce the load on the JavaScript string to improve map usage.

Benefits of React Native

There are a few React Native benefits of building mobile apps. Some of these are given below:

1. **Use of Cross-Platform**: Provide "Read and write everywhere" area, which works on both Android platforms and iOS devices.

2. **Class Performance**: React Native written code is integrated into native code, which enables it to work in both applications and to work parallelly in both forums.

3. **JavaScript**: JavaScript information is used to build mobile applications.

4. **Community**: The large React and React Native community nearby helps us get whatever feedback we need.

5. **Hot Reload**: Making a few changes to your app code will appear immediately during upgrades. When a business idea is changed, its display is reloaded live on the screen.

6. **Upgrade Time**: Some features of iOS and Android are not yet supported, and the community is constantly developing advanced processes.

7. **Indigenous Components**: We will need to write a specific code for the platform if we want to create a native design that is not yet designed.

8. **Presence Uncertain**: As Facebook develops this framework, its existence is uncertain because it retains all rights to execute the project at any time. As React Native thunderstorms rise, it is less likely to occur.

ADVANTAGES

Key Benefits

The benefits of React Native are numerous and varied and ensure that engineers enjoy a unique coding experience.

Community Support

As an open-source framework, React Native allows the entire developer community to browse all documentation related to this technology for free and allows them to contribute to it whenever they want.

A fully community-based, React Native organization can always access the guidance of other engineers, search for relevant information, and assist other engineers who are struggling with something. Engineers can also benefit the community by asking other engineers to review or provide appropriate feedback about their ongoing responsibilities. In addition, developers are encouraged to share their findings and lessons, making it a truly engaging experience for everyone involved. This is one of the most amazing benefits of using React Native.

Proper Performance

The performance of the platform lies in improving performance using traditional modules and controls. It works with native Android and iOS components and continues to generate codes in native APIs without interruption.

Performance enhancement and performance are a direct result of a framework that uses a clearly different thread, which differs from native APIs and UIs. You may also be open to other options such as WebView, but remember, it may adversely affect the performance of your application.

Reusable Code and Advanced Components

This helps to reduce project time and cost and is the god of all businesses and app developers. Even better is the situation where the business already has a request written in the React – in which case, the development costs are also reduced because a substantial portion of the existing code can be reused to create a new application.

Advanced features in the open library allow developers to access codes freely. These codes are already written and engineers will be preparing to use them. The result? Fast development!

Benefits of Live and Hot Reloads

Live uploads can include and read code-modified changes. It also provides a new file in the template, which then automatically reads the application from scratch.

Hot Reload, based on Hot Module Replacement (HMR), was introduced after the initial reloading process was performed. While retaining features and sequence of functions, Hot Load has an added advantage – after saving changes to the file, and the HMR architect then continues to keep the updated files in the required locations as the application continues to run in the background. The main advantage of using Hot Reloading lies in its ability to authorize changes to the source code in a way that allows the developer to view the codes, even if it does not reassemble the application.

Therefore, if a developer has two or more windows open with the code and screen of the app, he can see the results immediately after making the necessary changes to the code. Thus, Hot Relocation ensures that the waiting time is reduced.

Expensive Solution

Reusable Revenue Benefit provided by React Native helps to reduce the cost of creating the app on a large scale. With this framework, codes do not have to write different codes for iOS and Android and can even code codes in an existing language. This creates the need for a small team of indigenous engineers in all application development businesses and ensures a reduction in project completion time with the help of the React Native community.

Simplified UI

The motivating force behind the use of React Native Technology is that it ensures easy and seamless user interaction. The JavaScript library is more like an open-source framework than a standard framework. With the help of this technology, developers can achieve the right sequence of creating applications.

Typically, React Native-built applications have a responsive UI, a seamless UX, and take less time to download.

External Plugin Support

The main structure of React Native has no specific components. To address this deficiency, it ensures that developers have access to third-party plugins such as JavaScript modules and native modules.

Modular Architecture

A popular software design strategy, modular editing ensures the division of program functions into free and flexible blocks called modules. It makes the application build process easier by helping developers run each other's projects whenever needed. It also improves the team collaboration needed to produce and receive updates.

React Native engineers can benefit from its natural and accurate modular design, given its ability to improve applications quickly. Modules can be reused while working with mobile phones and web APIs.

Growing Stability and Reliability

React Native is also helpful in simplifying data binding in a way that protects the parent's data and does not allow it to be touched on the part of the child, thus making the apps stronger and more reliable. To make any changes to an item, engineers need to change their status first before systematically applying all the updates. This function will ensure that only approved components can be updated.

Access to Libraries and Ready-to-Do Solutions

React Native comes with a list of pre-made solutions and libraries available for free, so engineers can access them. Its solutions not only help simplify app building, but also help developers focus on creating more error-free code.

Now that you should be aware of the benefits of using React Native, let us know more about its drawbacks.

DISADVANTAGES OF NATIVE REACT

Below is a comprehensive list of React Native malpractices that developers should be aware of before choosing to create their own operating system.

Immaturity

React Native is a new programming language compared to its older Android and iOS counterparts. React Native life style cycles have not been fully explored, which is why they can sometimes have negative or unpredictable effects on app activities. Here are some similar examples:

1. The React Native framework is rapidly evolving, with new and updated updates being released weekly. So, app creators need to keep updating their apps regularly because each update introduces many changes. Failure to update the application for a few months will deactivate it. Popular apps like Airbnb have struggled with this challenge in the past.

2. Engineers also face the problem of writing additional native code for parts that do not comply with React Native, as well as working on existing codes that need to be written.

3. Sometimes, parts of React Native do worse than their traditional equality, as in the extensive list. It can be exceedingly difficult to use a detailed and complex list with React Native compared to other components related to a mature platform, which provides a better layout.

Hard to Learn

Learning React Native can be incredibly challenging, especially for new app developers who may find it difficult to create applications with JSX in the JavaScript syntax extension. In addition to React Native, app developers must know the app's native code as well. React Native has its libraries with native bridges for features such as maps, videos, etc., but it requires highly experienced engineers for the three forums. Developers who do not have experience of many platforms can find some inconsistencies in both iOS and Android platforms exceedingly difficult. The learning curve is steep and may delay growth.

Low Security

React Native is a JavaScript library and open-source framework because developers often face the challenge of keeping the application secure. JavaScript is very flexible, and this results in some developers experiencing lower security standards. If you are developing applications that require additional layers of security, such as banking or financial applications, you need to be extra careful. If not, malicious code captions may pose a serious threat to the security features of the application. That is why engineers sometimes avoid building financial applications in React Native.

Complex UI

According to many codes, React Native is not the right choice for applications that require complex touch, screen modification, animation, or require more interaction. Unless React Native has a touch response system, codes may continue to struggle with screens with complex touches because iOS and Android touch subsystems are different from others, and using a compact API can be a challenge.

Long Initialization Time

Another problem with coding that they have with React Native is that it takes a long time to start working time before it is professionally delivered for the first time. The problem exists even with hi-tech devices and can be caused because JavaScript threads usually take too long to get started.

Memory Management

React Native is not suitable for use on computer applications because it is totally based on JavaScript. It reduces performance and speed in these applications, and float counting is also handled in an inefficient way, making memory management and usage extremely difficult. These are some of the good and bad things that have been acknowledged about using React Native.

CONCLUSION

In this chapter, we learned about what React Native is, what are the advantages and disadvantages of it, and risks and drawbacks of it. Let us go forward with the next chapter and learn more exciting things about React Native.

Working with React Native

The previous chapter is about what React Native is, its advantages, and risks and drawbacks. In this chapter, we are going to work in app development with React Native.

HOW DOES REACT NATIVE WORK?

1. **UI Thread, also known as Main Series:** This is used for native rendering of Android or iOS UI. For example, on Android, this series is used for simulation/structure/drawing of Android.

2. **JS Thread:** A JS Thread or JavaScript thread is a thread where the mind will work. For example, this is a series where the JavaScript code of the application is used, the API calls are made, touch events are processed, and much more. Indigenous view updates are compiled and posted to the traditional side at the end of each event loop in the JS series (and released at the end of the UI series).

DOI: 10.1201/9781003310440-2

3. **Integrated Updates:** In order to maintain good performance, the JS series must be able to send integrated updates to the UI series prior to the next draft delivery deadline. For example, iOS displays 60 frames per second and this leads to a new frame every 16.67 ms. If you do complex processing in the loop of your JavaScript event that leads to a UI change and takes more than 16.67 ms, then the UI will appear lazy.

4. **Native View:** One exception is the native view that occurs entirely in the UI series for example, navigatorIOS or scroll view works fully in the UI series and therefore is not blocked due to the slow JS series.

5. **Native Module Thread:** Sometimes an application requires access to the platform API, and this happens as part of a series of traditional modules.

6. **Render Thread:** For Android L only (5.0), the traditional react series is used to generate real OpenGL commands used to map your UI.

PROCESS INVOLVED IN WORKING OF REACT NATIVE

1. At the beginning of the application, the main cable starts working and starts loading JS loads.

2. If the JavaScript code is successfully uploaded, the main thread sends it to another JS thread because when JS performs heavy calculations, it temporarily installs the cable, and the UI string will not suffer at any time.

3. When the React starts delivering, the Reconciler starts to "vary", and when it produces a new DOM (structure), it sends changes to another series (Shadow Cable).

4. The shadow string calculates the structure and sends the parameters/properties of the structure to the main sequence (UI). (Here you are wondering why we call it "shadow"? Because it produces shade nodes.)

5. Since only the main thread is able to render something on the screen, the shadow string must send the generated structure to the main series, and then the UI renders.

React Native Architecture

The cross-platform power of React Native is possible due to its unique properties.

A key feature of the React Native buildings is the bridge. This application uses the React library to provide applications to the device. Simply put, the bridge converts JS code into native parts and vice versa. The bridge translates JavaScript into specific domain-specific objects. Receives JS call, using APIs (Kotlin, Objective C, Java), which allows native application rendering. The process does not affect user self-awareness because these async leaders occur outside the main sequence.

However, if your application uses a lot of threads and a large amount of data, this structure can cause delays.

Development Process

React Native is based on React and uses a single JavaScript codebase to reuse code on a variety of platforms. Unlike Ionic and many other platform development frameworks, React Native provides traditional components by recruiting API-specific platforms. For example, to provide UI components on iOS, React Native uses Objective C or Swift APIs. As for Android mobile apps, it will be Java or Kotlin. In fact, a developer does not need to know Objective C or Java to create applications.

The React Native development process takes place in JavaScript, TypeScript, and JSX. Engineers can also use key components (up to 100%) of code.

Another unique feature of React Native is its component creation instructions. Replace HTML components such as <div> <span> <a> <p> etc. (React), RN has certain components that replace it:

Also, features such as 3d group library support, hot reload, and large UI libraries make the development process easier and more productive for developers. When the app is ready, you can connect it with a cloud or a local website to provide storage capacity.

React Native Features

Here, we will discuss the features of React Native that make the framework stand out.

NPM Repository Support

NPM (Node Package Manager) broadcasts the process of developing native React applications. NPM is a repository of prefabricated libraries that engineers can use to work with the React Native framework. This will make the development process much faster, allowing React Native developers to download code patterns from the NPM library.

Reuse of Code

This is a key feature of any different platform development framework. However, the % of code you can reuse varies depending on the platform. In the case of React Native, you can apply the entire code to all different forums. This will save a lot of time and reduces costs.

Flexible Planning Language

Language planning and its flexibility play a significant role in the functioning and success of the framework. When the primary language becomes the most common framework for cross-field development, the learning process becomes faster and easier. It means you will have no problems training your JS developers to work with React Native. While, if you want to create a new app quickly, it makes sense to hire experienced React Native engineers.

Alternatively, React Native uses JavaScript as a base and supports TypeScript out of the box. These features make the React Native platform accessible to a large group of engineers. According to a recent developer study, JS is the most popular programming language, with about 70% of engineers using it.

A Powerful Community

The React Native framework became popular among engineers around the world soon after its launch in 2015. Since then, the community has been growing and contributing to an open-source framework, expanding its operations, and accelerating it. This feature protects the future of the React Native cross-platform framework and makes it attractive to other engineers.

Supports 3D Group Libraries

Another feature that makes React Native stand out from other platforms is the support of 3d group libraries. Integration with 3d team libraries empowers developers with out-of-the-box solutions and increases development opportunities.

Use High Performance in Mobile Environments

React Native has been working with mobile platforms such as iOS and Android since its first day of existence. Not surprisingly, it has excellent performance in the development of mobile applications. React Native developers can also use more code in the mobile space than any other, making it the fastest platform for mobile apps right now.

HMR (Hot Module Replacement)

The HMR (Hot Module Replacement) allows React Native to modify, add, and modify modules while the system is in operation. As a result, this feature informs the application development process in the following ways:

- Save time by updating only modified code;

- Maintains application status (lost during reload);

- Updates the browser as soon as changes are made to the JS code.

The React Native live feature lets changes on the screen you change them. This feature is especially useful in the development of mobile applications.

UI-rich Skills

The React Native framework is an option to go to if you pay close attention to the UI of your app. The framework has special render capabilities as well as many UI libraries for all types of applications.

The Future of React Native

The Facebook team, along with all stakeholders from the developer community, continue to develop the React Native environment. They can add new features, expand React Native functionality, and expand its multiplatform capacity.

There is no doubt that with high performance and a community of dedicated engineers behind you, React Native is here to stay and will continue to emerge. Currently, the React Native framework emerges in the following ways:

Development of Broadcast Model

Currently, the React Native community is reviving the Fabric project which should change the way it is at last. It will allow developers to request JavaScript by synchronizing in each series. This feature will reduce the loading time of a large series without blocking the response.

Advances in Platform-Agnosticism

Platform-agnosticism is a specific application development philosophy aimed at creating cross-platform applications. In hindsight, a good app is one that you can make once and use it across the platform without the added deception of code. Although it is not easy to achieve, the React Native community strives to enable the framework to create completely different applications.

Ease of the Bridge

The next step in developing the React Native community you go to is to make the bridge easier. This will improve the direct interaction between native and JavaScript and allow for the creation of new debugging tools.

Async Skills Expansion

The development of Async aims to improve the harmonious delivery of the React Native framework. This, in turn, will facilitate compliant and consistent data management.

What Does the Development Process Look Like?

We now understand the basics of React Native structures. It would be interesting to examine what the development process looks like. We start by opening our project using our favorite editor. Suppose we have a section called Greetings, which only shows the text "Hello!"

To start the iOS app, we need to run "run-ios" from the command line. This will start the application in the simulator or on the actual device if we have it connected to a computer. The result will look like this:

If you want the app to say "Hello!" instead of "Hello!" you can open the editor and change the text. Then, in the template, we can press Command + R, as we do when reloading a web page. Change will soon appear! Instead of waiting for a construction process that can take a minute or more, we have a quick response. This makes development much faster.

To launch our Android app, we need to make run-android react-native. With it, we can also use our part of the greeting completely. This is because the component does not have a field-specific code. React Native will ensure that it provides AndroidTextView instead of iOSU-IView. This code re-operation is one of the strongest aspects of this technology.

But, the interesting part is how we can fix bugs in our app. From the device developer menu, we can select "Remove JS error remotely." This will open Google Chrome and launch our JavaScript in the browser instead of opening it on the device. React Native sets up a web socket connection between the device and browser. This will enable us to use the powerful developer console. By using it, debugging becomes easy, especially if you come from a web development domain.

REACT NATIVE COMPONENT LIFE CYCLE PHASES

A component's life cycle in React Native can be divided into four phases.

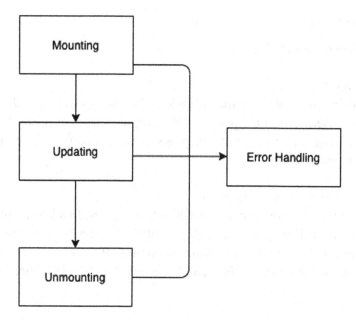

Life cycle of React Native.

1. **Mounting**: In this section, a partial model is created and installed in the DOM.

2. **Updating**: In this phase, the reaction component is said to be born and begins to grow with the latest updates.

3. **Unmounting**: At this stage, part of the react is removed from the actual DOM.

4. **Error Handling**: It is called in case any error occurs while assigning a part.

Now let us talk about the separate ways in which these categories are defined.

Mounting Phase

Below are some ways in which a component model is created and installed in the DOM.

- Constructor ()

- static getDerivedStateFromProps()

- render ()

- ComponentDidMount()

Constructor()
It is the first method called the life cycle of the traditional part of the reaction. It is used to start the part with the original shape. In the builder no UI rendering is performed. It gets props as an argument and we can set the situation this way.

static getDerivedStateFromProps()
It is called just before the delivery method, both at the first launch and the next update. It is to replace the componentWillReceiveProps method. We could not update the status within this method. If we want to review the situation, we have to come back, and another object of opposition is also empty.

render()
It is the only method required in the reaction component. Say what should be displayed on the screen. render () method is pure function which means it does not change the state. It returns the same result every time it is requested and does not link directly to the browser.

ComponentDidMount()
This method is called when the native part of the react has finished supplying. It is a wonderful place to upload data from remote storage and update the status as a result. This will update the UI of our mobile screen. Whenever we make any changes to the situation and provide () the so-called methods that will reflect the changes on the screen.

Updating Phase

Whenever there is any change in their status or props, the partial review process begins. Below are the methods used to update sections of the react component.

Static getDerivedStateFromProps()
As we have discussed above, this method is used whenever any changes in the situation or props occur.

shouldComponentUpdate()

It is used before the dedication when new buildings or circuits are adopted. The default value for this method is approximate. This method is not used the first offer or when forceUpdate is used. If we wish to discontinue rewriting to change status or props, we may return the lie in the manner of shouldComponentUpdate ().

render()

Whenever there is any change in the state or props then render methods are used again.

getSnapshotBeforeUpdate()

This method is used before the newly released output. Allows our component to retrieve certain information from DOM before it is modified.

componentDidUpdate()

componentDidUpdate () method is used immediately after partial rewriting is complete. It is important to note that it is not called the first offer.

Unmounting Phase

componentWillUnmount()

componentWillUnmount () method is used when a component is removed from DOM. We can perform cleanup tasks in this way, such as doing illegal things, canceling an ongoing network request.

Error Handling Phase

Whenever any error occurs after a part is assigned, then the response error response phase is used following the method below.

- static getDerivedStateFromError()

- componentDidCatch()

getDerivedStateFromError()

It is used whenever an error occurs while delivering. It detects an error as a parameter and returns the value to update the status.

componentDidCatch()

This is requested if any error is cast on the genealogy. It gets two parameters.

1. **error**: The error that was thrown

2. **info**: It is an object having information about which component threw that error.

Creates Components in a Traditional Responsive Way

React Native has all the features and functionality that work very well in app development, but both Android and iOS work differently in the design language. Satisfying both design language and making both look like a traditional app, custom components play a key role in application development.

Let's start with a section for Custom Text field for Android & platform iOS that will look similar in their design language.

Step 1: Create a Custom section and specify props that will customize our Custom section.

```
export default class CustomTextInput extends
Component {
  static propTypes = {
  containerStyle: PropTypes.style,
  style: PropTypes.style,
  autoFocus: PropTypes.bool,
  editbale: PropTypes.bool,
  textColor: PropTypes.string,
  onChangeText: PropTypes.func,
  value: PropTypes.string,
  placeholder: PropTypes.string,
  }
}
```

Step 2: Then let us start with the render() method

```
import React, { Component } from 'react';
import {
View,
Platform,
TextInput
```

```
} from 'react-native';
import CustomTextInputStyle from './
CustomTextInputStyle';
import { TextField } from
'react-native-material-textfield';
export default class CustomTextInput extends
Component {
 render() {
  if(Platform.OS === 'ios') {
   return(
    <View style={ [CustomTextInputStyle.mainBlock,
                  this.props.containerStyle]}>
     <View style={CustomTextInputStyle.
                  textboxBlock}>
      <TextInput
       textColor={Colors.brandText}
       style={ [CustomTextInputStyle.textInput,this.p
            rops.style]}
       labelFontSize={12}
       autoCapitalize={false}
       editable={this.props.editable}
       value={this.props.value}
       onChangeText={this.props.onChangeText}
       placeholder={this.props.placeHolder}
       placeholderTextColor={Colors.placeHolderText}
       autoFocus={this.props.autoFocus} />
     </View>
    </View>
   )
  } else {
   return(
    <View style={ [this.props.containerStyle,
CustomTextInputStyle.mainBlock]}>
     <TextField
      textColor={Colors.brandText}
      style={ [CustomTextInputStyle.textInputAndroid
            ,this.props.style ]}
      labelFontSize={12}
      value={this.props.value}
      editable={this.props.editable}
      activeLineWidth={1}
      autoCapitalize={false}
      labelTextStyle={{fontFamily: 'Roboto-Regular'}}
```

```
    tintColor={Colors.brandSecondaryText}
    onChangeText={this.props.onChangeText}
    renderAccessory={this.renderIcon.bind(this)}
    label={this.props.placeHolder}
    placeholderTextColor={Colors.placeHolderText}
    autoFocus={this.props.autoFocus} />
  </View>
 )
 }
 }
}
```

Here the Platform item separates the iOS and Android code but the Components are controlled by various utilities. For the native part, we are unable to access the essential Android Text Field which can be solved by installing and importing android "react-native-material-textfield."

Step 3: Import the Custom Text field section to the parent section and make sure you provide the correct part of the section.

```
import CustomTextInput from './CommonComponents/
CustomTextInput';
```

Step 4: Enter the Custom Section within the render () path of the parent section where we want the display to go.

```
<CustomTextInput
 textColor='#111111'
 style={style.textInput}
 containerStyle={style.textInputContainer}
 editable={true}
 value={this.state.username}
 onChangeText={this.setUsername.bind(this)}
 placeHolder="Username"
 autoFocus={true} />
 }
 }
```

You can now use this on iOS and Android to see the difference in the text field which is often difficult to automatically access part of the traditional text response field. You can create a custom section for Button, Text Label, Search Bar etc. You can use the reusable code in React Native.

WHAT IS THE COMPONENT OF REACT NATIVE?

Traditionally, a section is a place where we add our real-time active code, just as we add all of our code to the body tag on a web page. In the traditional way, we add all the active code and other components to our basic component (class/function).

Let's understand both classroom-based and work-based aspects with examples.

React Native – Class Component

Here is a simple example of a classroom-based component that just prays Hello, React Native on screen

```
import React, { Component } from 'react';
import { Text } from 'react-native';
class New extends Component {
 render() {
  return (
   <Text>Hello, React Native</Text>
  );
 }
}
export default New;
}
```

Description

In the code above, we imported the ReactandComponent from the react library. These are used to form part. Then, we introduce a Text component which is an integral part of the react-native.

Then we create a classroom with a new name that expands the Building phase. Then we present the Text component as a response to a new class, which is returned that way. Remember, for example, the class must have a sub-method and a retrieval method to be used.

Then we export New class as default. So, anytime any other part uses this file then it will automatically replace part of the class as part of the default.

React Native – Function Component

Here is a simple example of a work-based component that simply returns a Hello, React NativeText.

```
import React from 'react';
import { Text } from 'react-native';
const New = () => {
 return (
  <Text>Hello, React Native</Text>
 );
}
export default New;
```

Description

In the code above, we announced functionNew that restores the text feature. Remember, any part of the return function is provided as a response. Therefore, no need to use the render() method within it.

HOST PLATFORM APIS

When you create mobile applications, you will naturally want to take advantage of certain forum APIs. React Native makes it easy to access things like phone camera, location, and ongoing storage. These platform APIs are made available to React Native through the included modules, providing us with JavaScript links that are easy to use for these tasks.

React Native does not bind the functionality of the default platform; some APIs require writing modules, or can use modules written in the React Native community. We will cover that process in Chapter 7. Documentation is the best place to test whether the API is supported.

This chapter covers some of the available APIs. As our example, we will make some changes to the weather system from the beginning. We will add geolocation to the application so that it can detect the user's location automatically. We'll also add "memory" to the app, so it can remember your previously searched locations. Finally, we will use the camera roll to transform the background image into one of the user's photos.

When you create a cross-platform application, you want to reuse as much code as possible. Circumstances may arise where it makes sense that the code is different, for example, you may want to use different visual components for Android and iOS.

React Native provides two methods to organize code and separate it by platform:

1. Using the Platform module.

2. Using platform-specific file extensions.

Some components may have properties that operate in only one location. All of these properties have annotations via the platform and have a small badge next to them on the website.

Platform Module

React Native provides a platform that detects the platform on which the application operates. You can use the discovery mind to use a field-specific code. Use this option when only a small portion of the part is facing the field

```
import { Platform, StyleSheet } from 'react-native';
const styles = StyleSheet.create({
 height: Platform.OS === 'ios' ? 200 : 100
});
```

Platform.OS will work when running on iOS and android when running on Android.

There is also a Platform. 'android' | 'traditional' | 'default', which returns the most appropriate value for the field you are currently working on. This means that when you use the phone, iosandandroid keys will choose your preference. If that is not specified, the native key will be used and then the default key.

```
import { Platform, StyleSheet } from 'react-native';
const sty = StyleSheet.create({
 container: {
  flex: 2,
  ...Platform.select({
  ios: {
   backgroundColor: 'yellow'
  },
  android: {
   backgroundColor: 'red'
  },
```

```
default: {
// other platforms, web for example
backgroundColor: 'blue'
}
})
}
});
```

This will result in the container being flexible: 1 on all platforms, red background on iOS, green background on Android, and blue background on some platforms.

Since it accepts a limited amount, you can also use it to replace field-specific components, such as below:

```
const Component = Platform.select({
ios: () => require('ComponentIOS'),
android: () => require('ComponentAndroid')
})();
<Component />;
const Component = Platform.select({
native: () => require('ComponentForNative'),
default: () => require('ComponentForWeb')
})();
<Component />;
```

Detecting Android version

For Android, the Platform module can also be used to get the Android Platform version where the app is running.

```
import { Platform } from 'react-native';
if (Platform.Version === 25) {
console.log('Running on Nougat!');
}
```

Getting iOS Version

For iOS, Version is the result of [UIDevice systemVersion], which is a series with the current version of the operating system. An example of a system version is "10.3". For example, getting a larger version of iOS:

```
import { Platform } from 'react-native';
const majorVersionIOS = parseInt(Platform.Version, 10);
if (majorVersionIOS <= 9) {
 console.log('Work change in behavior');
}
```

Platform-Specific Extensions

If your domain code is too complex, you should consider splitting the code into separate files. React Native will get when the file has a -i.ios. noma. android. Expand and upload the appropriate platform file if needed in other sections. For example, it says you have the following files in your project.

```
BigButton.ios.js
BigButton.android.js
```

You can require the component as follows:

```
import BigButton from './BigButton';
```

React Native will pick up the file based on the running platform.

Native-specific Extensions (i.e. Sharing Code with NodeJS and Web)

You can also use .native.js extension if you want the module to be shared between NodeJS and React Native, because it does not have Android/iOS differences. This is especially helpful for projects with a common code shared between React Native and ReactJS.

For example, it says you have the following files in your project:

```
Container.js # picked up by Webpack, Rollup or any
other Web bundler
Container.native.js # picked up by the React Native
bundler for both Android and iOS (Metro)
```

You can use it without the .native extension, as follows:

```
import Container from './Container';
```

Pro tip: You can configure the bundler to ignore.native.js extensions to avoid code in your production bundle, thus reducing the final bundle size.

CONCLUSION

In this chapter, we learned about how React Native works, rendering life cycle, creating components in React Native host platform, etc. In the next chapter we are going to learn about building the first application in React Native.

## CHAPTER 3

Building Your First Application

IN THIS CHAPTER

➤ Building your first application

➤ Setting up your environment

➤ Creating a new application

➤ Exploring the sample code

➤ Building an app

In the previous chapter, we learned about how React Native works and the rendering of the life cycle etc. In this chapter, we will learn about building our first project with React Native, so let us get started.

In this chapter, you build on the beginnings of a desktop app and create some rich features that make the app a usable, minimally viable product. You also had a chance to explore how you can evolve a desktop app's codebase to remain readable and how you can organize the code for a desktop app.

INSTALLATION OF REACT NATIVE CLI

In this section, we will learn how to setup your React Native CLI environment on your Windows machine. Also, we will cover everything from the installation of node.js dependencies and other prerequisites, including

DOI: 10.1201/9781003310440-3

Android Studio and Rack Native CLI that we will need in our development process, so without further delay, let us get started.

What do we do next?

Installing Windows Terminal

You will learn many ways to uninstall and install Windows Terminal on your computer. Let us take a look at some of the basics of Windows Terminal and installation steps.

When you open Windows 11, Windows Terminal is installed automatically. To launch Windows Terminal in Windows 11, right-click the Start button and select "Windows Terminal" from the menu.

According to Microsoft, Windows Terminal is a modern, fast, powerful, and efficient application of command-line tools and shell tools, such as Command Prompt, PowerShell, and WSL. It can run any command-line program, including all Windows terminal emulators, in another tab. In simple terms, Terminal combines Command Prompt (cmd), PowerShell, Azure Cloud Shell, and WSL into one. If you have Windows 10 open, you must install Windows Terminal. Windows Terminal needs Windows 10 1903 (build 18362) or later. In Windows 11, Windows Terminal will be installed automatically.

Ways to Install Windows Terminal

There are several ways to install Windows Terminal on a PC, and they are listed below.

- **Installing Windows Terminal on Microsoft Store**: This is the preferred way to install Windows Terminal on your computer. When you install it in a Microsoft store, it lets you keep up to date with the latest updates.

- **Windows Terminal Installation using PowerShell**: If you do not want to use the Microsoft store, you can use PowerShell. It will require you to install Chocolatey first and then install Windows Terminal.

- **Get Windows Terminal from GitHub**: It involves downloading Windows Terminal from GitHub and then installing it. If you install from GitHub, the terminal does not update with newer versions.

Method 1: Installing Windows Terminal from Microsoft Store
On your Windows computer, click Start and open the Microsoft Store
(MS). In the MS Store, click the "Search" option and type Windows
Terminal. Select the Windows Terminal app and click Discover.

You do not need to sign in to the Microsoft Store to download Windows
Terminal. When you are asked to sign in, just select No, and the Windows
Terminal download starts and is installed.

Method 2: Install Windows Terminal using PowerShell | Chocolatey
Chocolatey is a high-performance Windows automation management
software that integrates installer, usable, zips, and text into integrated
packages. This is a very popular tool which is one of the tools of many
PowerShell users.

If you have not yet installed Chocolatey, you can install it in
PowerShell. Launch PowerShell as administrator and use the following
command.

```
Set-ExecutionPolicy Bypass -Scope Process -Force;
[System.Net.ServicePointManager] :: SecurityProtoco
l = [System.Net.ServicePointManager] ::
SecurityProtocol -bor 3072; iex ((New Object System.
Net.WebClient) .DownloadString ('https://chocolatey
.org/install.ps1'))
```

After installing Chocolatey, let us install Windows Terminal in the
same PowerShell window.

```
>>> choco install microsoft-windows-terminal
```

If you use the command above, the tool downloads the latest version
of Windows Terminal. The latest version of Windows Terminal has been
downloaded and installed on your computer.

Method 3: Download and install Windows Terminal from GitHub
For anyone who can install Windows Terminal in the Microsoft store, you
can download it yourself at the GitHub Uninstall page. On the GitHub
Windows Terminal release page, you will get both stable versions, preview
versions of Windows Terminal. Select a stable Windows Terminal release
and scroll down to Assets, download the file ending in .msixbundle. To

install Windows Terminal on your computer, right-click on Microsoft. WindowsTerminal.msixbundle and select Open.

In the Install Windows Terminal window, click Install. Terminal installs now. The tool should start after installation.

Installing Git

To use Git, you will need to install it on your computer. Even if you have already installed Git, it is to upgrade to the latest version. You can install it as a package or use another installer or download it from its official site.

Now the inquiry arises as to how to download the Git Installer package. Below is a slow installation process that helps you download and install Git.

How to Download Git?

Step 1: To download Git Installer, visit the official Git site and go to the download page. The download page link is https://git-scm.com /downloads. Click the package provided on the page as the release version (version can be changed) in windows. The download will start after selecting the package.

Now, the Git Installer pack has been downloaded.

Install Git

Step 2: Click on the downloaded file and select yes to continue. After selecting yes installation first. Click on the following to continue.

Step 3: By default, the components are automatically selected in this step. You can also select your required component. Click next to continue.

Step 4: Git command-line options are selected automatically. You can choose your preferred preferences. Click next to continue.

Step 5: The default transport backend options are selected in this step. Click next to continue.

Step 6: Select the required end line option and click next to continue.

Step 7: Select your favorite emulator and click next to continue.

Step 8: This is the last step that provides some additional features such as system temporary backup, verification management, and symbolic link. Select the features and click on the following option.

Step 9: Files are removed from this step. Therefore, Git installation is complete. You can now access Git Gui and Git Bash.

It helps with three aspects.

1. Create a New Store

2. Clone Archive Existing

3. Open Existing Archive

Installing Node.js and NPM package manager

Introduction

Node.js is a workspace that covers everything you need to run a JavaScript program. Used to use scripts on a server to deliver content before being delivered to a web browser.

NPM is known for Node Package Manager which is a repository and application for developing and sharing JavaScript code.

This guide helps you to install and update Node.js and NPM in the Windows operating system along with other useful Node.js instructions.

Requirements

User account with administrator rights (or the ability to download and install software).

Windows command-line access (search> cmd> right click> use as administrator) OR Windows PowerShell (Search> Powershell> right click> use as administrator).

Installing Node.js and NPM on Windows System

Step 1: First, download Node.js Installer

In a browser, navigate to https://nodejs.org/en/download/. Click on the Installer button to download the latest version. At the time of writing, version 10.16.0-x64 was the latest version. The Node.js installer includes an NPM package manager.

Step 2: Install Node.js and NPM from the Browser

1. When the installer has finished downloading, launch it. Now open the download link in the browser and click on the file. Browse file to the location where you saved the file then double-click to launch it.

2. The program will ask if you want to use the software – click Run.

3. You will be accepted into the Node.js Setup Wizard – click Next.

4. On the next screen, update the license agreement. Click the "Next" button when you agree to the terms and conditions, then installation of the software begins.

5. The installer will tell you the installation location. Leave the default location until you have a need to relocate it – then click Next.

6. The wizard will allow you to select the components to install or remove from the installation. Also, unless you have a specific need, accept the default by clicking Next.

7. Finally, click the Install button to launch the installer. When done, click Finish.

What Is NPM?

NPM is the default package manager for your projects. NPM includes a command-line (CLI) tool that gives you access to the NPM package register. The register stores most JavaScript packages made available through NPM CLI, as well as its metadata. The NPM website gives you an effortless way to search for JavaScript packages and learn information about them. The package.json file created by NPM CLI helps to manage project dependencies. It also ensures consistent project implementation in all areas.

How to Install or Update NPM

The steps show you how to install NPM and Node.js. It also gives you ways to update your NPM installation.

How to Install NPM

Since NPM is integrated with Node.js, you need to install Node.js. The NPM recommended installation method uses Node Version Manager (NVM). This version manager helps to avoid permissions and conflict issues with NPM packages. To install NPM, follow the steps in their guide.

How to Install and Use Node Version Manager NPM
Using NPM, you can install the stable version of Node.js, the same version
of NPM using the following command:

```
npm install node
```

To confirm your NPM installation, check the installed NPM version.
```
npm -v
```

How to Update NPM
When working with NVM to manage Node.js versions, updating your
NPM version requires you to update your Node.js version. To verify that
you are the latest version of NPM, use the NPM installation command to
install the stable version of Node.js.
Then, tell NPM to use the latest version.

```
npm install node
```

If you want to update NPM, use the dedicated NPM command without
updating,

```
npm install-latest-npm
```

NPM offers two main ways to incorporate specific packages into your
project. You can install a specific package with the NPM installation command. In the example below, NPM installs the latest stable version of the
package. An example includes the Express web application framework.

```
npm install express
```

Alternatively, you can specify the version of the package you want
installed on your system.

```
npm install express@4.17.1
```

You can specify the width of the version of the package you want to
install. Put the translation sentence between quotes, and precede the
translation number with the comparison operator you want to use. You
can use multiple boundary versions, separating them from spaces.

```
npm install express @ ">=4.1.0<4.17.1"
```

The above command includes the latest available version of the Express JS package equal to or larger than 4.1.0 and below 4.17.1.

Step 3: Confirm Installation

Now, open the prompt, and enter the following:

```
C:\Users\PC>node -v
v14.15.0
```

The program should display a version of Node.js installed on your system. You can do the same with NPM:

```
C:\Users\PC>npm -v
8.5.3
```

Installing React Native CLI

Now we will see how we can install and configure the React Native development environment on Windows. If you want how to install React Native on Mac, check out the blog post below. You can use Expo CLI & also React Native CLI to improve the React Native app on Windows.

Expo CLI is a package that incorporates many native features (location, camera, etc.) when developing an application with React Native. For the first time, when you develop a traditional reaction with the Expo CLI, you can feel comfortable. However, this package includes many native features that you do not use, and that makes the system build process even bigger. Also, if you want to integrate a native feature that does not include Expo CLI, it is difficult to do. Therefore, we do not recommend using Expo CLI.

This section is about how to install and configure the React Native CLI site. Also, we will create a React Native project with React Native CLI and test its effectiveness.

We need to install Nodejs, Watchman, Xcode, etc., to improve the application with native responses. Let us see how we can put them one by one.

Installing Python

The React Native building system uses Python. Python is basically installed on Mac, so this process is not required, but for Windows, this is required.

Open Command Prompt (cmd) as Administrator, then execute the Chocolatey command below to install Python.

```
choco install -y python2
```

After installation, we need to restart the computer in order to use Python. After a reboot, open Command Prompt (cmd), and then execute the command below to check if Python is properly installed.

```
python --version
```

React Native CLI

Let us install React Native CLI to improve the application with native responses. Use the NPM command below to install React Native CLI worldwide.

```
npm install -g react-native-cli
```

After installation, download the command below to check the React Native CLI is properly installed.

```
npx react-native --version
```

If the React Native CLI is properly installed, you can see the React Native CLI version as below.

```
react-native-cli: 2.0.1
```

Installing Android JDK

We need to install JDK (Java Development Kit) to upgrade the Android application with React Native. Open Command Prompt (cmd) as Administrator, then use the Chocolatey command below to install JDK.

```
choco insert -y jdk8
```

After installation, restart Command Prompt (cmd) and then execute the command below to check that Java is installed properly.

```
Java -version
```

If Java is installed by installing JDK, you can see the Java version below.

```
OpenJDK version "1.8.0_222"
```

```
OpenJDK Runtime Environment (AdoptOpenJDK) (build
1.8.0_222-b10)
OpenJDK 64-Bit Server VM (AdoptOpenJDK) (build
25.222-b10, mixed mode)
```

If JDK is installed, Java compiler is installed. Perform the command below to check that the Java compiler is installed properly.

```
Javac -version
```

JAVA_HOME FLEXIBLE ENVIRONMENT

The next step is to set the variable JAVA_HOME to point to the input list. We have marked down the Installation directory in the previous step, located in the C: \ Program Files \ Java \ jdk1.8.0_bxx folder where bxx is the update number. Follow these steps:

- Go to Control Panel -> System (Control Panel -> System and security)

- Click on Advanced System Settings

- Under the Advanced tab, Select Local Variables

- Under the System Variables tab (in the window below), check to see if JAVA_HOME is available. Once found, double-click on it or click new

- Enter a Font Name = JAVA_HOME & Folder = C: \ Program Files \ Java \ jdk1.8.0_181.

- Click OK when done.

Installing Android Studio

We need to install Android Studio to upgrade the Android app with React Native. Click the below-given link to go to the Android Studio official site and download the installation file.

Android Studio: https://developer.android.com/studio
After downloading, use the installation file to install Android Studio.

Android Studio Configuration

- You can see the screenshot below after using the Android Studio installation file.

- Click the Next button and go to the next screen. When you go to the next screen, you can see the Select Components screen as below. Select the Android Device and click the Next button and go to the next screen.

- If you go to the next screen, you can see the Android Studio Install Path screen as below. Set the Install Method or save default, click the Next button to go to the next screen.

- When you go to the next screen, you can see the startup menu screen as below. Just click the Apply button to install.

- After installation, you can see the screen below. Click the Next button to complete the installation of Android Studio.

- When you click the Next button to complete the installation, you will see the screen. Check Start Android Studio and click the Finish button to complete the installation of Android Studio.

- When you click the Finish button, you can see Android Studio done below. Select Do Not Enter Settings, then click the OK button to sign up for Android Studio.

- If you click the OK button to use Android Studio, you can see the Android Studio Setup Wizard below. Click the Next button and go to the next screen.

- When you go to the next screen, you can see the input type screen as below. Select Custom, then click the Next button to go to the next screen.

- When you go to the next screen, you can see the Select Theme UI screen as below. Select your favorite theme, then click the Next button to go to the next screen.

- When you go to the next screen, you can see the SDK component setup screen as below. Select the operating option (Intel ® HAXM) and the Android Virtual Device option, then click the Next button.

- On the next screen, they will see the Emulator settings screen as below. Click the Next button without changing the particular.

- The next process is the installation of a standard system, so I do not explain the details. Just click the Finish button to proceed with the installation of the Android Studio to complete it.

After the installation of the Android Studio, you can see the Android Studio being created below.

Installing Android SDK

Android Studio SDK configuration

Click Configure> SDK Manager Menu in the right pane to go to the Android SDK configuration.

If the screen is displayed at the top as below, select the Show Details Package option at the bottom right. Find and select an option below the list.

```
Android SDK Platform 29
Image of Intel x86 Atom System
Google APIs Intel x86 Atom System Image
Google APIs Intel x32 Atom_64 System Image
```

When you have selected all of the options above, click the OK button at the bottom right to enter them.

Configure the Android Studio Environment variable.

Android Studio installation and adjustment done. Now, we need a flexible setup environment. Right-click The PC and then click the Properties menu as below.

When you click the Properties menu, you can see the System and Security screen. Click Advanced Settings in the menu on the left.

When you click the Advanced System Settings menu, you can see the system objects screen as below. Click the Advanced tab, then select the Environmental Variables button under Advanced.

When you click the local variable, you can see the box below. Click the new button for user variables in your wording.

When you see the box above, enter the ANDROID_HOME name in the Variable name, along with your Android Studio SDK path to the Variable value. If you do not know your Android Studio SDK path, use the Android Studio SDK debug screen as below. You can see the Android Studio SDK location at the top of the Android Studio SDK configuration screen.

If you have added the ANDROID_HOME flexible environment, you need to set the Android Studio field tools path. Click through the user interface to get a list of your names to go to the edit dialog.

If you can see the screen as above, enter the paHt tools tool folder along the Android SDK such as C: \ Users \ [username] \ AppData \ Local \ Android \ Sdk \ platform-tools at the bottom of the list and click the OK button.

After that, open Command Prompt (cmd) and execute the command below.

```
adb
```

If the natural variable is properly configured, you can see the result below.

```
Version of Android Debug Bridge 1.0.41
Version 29.0.1-5644136
Installed as / Users / jeonghean_kim / Library /
Android / sdk / platform-tools / adb
```

Installing Visual Studio Code (IDE)

In this section, we will have a look at the steps for how to download and install Visual Studio Code for Windows and Mac operating systems.

To improve each programing language, there are IDEs (Integrated Development Environments) available. In JavaScript, there are also many IDEs, the Visual Studio editor is one of them. It is a lightweight and robust source code editor that works on your desktop and is available for Windows, macOS, and Linux. Visual Studio Code has built-in JavaScript, TypeScript, Node.js support. It has an extensive ecosystem for extensions for other languages (such as C++, C #, Java, Python, PHP, Go) and operating times (such as .NET and Unity). At ToolsQA we use VS Code for Protractor, Cypress, JavaScript, etc.

How to Download and Install Visual Studio Code?

Getting up and working with Visual Studio Code is fast and straightforward. It is a download so you also install it quickly & also try VS Code. VS Code is a free code editor. Additionally, it works on macOS, Linux, and Windows operating systems. Let us see how we can set the same ones on different platforms that we use.

The first step is shared across all platforms regardless of which OS you are using.

Download Visual Studio Code

You can download the Visual Studio code at the URL "https://code.visualstudio.com/download" by selecting the appropriate field:

You can click on the icons depending on the operating system you plan to download for the visual studio code editor.

How to Install VStudio Code on Windows?

- First, download the Visual Studio Code installer for Windows. Once downloaded, use the installer (VSCodeUserSetup- {version} .exe). It will only take a minute.

- Second, accept the agreement and click next.

- Third, click on "create desktop icon" to access the desktop and then click Next.

- After that, click the install button.

- Finally, after completing the installation, click the end button, and the virtual studio code will open.

- By default, VS Code under C: \ users {username} \ AppData \ Local \ Programs \ Microsoft VS Code.

- After successful installation, let us move on to the next section to understand the various components of the Visual Studio User Code Editor.

Why Do You Use React Native?
Yes, there are methods other than React Native like ionic and flutter, but ionic is used to create a blended application that does not give us a natural feeling. It is just a sugar-coated HTML with JavaScript wrapped and the flutter experience is better than the native because it does not require a bridge to communicate with native objects, but flutter uses Dart, which is also a new programming language you need to learn to create applications. in flight. However, the enquiry arises as to why we should use React Native? Examine the points mentioned below.

Things we have covered include the following:

- Refactoring the code by using Node.js's module functionality

- Using third-party libraries to implement search features

- Applying Electron and NW.js's shell API to handle opening files with their default applications

- Improving app navigation to make the desktop app more usable

The main thing to take away from this chapter is that with a couple of hundred lines of code and some external files, you can build an app that replicates what a native desktop app can do (and one that has relatively complex functionality). Not only that, you have been able to use third-party libraries like lunr.js to help provide this functionality and structure the code in such a way that it can be used in web apps and allow for building apps for both the web and desktop from the same source code.

SETTING UP YOUR ENVIRONMENT

This page will help the user to install and build the first React Native app.

If you are new to mobile development, an easy way to get started is with Expo CLI. Expo is a set of tools that are built around React Native and, although it has various features, the main thing for us now is that it allows you to write a React Native app within minutes. You will only need the latest version of Node.js as well as a phone or emulator. If you like to try React Native directly in the browser before installing any tools, you can try Snack.

Once you are familiar with mobile development, you may want to use the React Native CLI. It requires Xcode or Android Studio to get started. If you have one of these tools installed, you can get up and work within a few minutes. If not installed, you should expect to spend about an hour re-installing them.

- Expo CLI Quickstart

- React Native CLI Quickstart

Assuming that you have Node 12 LTS or greater installed, you can use NPM to install the Expo CLI command-line utility.

- NPM

- Yarn

    >>>npm install -g expo-cli

Then run the commands to create the latest React Native project called "AwesomeProject":

- **npm**

- Yarn

```
>>>expo init MyProject
cd MyProject
npm start # you can use: expo start
```

This starts a development server for you.

Running React Native Application

Then, install the Expo client app on your iOS or Android phone and connect to a wireless network like your computer. For Android, use the Expo app to scan a QR code on your terminal to unlock your project. For iOS, use the built-in QR code scanner for the Camera app.

Modifying Your App

Now that you've successfully used the app, let's fix it. OpenApp.js in the text editor of your choice and edit specific lines. The app should automatically reload once you have saved your changes.

Now, it is running app on a simulator or virtual device.

Expo CLI allows you to use your React Native application on a mobile device without having to set up an upgrade. If you want to run the app on iOS or Android Device, please refer to use the "React Native CLI Quickstart" instructions and learn how to install Xcode or set up your Android upgrade.

Once you set these up, you can launch your app on the Android Visible Device using runnpm use android, or in iOS Simulator with runnpm run iOS (macOS only). Here are some of the descriptive elements:

Exploring the Sample code

React Native is starting to change the game in the world of mobile development. By using the skills, you already have, as a web developer, you can find a set of common ways to build user links on mobile devices. In this section, we shall talk about many aspects of React Natives as we develop a note-taking app, which we call React notes. While building up key features, such as taking notes, saving notes to the device, viewing a list of saved notes, and navigating between screens, you will learn the basic skills you have to improve your app. You will have the chance to go beyond the basics by adding the ability to store images and geolocation data in notes. Performance is just part of what makes an app great – it should look good too, so we made sure to provide you with a complete understanding of structure and styles. By the end of this book, you will have launched a fully installed app from start to finish and have all the skills you need to share with the world your React Native apps!

BUILDING AN APP

Building a modern app requires modern tools. That's why we've seen a trend in the use of React Native. JavaScript frameworks, for example, provide excellent features beyond the use of basic development methods. Frames open up a new way to deal with problems associated with the development of a mobile app.

React Native allows you to make direct calls using APIs that offer additional customizable liquid upgrades. React Native can be used well to build native Android and iOS apps. This is done by using React on the server side rather than in the browser. Technically, React Native starts working on an embedded JavaScript Core model, and then advanced components provide it.

In section, we will focus on how to build an Android app with React Native. We will be developing a basic "movidedb" application that will include a list of movies and related information. So, let's get started.

Building an Android App with React Native

STEP 1: Blank React Native Project Creation
Our step is to create a blank React Native project. To do so, you need to install a Node on your system that will build your Android app. Once the Node is installed, you now need to create a project in the directory of your choice. npm install -g react-native-cli

Are you still confused? Then, follow the guide to get a better understanding.

Once it is installed, you have to create the new project in the directory of choice. If you are in the folder, type the command to install the required modules.

>>>react-native init Movies

This will create a new folder named "Movies" and the required modules within it.

As React Native is used for iOS and Android apps together, JavaScript code can share between the two files, index.ios.js, index.android.js. As we are building an Android application, we will use index.android.js

STEP 2: Connect Android Device
It is time to connect the Android device to the system. After connecting, you need to run the following command.

>>>react-native run-android

If you did it well, you will see the blank app on the device.

STEP 3: Getting Information from the Moviedb API
It is time to setup the app to connect to the *themoviedb database.* To get started, you first need to get the required API. Once you get the API, you can start to write your app code. The Moviester class should look like the below.

```
class Moviester extends Component {
 render() {
  return (
   <View style={styles.container}>
    <Text style={styles.welcome}>
     Welcome to React Native Android App
Development!
    </Text>
    <Text style={styles.instructions}>
     To get started, edit index.android.js
    </Text>
    <Text style={styles.instructions}>
     Press menu button for Menu List
    </Text>
   </View>
  );
 }
}
```

The basic code initializes the Moviester module, however, it still needs a constructor to work effectively. A constructor will also initialize the variables. For now, we will focus on moviesData array as it will store all the JSON data that is fetched using the API.

```
constructor(props) {
  super(props);
  var ds=new ListView.DataSource({rowHasChanged:
(r1, r2)=>r1 !==r2});
  this.state={
  movieData: ds.cloneWithRows([]),
  };
}
```

STEP 4: Defining the fetchMoviesData Method
Now, we need to code the module for fetching the data using the API. For the same, we will use the code below.

```
fetchMoviesData() {
  var url='http://api.themoviedb.org/2/movie/now
_playing?api_key=API_KEY';
  fetch(url)
    .then(response=>response.json())
    .then(jsonData=>{
    this.setState({
      movieData: this.state.moviesData.cloneWithRows
(jsonData.results),
    });
    })
    .catch(error=>console.log ('Error: '+error));
}
```

STEP 5: Creating the Life Cycle componentDidMount Method
Lastly, we create the componentDidMount method that will act as a life cycle method. It will be executed once the first rendering takes place.

```
componentDidMount() {
  this.fetchMoviesData();
}
```

STEP 6: View Creation
The last few steps are to create the front end of your app. To do so, you need to import some components. These components will be used to create the view for your React Native Android app.

```
import {
AppRegistry,
```

```
StyleSheet,
Text,
View,
ListView,
Image
} from 'react-native';
```

The few components that we need to learn about include the following:

1. **ListView**: It is used to show the vertical scrolling lists in an app effectively.

2. **Image**: The component is used to display various types of images on the app. It includes static resources, network, temporary local images, and so on.

STEP 7: Reconstructing the Return Method

Now, that we have written others modules which handle the various aspect of the application, we now need to edit the return() method and make it readable.

```
render () {
  return (
   <ListView
    dataSource={this.state.moviesData}
    renderRow={this.renderRow}
    style={styles.container}
   />
  );
 }
```

We have written the code for the dataSource method which will fetch the movie data from the moviedb using the API. However, the "render-Row" method takes the template required to be rendered for each row. We will now define it below. Also, the renderRow method should be defined within the Moviester module.

```
renderRow(rowData){
  return (
   <View style={styles.thumb}>
    <Image
     source={{uri:'PUT URL HERE'}}
```

```
    resizeMode='cover'
    style={styles.img} />
    <Text style={styles.txt}>{rowData.title}
(Rating: {Math.round(rowData.vote_average * 10) /
10}) </Text>
    </View>
  );
}
```

You need to put the source URI correctly for the above code to work properly. We are set to make the app work as intended. However, we need to create some style sheets to give the application some looks. You can do this by using the following code.

```
var styles=StyleSheet.create({"Code part"});
```

STEP 8: Running the App
The step is to run the app using the following command.

```
>>> react-native run-android
```

This will start your app on smartphone/device.
Wow! You have created the app successfully.

Conclusion
In this section, we learned about Setting Up Your Environment, creating a New Application, Exploring the Sample Code, Building an App. In the next section, we will learn about components for mobile.

React Native – Default Application
If you double click on the default app you can feel that the app.js file looks like

```
import React from 'react';
import {StyleSheet, Text, View} from 'react-native';
export default class App extends React.Component {
  render() {
   return (
     <View style={styles.container}>
       <Text>Open up App.js to working on your app!</
Text>
       <Text>Changes you make will automatically
reload. </Text>
```

```
<Text>Shake phone to open the menu.</Text>
</View>
);
```

To display a normal message saying "Welcome to World" remove the CSS code and add the message to be printed wrapped inside the <text> </text> tags inside <view></view> as shown below.

The rest of the code is the same as react application basic code.

```
import React from 'react';
import {StyleSheet, Text, View} from 'react-native';
export default class App extends React.Component {
  render() {
   return (
    <View>
      <Text>Welcometo World</Text>
     </View>
    );
  }
 }
 }
}
const styles = StyleSheet.create({
  container: {
   flex: 1,
   backgroundColor: '#fff',
   alignItems: 'center',
   justifyContent: 'center',
  },
});
```

The data inside React Components are handled by state and props. In this section, you will learn about the state.

Props and State Definition

Props is a JavaScript object that React components receive as a non-compliant installation to produce a React element. They provide data flow between components. Transferring data (props) from one component to another as a parameter:

In the class section you need to define custom HTML attributes to which you assign your data and transfer it via the special React JSX syntax:

```
import React, {Component} from 'react';
class App extends Component {
 render() {
  const greeting = 'Welcome to React';
  return (
   <div>
    <Greeting greeting={greeting} />
   </div>
  );
 }
}
class Greeting extends Component {
 render() {
  return<h1>{this.props.greeting}</h1>;
 }
}
export default App;
```

To receive props class components, you can use the JavaScript keyword this. For functional component props are passed as an argument to a function:

```
import React, {Component} from 'react';
class App extends Component {
 render() {
  const greeting = 'Welcome to React';
  return (
   <div>
    <Greeting greeting={greeting} />
   </div>
  );
 }
}
const Greeting = props => <h1>{props.greeting}</h1>; //
here an arrow function receives with the name
greetings
export default App;
```

In our example, data was a string variable. But props can be anything such as integers, objects, arrays, and even React components.

State

State is a JavaScript object that contains data that influences how a component looks in a particular area at a time. The second part is what makes the world different compared to resources. The world is just a picture of an app at a time. All user interaction with your app may result in a change in the default state and the overall UI as a result. The situation changes during the life span of the React section. Examples of status:

To get part of the class you need to call the class builder within the React section:

```
Import React, {Part} from 'react';
Class button expands {
 builder (resources) {
  super (buildings);
  this.state={counter: 1};
 }
 give () {
  return (
   <button>{this.state.counter}</ton>>
  );
 }
}
```

Release the default button.

To get the active part you need to use the State Hook:

```
Import React from 'react';
Activity counter () {
 const [count, setCount]=React.useState (1);
 return (
  <div>
   <p>You clicked {count} times</p>
   <button onClick={() => setCount (count+1)}>
   Click me
   </button>
  </div>
 );
}
export Default Counter;
```

The state breathes life into your app and is something that makes your app work. The status may be Boolean, numbers, character units, or more complex JavaScript objects.

Stateful and stateless componentsStateless Component may only contain props, no status. Such a component can be linked with a function: it receives an input ('object' object) and returns the result (React object). Non-standard parts are used if you want to represent props and the part does not need to be connected. They are easy to use and test.

The Stateful Component may contain props but must-have status. The decent part owns its status and can change it. When a component changes position, it reloads. Official components help when the application needs to respond to user input and actions. They provide flexible user interaction through client-server communication and help create interactive pages. The parts that work normally have no shape, while the parts of the class add deception to the world. However, it has changed with the introduction of Hooks inactive components. The State was one of the most important advantages of class parts, but today the Hooks have added state administration and life cycle systems to the functional parts, so they can also be called independent components.

- React components give a reset if props or conditions have changed. Any update from anywhere in the code change the redeployment of the appropriate part of the user interface.

- Props and conditions are JS objects, which means they both contain the many structures and methods we need.

- The same combination of props and state locations should produce the same output.

Difference between State and Props
The state is mutable, while props are immutable. This means that the state can be updated further while props cannot be updated.

Using State
This is our root component. We are importing components Home which will be used in most of the chapters.

App.js

```
import React from 'react';
import {StyleSheet, Text, View} from 'react-native';
export default class App extends React.Component {
  state = {
    myState: laboris nisi ut aliquip ex ea consequat.
```

```
  Duis aute irure dolor reprehenderit in voluptate
velit esse dolore eu
  fugiat nulla pariatur. sint occaecat cupidatat
non, sunt in
  qui officia deserunt mollit id est .'ipsum dolor
sit amet, consectetur.
 }
  render() {
  return (
  <View>
   <Text>{this.state.myState}</Text>
  </View>
  );
 }
```

Updating State

Since state is mutable that means we can update it by adding function deleteState and call it using the onPress={this.deleteText} event.

App.js

```
import React, {Component} from 'react'
import {Text, View} from 'react-native'
class App extends Component {
  state={
  myState: 'Lorem dolor sit amet, adipisicing elit,
sed
     do eiusmod incididunt ut et dolore aliqua.
     Ut enim ad minim veniam, quis nostrud ullamco
laboris nisi
     ut aliquip ex ea consequat. Duis aute irure in
     in velit esse eu fugiat nulla pariatur.
     mollit anim id est laborum.'
 }
  updateState=() ⇒ this.setState({myState: 'Updated
State'})
  render() {
  return (
   <View>
    <Text onPress={this.updateState}>
     {this.state.myState}
```

```
    </Text>
    </View>
    );
  }
}
export default App;
  }
```

We will use class syntax for mean parts (container) and functional syntax for seamless parts (presentations). We will learn more about that in the next chapter. We will also learn how to use the syntax of the updateState arrow function. You should remember that this syntax uses lexical scope, and this keyword will be tied to a natural object (Class). This will sometimes lead to unexpected behavior.

Another way to describe the methods is to use the EC5 functions, but in that case, we will need to tie this by hand to the builder. Consider the following example to understand this.

```
class Home extends Component {
  constructor() {
    super()
    this.updateState=this.updateState.bind(this)
  }
  updateState() {
    //
  }
  render() {
    //
  }
}
```

Build Your First App with React Native

Once React is installed, it starts with Folder Layout

- Add a folder to the root and name its 'application.'

- Now move the App.js file to the root of the 'application.'

- Then update index.js import statement to 'import Application from ./app/App.js.'

- Finally, create folders within the 'app.'

A few words and their functions you need to be aware of:

- **Screens**: These are known as our main ideas.
- **Assets**: There are two folders in this directory called images and animations.
- **Components**: This is the place where you will put all your shared parts.
- **Configure**: You can set the color scheme of your application in the colors.js file to keep things in control.

Creating an App

First, install it once worldwide:

```
$ npm install -g create-react-native-app
or
$ yarn global add create-react-native-app
```

You need to make sure that you are using Node v6 or a later version with npm v3 or narn v4 version of Yarn. We are not asking you to use npm v5 because of the big problems you are experiencing in that npm version.

Then to create an app, use:

```
$ create-react-native-app my-application
$ cd my-application
```

After applying the above-mentioned line of codes, the directory will be created with the word 'my-app' within the current active directory. This will also produce the initial design of the project within "my plan" so keep adding all the basics. If you have previously worked with React Native, you will know that you will not see any "android" or "ios" directories. Therefore, once the installation is complete, further instructions will be executed by you in the project guide:

At the Start of NPM

It will run your application in the development mode with interactive command, and to launch it without notice, use the '- and interactive' flag. If you want to watch it, open it in the Expo app on your phone to view the file. And it will reload if you save the edits to your files. With this, you can also see construction errors appear and log in to the terminal.

What Is Cross-Platform Development?

React Native is a separate open-source development software developed in Javascript and differs from other platforms for different platforms. React Native apps are usually developed in key languages such as Javascript for Android and Objective C or Swift for iOS. This is the reason for the rapid operation of native applications. React Native was launched on Facebook's internal hackathon in 2013. Since then, it has been available for testing in January 2015 and has been moving to the current mobile development platform.

Cross-platform development is the practice of making software that is compatible with more than one type of hardware platform. The cross-platform application can run on Microsoft Windows, Linux, and macOS, or both. A good example of a cross-platform app is a web browser or Adobe Flash that does the same, regardless of which computer or mobile device you are using.

Cross-platform is considered a sacred software development tool – you can build your own codebase once and run it on any platform, as opposed to software traditionally built for a particular platform. Engineers can use the tools they know well, such as JavaScript or C #, to build anonymous forums. Software owners are also interested in you as product development, in terms of marketing time and cost, slows down.

What Are Some of the Features of Cross-Platform Development?

A Lot of Listeners

You do not have to decide which audience to target, that is, iOS or Android users, as different platform software works on both, giving you access to a wider user base.

Stability of the Court

There is a difference between roaming and design between iOS and Android, which – in the development of the platform – is handled automatically, thanks to a shared codebase. This helps to create app brand ownership in both forums with less effort than the native one.

Reusable Code

This is one of the biggest benefits of platform development – you can create your own codebase for Android and iOS at the same time. Indigenous app development requires coding separately and usually requires two different software developers to do the job – one for iOS and the other for Android.

Rapid Development
With only one codebase required to manage iOS and Android, and when everything is in one place, product development is very fast. Cross-platform applications are built as single projects, although they can support various devices, a large amount of code can be reused between platforms.

Reduced Costs
Building cross-platform applications can be 30% cheaper than building traditional applications, all thanks to the ability to reuse code and rapid development, which directly contributes to costs.

What you have learned so far may lead you to conclude that cross-platform development is flawless – no, it is not. Let us get into them right now.

Requires Additional Technology to Ensure High Performance
It is a common myth that cross-platform applications don't work as well as their native counterparts. For example, both Flutter and React Native's goal is to run at 60 frames per second. In most cases, cross-platform applications can work in the same way as native applications as long as the developers have sufficient skills and expertise.

As cross-platform applications have to respond to a variety of devices and platforms, it makes encoding extremely difficult. This creates a lot of work for engineers who have to incorporate variables into different devices and platforms to account for differences – especially when it comes to more complex aspects.

CHAPTER SUMMARY

This chapter covered React Native fundamental installation. This allows the creation of a multiplatform application using the same codebase. Essentially it enables the developers to use the React Native framework along with the other native platform capabilities. It also explains its features.

## CHAPTER 4

Components for Mobile Development

IN THIS CHAPTER

➤ Components for mobile

➤ Analogies between HTML elements and native components

➤ Working with touch and gestures

➤ Working with organizational components

➤ Platform-specific components

In the previous chapter, we learned about building the first application with React Native. In this chapter, we are going to learn about the components for mobile application development.

COMPONENTS FOR MOBILE

Analogies between HTML and Native Components

When you are developing for the web, we make use of various basic HTML elements. These include <span>, <div>, and <img>, as well organizational elements such as <ol>, <ul>, and <table>. (You could include a consideration of HTML elements such as <audio>, <svg>, <canvas>, and so on, but we will ignore them for now.)

DOI: 10.1201/9781003310440-4

When dealing with React Native, we do not use these HTML elements, but we use various components that are nearly analogous to them.

HTML	React Native
div	View
img	Image
span, p	Text
ul/ol, li	ListView, child items

Although these elements serve almost the same purpose, they do not change. Let us take a look at how these components work on mobile with React Native and how they differ from their browser-based counterparts.

The Text Component

Rendering text is a basic function; any application needs to render text somewhere. However, text within the context of React and mobile development work separately from text rendering for the web.

When working with text in HTML, you could include raw text strings in a variety of elements. More, you can style them with child tags like <strong> element and <em> element. So, you end up with a snippet (HTML) that looks like this:

For example,

```
<p>The quick <em>brown</em> over the lazy
<strong>dog</strong>.</p>
```

In React Native, the <Text> element components can have plain text nodes as children. In other words, this is not valid:

```
<View>
 Text does not go here!
</View>
```

Instead, wrap the text in a <Text> component:

```
<View>
 <Text>This is OK!</Text>
</View>
```

When you deal with <Text> components in React Native, you will no longer have access to subtags such as <strong> and <em>, and you can apply styles to achieve similar effects through the use of attributes such as fontWeight and fontStyle. Here is how you might achieve an effect by making use of inline styles:

```
<Text>
  The quick <Text style={{fontStyle: "arial
"}}>brown</Text> fox
  jumped over the lazy <Text style={{fontWeight:
"bold"}}>dog</Text>.
</Text>
```

This approach could quickly become verbose. You will likely want to create styled components as a sort of shorthand when dealing with text, as shown in Example 4.1.

Example 4.1. Creating reusable components for styling text

```
var styles = StyleSheet.create({
  bold: {
    fontWeight: "bold"
  },
  italic: {
    fontStyle: "italic"
  }
});
var Strong = React.createClass({
  render: function() {
    return (
    <Text style={styles.bold}>
    {this.props.children}
    </Text>);
  }
});
var Em = React.createClass({
  render: function() {
    return (
    <Text style={styles.italic}>
    {this.props.children}
    </Text>);
  }
});
```

Once you have declared these styled components, you can easily make use of styled nesting. Now the React Native version quite similar to the HTML version (see Example 4.2).

Example 4.2. Using styled components for rendering text

```
<Text>
The quick <Em>brown</Em> fox jumped
over the lazy <Strong>dog</Strong>.
</Text>
```

Similarly, React Native does not inherently have a concept of header elements (h1, h2, etc.), but it is easy to declare own styled <Text> elements and use them as needed.

In general, when dealing with styled text, React Native allows you to change your approach. Style inheritance React Native is limited, so you lose the default font settings for nodes in the tree. Once again, Facebook recommends solving this by using styled components:

You have probably noticed a pattern here: React Native is very opinionated in its preference for the reuse of styled components over the reuse of styles. We will further discuss this in the next chapter.

THE IMAGE COMPONENT

If text is the basic element in an application, images are closed for both the mobile and the web. When writing HTML and CSS for the Webpage, we include images in various ways. Sometimes we use the <img> tag, while we apply images using CSS, such as when we use the background-image property. But in React Native, we have a similar <Image> component, but it behaves differently.

The simple usage of the <Image> component is easy and straightforward; just set the source prop:

```
<Image source={require('image!puppies')} />
```

It is worth that it is also possible to include web page-based image sources instead of bundling assets with any application. The Facebook application does this as one of the examples in the UIExplorer application:

```
<Image source={{uri: 'https://facebook.git.io/react
/img/logo_log.png'}}
    style={{width: 300, height: 300}} />
```

When utilizing network resources, you need to specify dimensions manually.

Downloading images via the network rather than as assets has some advantages. During development, for example, it may be easier to use this approach while prototyping rather than importing all of the assets ahead of time. It changes the size of your bundled mobile application so that users need not download all of your assets. However, it means that you will be relying on the user's data plan whenever they access your application in the future. For most cases, you will want to avoid using the URI-based method.

If you are wondering about working with the user's own images, we will cover the camera roll in Chapter 6.

Because React Native for mobile emphasizes a component-based approach, images include as an <Image> component instead of being referenced via styles. For instance, we wanted to use an image as a background for weather application. Whereas in HTML and CSS you would like to use the background-image property to apply a background image, in React Native you use the <Image> as a container component, like so:

```
<Image source={require('image!puppies')}>
{/* Your content here... */}
</Image>
```

Styling the images is fairly straightforward. In addition to using styles, certain props control how the image will be rendered. You will usually use resizeModeprop, for example, which can be set to enlarge, cover, or contain. The UIExplorer app demonstrates this well.

The <Image> component is easy to work with and very flexible. You will make extensive use of it in your own applications.

WORKING WITH TOUCH AND GESTURES

Web-based interface is often designed for mouse-based controls. We use features such as high-speed status to show interaction and respond to user interaction. For mobile, this is an important touch. Mobile forums have their own rules around the interaction you would like to design. This varies in some ways from one platform to another: iOS behaves differently than Android or Windows.

React Native provides a number of APIs for you to use as you create links ready to touch. In this section, you get to look at the <TouchableHighlight> container section, as well as the low-level APIs offered by PanResponder and the Gesture Responder program.

USING TOUCHABLEHIGHLIGHT

Any interface elements that respond to the user's touch (like buttons, control elements, etc.) should usually have a <TouchableHighlight> wrapper. <TouchableHighlight> causes overlay when the view is touched, giving the user a visual response. The important interactions that cause a mobile app to feel, as opposed to a mobile-optimized website, where touch response is limited. As a general rule, you should use <TouchableHighlight> wherever there may be a button or link on the web.

For its basic functionality, you just need to wrap your part in the <TouchableHighlight>, which will add a simple overlay when pressed. The <TouchableHighlight> section also gives you hooks for events like asonPressIn, onPressOut, onLongPress, and so on, so you can use these events in React programs.

Example 4.3 shows how to wrap a component data in a TouchableHighlight so that the user can give feedback.

Example 4.3. By using the TouchableHighlight component

```
<TouchableHighlight
 onPOut={this._onPressOut}
 onPressIn={this._onPressIn}
 style={styles.touchable}>
  <View style={styles.button}>
   <Text style={styles.welcome}>
    {this.state.pressing ? 'EEK!' : 'PUSH ME'}
   </Text>
  </View>
</TouchableHighlight>
```

When a user presses a button, an overlay appears, and the text changes to <TouchableHighlight> to give the user a visual response – the left-handed (left) and the highlighted right (right).

This is a built-in example, but it shows the basic interaction that makes the "world" button affect the mobile. Overlay is an important piece of feedback that lets the user know that something can be pressed. Note that in order to use overlay, there is no need to apply any logic to our styles; <TouchableHighlight> carries with us what is logical.

Touch/PressDemo.js illustrates the use of TouchableHighlight

```javascript
'use strict';
var React = require('react-native');
var {
 Text,
 View,
 StyleSheet,
 TouchableHighlight
} = React;
var Button = React.createClass({
 getInitialState: function() {
  return {
   clicking: false
  }
 },
 _onPressIn: function() {
  this.setState({clicking: true});
 },
 _onPressOut: function() {
  this.setState({clicking: false});
 },
 render: function() {
  return (
   <View style={styles.container}>
    <TouchableHighlight
     onPressIn={this._onPressIn}
     onPressOut={this._onPressOut}
     style={styles.touchable}>
     <View style={styles.button}>
      <Text style={styles.welcome}>
       {this.state.pressing ? 'EEK!' : 'PUSH ME'}
      </Text>
     </View>
    </TouchableHighlight>
   </View>
  );
 }
});
```

```
var styles = StyleSheet.create({
 container: {
  flex: 1,
  justifyContent: 'center',
  alignItems: 'center',
  backgroundColor: '#F5FCFF',
 },
 welcome: {
  fontSize: 20,
  textAlign: 'center',
  margin: 10,
  color: '#FFFFFF'
 },
 touchable: {
  borderRadius: 100
 },
 button: {
  backgroundColor: '#FF0000',
  borderRadius: 100,
  height: 200,
  width: 200,
  justifyContent: 'center'
 },
});
module.exports = Button;
```

Try setting this button to respond to other events using hooks such as Press and on LongPress. The way to get an idea of how these events relate to user interaction is to test using a real device.

GESTURERESPONDER SYSTEM

What if you want more than just to make things "fun"? React Native also introduces two custom touch management APIs: ActionResponder and PanResponder. GestureResponder is a low-level API, while PanResponder provides useful captions. We will begin by looking at how the GestureResponder system works because it is the basis of PanResponderAPI.

Touch on mobile is very complex. Most mobile platforms can only support multitouch, which means that there can be multiple active touch points on the display at the same time. (However, not all of these finger-prints; consider the difficulty of, for example, finding the palm of the user in the corner of the screen.) Additionally, there is a problem of which view should handle a given touch. This problem is similar to the way mouse events are handled on the web, and the default behavior is also the same: the top child has an auto-touch event. With React Native's touch system, however, we can reverse this behavior if we choose to do so.

The touch responder is an idea that captures a given touch event. In the last section, we saw that the <TouchableHighlight> section acts as a touch response. We can make our parts a touch response, too. The life cycle discussed in this process is a bit complicated. The idea you want to get in touch with the touch responder should use four accessories:

1. View.props.onStartShouldSetResponder

2. View.props.onMoveShouldSetResponder

3. View.props.onResponderGrant

4. View.props.onResponderReject

A view can request to be the responder during the *begin* or the move phase. This behavior is by onStartShouldSetResponder and onMoveShouldSetResponder. When these functions return true, the view attempts to claim responder status.

After an idea has been attempted to claim respondent status, your attempt has been rejected. Appropriate callback or RResponderGrantoron ResponderReject – will be requested.

The responder ignores functions that are called in a bubbling pattern. If more views try to find the status of the respondent, the deeper part will be the respondent. This is usually the desired behavior; if not, you will have difficulty adding the affected parts as buttons to the larger view. If you want to write over this behavior, parent sections can use onStartShouldSetResponderCapture and onMoveShouldSetResponderCapture. Returning the truth from any of these will prevent the children of the party from being a touch response.

After the view successfully seeks out the status of the touch responder, it is appropriate holders can be called. Here is an excerpt from the GestureResponder:

```
View.props.onResponderMove: It is responder is works
when user is moving her finger
```

```
View.props.onResponderRelease: It is responder is
works when user fired at the end of the touch (i.e.,
"touchUp")
View.props.onResponderTerminationRequest: If
something else you want to become responder. Should
the view release the responder?: Returning true
allows release
View.props.onResponderTerminat:Responder removed
from view. It may take another 1 look after the call
toonResponderTerminationRequest, or OS without
question (happens via the control center /
notification center on iOS).
```

In most cases, you will be more concerned with RespondingMoveReport. All of these methods get the action of the touch event, attached to the following format (again, quoted in documents):

```
changedTouches: It is an array of all touch events
that have changed since the last event
Identifier: The ID of the touch
location: The X position is relative to the element
location: The Y position is relative to the element
pageX: The X position is relative to the screen
pageY: The Y position is relative to the screen
Target: The node id of receiving the touch event
Timestamp : A time identifier is useful for velocity
calculation
 It touches Array of all current touches on the
screen
```

You can use this information when deciding whether to respond to an event. Maybe your vision only cares about the touch of two fingers, for example. This is a low-level API; if you want to find and respond to touch in this way, you will need to spend a good time adjusting the correct parameters and finding out what values you should be concerned about. In the section, we will look at PanResponder, which provides high-quality user friendly interpretation.

PanResponder

Unlike <TouchableHighlight>, PanResponder is not a part but a class assigned to React Native. It provides a higher-level API than the basic events detected by the Gesture Responder program while still providing access to those green events. A PanResponder gesture Stateobject provides you access to the following, in accordance with PanResponder documents:

```
stateID: ID of the gestureState (there at least
single touch on screen)
moveX: The screen coordinates of the moved touch
recently
moveY: The screen coordinates of the moved touch
recently
x0: It is a screen coordinates of the responder
grant for x axis
y0: It is a screen coordinates of the responder
grant
```

for y axis

```
dx: It accumulated distance of the gesture since the
touch started
dy: It accumulated distance of the gesture since the
touch started
vx: It is a current velocity of the gesture
vy: It is a current velocity of the gesture
numberActiveTouches: It is a number of touches
currently on screen
```

As you can see, in addition to the green area data, a gesture Stateobject also includes information such as current touch speeds and aggregated distances.

In order to use the PanResponder in component, we need to create a PanResponder object and attach it to the component in a subformat.

To create a PanResponder we need to specify the appropriate PanResponder events holders

Creating a PanResponder requires us to pass a set of callbacks

```
this._panResponder = PanResponder.create({
# this._handleStartShouldSetPanResponder,
# this._handleMoveShouldSetPanResponder,
#  onStartShouldSetPanResponder:
# onPanResponderMove: this._handlePanResponderMove,
```

```
# onPanResponderTerminate:
this._handlePanResponderEnd,
});
```

Then, we use syntax to attach the PanResponder to the view in the component's render method

Attaching the PanResponder using spread syntax

```
render: function() {
 return (
  <View
   {...this._panResponder.panHandlers}>
   { /* View contents here */ }
  </View>
  );
}
```

After this, the holders you have transferred to PanResponder.create call will be requested during the appropriate action events if a touch appears within this view.

Example 4.7 shows a modified version of the PanResponder model code provided for React Native. This version listens to touch events in the container view, in contrast to just a circle, so the values are printed on the screen as you interact with the app. If you plan to use your touch sensors, I suggest you try this app on a real device to get a feel of how these values respond. It shows a screenshot of this example, but you will need help with a device with a real touch screen.

Touch/PanDemo.js explain the use of PanResponder

```
// Adapted from below github link
// xlink:href="https://github.com/facebook/react
-native/blob/master/">https://github.com/facebook/
react-native/blob/master/
// Examples/UIExplorer/PanResponderExample.js
'use strict';
var React = require('react-native');
var {
 StyleSheet,
 PanResponder,
```

```
View,
Text
} = React;
var CIRCLE_SIZE = 40;
var CIRCLE_COLOR = 'blue';
var CIRCLE_HIGHLIGHT_COLOR = 'green';
var PanResponderExample = React.createClass({
// Set some initial values.
_panResponder: {},
_previousLeft: 0,
_previousTop: 0,
_circleStyles: {},
circle: null,
getInitialState: function() {
 return {
  numberActiveTouches: 0,
  moveX: 0,
  moveY: 0,
  x0: 0,
  y0: 0,
  dx: 0,
  dy: 0,
  vx: 0,
  vy: 0,
  }
},
componentWillMount: function() {
 this._panResponder = PanResponder.create({
  onStartShouldSetPanResponder:
  this._handleStartShouldSetPanResponder,
  onMoveShouldSetPanResponder:
  this._handleMoveShouldSetPanResponder,
  onPanResponderGrant:
  this._handlePanResponderGrant,
  onPanResponderMove: this._handlePanResponderMove,
  onPanResponderRelease:
   this._handlePanResponderEnd,
  onPanResponderTerminate:
  this._handlePanResponderEnd,
  });
 this._previousLeft = 20;
 this._previousTop = 84;
```

```
   this._circleStyles = {
    left: this._previousLeft,
    top: this._previousTop,
   };
  },
  componentDidMount: function() {
   this._updatePosition();
  },
  render: function() {
   return (
    <View style={styles.container}>
     <View
      ref={(circle) => {
       this.circle = circle;
      }}
      style={styles.circle}
      {...this._panResponder.panHandlers}/>
     <Text>
      {this.state.numberActiveTouches} touches,
      dx: {this.state.dx},
      dy: {this.state.dy},
      vx: {this.state.vx},
      vy: {this.state.vy}
     </Text>
    </View>
   );
  },
  // It is _highlight and _unHighlight get called by
  PanResponder methods,
  // It is providing visual feedback to the user.
  _highlight: function() {
   this.circle && this.circle.setNativeProps({
    backgroundColor: CIRCLE_HIGHLIGHT_COLOR
   });
  },
  _unHighlight: function() {
   this.circle && this.circle.setNativeProps({
    backgroundColor: CIRCLE_COLOR (any color passed
  as arguments)
   });
  },
```

```
// We are controlling the circle's position
directly with setNativeProps.
_updatePosition: function() {
 this.circle && this.circle.setNativePr
ops(this._circleStyles);
 },
 _handleStartShouldSetPanResponder:
 function(e: Object, gestureState: Object): boolean
{
 // It should become active when the user presses
down on the circle.
 return true;
 },
 _handleMoveShouldSetPanResponder:
 function(e: Object, gestureState: Object): boolean
{
 //It should we become active when the user moves a
touch over the circle.
 return true;
 },
 _handlePanResponderGrant: function(e: Object,
gestureState: Object) {
 this._highlight();
 },
 _handlePanResponderMove: function(e: Object,
gestureState: Object) {
 this.setState({
  stateID: gestureState.stateID,
  moveX: gestureState.moveX,
  moveY: gestureState.moveY,
  x0: gestureState.x0,
  y0: gestureState.y0,
  dx: gestureState.dx,
  dy: gestureState.dy,
  vx: gestureState.vx,
  vy: gestureState.vy,
  numberActiveTouches: gestureState.
numberActiveTouches
 });
 // Calculate current position using deltas
 this._circleStyles.left = this._previousLeft +
gestureState.dx;
```

```
    this._circleStyles.top = this._previousTop +
gestureState.dy;
    this._updatePosition();
  },
  _handlePanResponderEnd: function(e: Object,
gestureState: Object) {
    this._unHighlight();
    this._previousLeft += gestureState.dx;
    this._previousTop += gestureState.dy;
  },
});
var styles = StyleSheet.create({
  circle: {
    width: CIRCLE_SIZE,
    height: CIRCLE_SIZE,
    borderRadius: CIRCLE_SIZE / 2,
    backgroundColor: CIRCLE_COLOR,
    position: 'absolute',
    left: 0,
    top: 0,
  },
  container: {
    flex: 1,
    paddingTop: 64,
  },
});
module.exports = PanResponderExample;
```

CHOOSING A TOUCH MANAGEMENT METHOD

You should decide when to use the touch and APIs discussed in this section. It depends on what you want to build. To give the user a basic response and to indicate that the button or other element is "touching," use the <TouchableHighlight> section. To use your custom touch links, use the green GestureResponder system, or PanResponder. Chances are you will always love the PanResponder method because it also gives you access to the simple touch events offered by the GestureResponder system. If you begin designing a game, or an application with interactions, then you need to spend time building the interaction you want by using these APIs.

For other applications, you do not need to implement any custom touch handling with either the Gesture Responder system or the PanResponder. In the next section, we have looked at some of the higher-level components that implement common UI patterns for you.

WORKING WITH ORGANIZATIONAL COMPONENTS

In this section, we will look at parts of the organization that you can use to control the normal flow within your application. This includes <TabView>, <NavigatorView>, and <ListView>, all using some of the most common mobile interactions and navigation patterns. Once you have set up your app navigation flow, you will find that these components are very helpful in making your application more realistic.

Using ListView

Let us start with the <ListView> component. In this section, you will create an app that lists *The New York Times'* bestsellers list and allows us to view data about each book. If you would like, you can claim your API token from *The New York Times*. If not, use the API token encoded in the sample code.

The list is very useful for mobile development, and you will notice that many mobile user links include them as a central object. A <ListView> is simply viewing, optional with special viewers of categories, titles, or footer. For example, you can see the interaction pattern in Dropbox, Twitter, and iOS apps.

<ListView> is a good example of where React Native shines because it can use its host domain. For mobile, the traditional part of <ListView> is often greatly improved so that the presentation is smooth and language free. If you expect to give a very large amount of items to your <ListView>, you should try to keep the child's view easy, to try to minimize stuttering. The basic React Native <ListView> component has two props: dataSource and renderRow data. The source, as the name implies, is a source of information about the data that needs to be provided. The renderRow should return the data-based component from a single data source element.

This basic usage is explained in SimpleList.js. We will start by adding a dataSource to our <SimpleList> component. A ListView.DataSource needs to implement the rowHasChanged method. Here is a simple example:

```
var ds = new ListView.DataSource({rowHasChanged:
(r1, r2) => r1 !== r2});
```

To set the right contents of a dataSource, we use cloneWithRows. Let us return the dataSource in our getInitialState call:

getInitialState: **function**() {

```
var ds = new ListView.DataSource({rowHasChanged:
(r1, r2) => r1 !== r2});
return {
 dataSource: ds.cloneWithRows(['a', 'b', 'c', 'a
longer example', 'd', 'e'])
 };
}
```

Another prop we need is renderRow, which should be a function that returns some of the JSX-based data for a given row:

```
_renderRow: function(rowData) {
 return <Text style={styles.row}>{rowData}</Text>;
}
```

Now we can put it all together to see a simple <ListView>, by rendering a <ListView> like so:

```
<ListView
 dataSource={this.state.dataSource}
 renderRow={this._renderRow}
/>
```

Let us create a <ListView> with more complex data. We will use the NY Times API to create a Sellers application, which renders the NY Times Seller list.

First, we initialize the data source to be empty because we will need to fetch the data:

```
getInitialState: function() {
 var ds = new ListView.DataSource({rowHasChanged:
(r1, r2) => r1 !== r2});
 return {
  dataSource: ds.cloneWithRows([])
 };
}
```

Then, we can also add a method for fetching and updating the data once we have it. The method gets called from componentDidMount:

```
_refreshData: function() {
 var endpoint =
```

```
'http://api.nytimes.com/svc/books/v3/lists/
hardcover-fiction?response-format
=json&api-key=' + API_KEY;
fetch(endpoint)
  .then((response) => response.json())
  .then((rjson) => {
  this.setState({
    dataSource: this.state.dataSource.cloneWithRow
s(rjson.results.books)
    });
  });
}
```

Each book returned by the NYTimes APIs has three properties: cover-URL, author, and title.

We update the <ListView> function to return a component based on those props.

For _renderRow, we only pass along the suitable data to the <BookItem>

```
_renderRow: function(rowData) {
  return <BookItem coverURL={rowData.book_image}
          title={rowData.title}
          author={rowData.author}/>;
},
```

We will also toss in a header and footer component and how these work. Note that for a <ListView>, the header and footer are not that sticky; even they scroll with the rest of the list. If you want a sticky header or footer, it is probably easiest to render them separately from the <ListView> component.

Adding methods render to header and footer elements in BookListV2.js

```
_renderHeader: function() {
  return (<View style={styles.sectionDivider}>
  <Text style={styles.headingText}>
  Bestsellers in Hardcover Fiction
  </Text>
  </View>);
},
```

```
_renderFooter: function() {
 return(
  <View style={styles.sectionDivider}>
   <Text>
    The data from the New York Times Seller list.
   </Text>
  </View>
  );
},
```

Altogether, the Sellers application consists of two files: BookListV2.js and BookItem.js. BookListV2.js is shown in Example 4.10. (BookList.js is a simpler file that fetches data from an API, and also included in the GitHub repository for your reference.)

Bestsellers/BookListV2.js

```
'use strict';
var React = require('react-native');
var {
 Text,
 View,
 Image,
 StyleSheet,
 ListView,
} = React;
var BookItem = require('./BookItem');
var API_KEY = '73b19491b83909c7e07016f4bb4644f9:2
:60667290';
var QUERY_TYPE = 'hardcover-fiction';
var API_STEM = 'http://api.nytimes.com/svc/books/v3/
lists'
var ENDPOINT = `${API_STEM}/${QUERY_TYPE}?response
-format=json&api-key=${API_KEY}`;
var BookList = React.createClass({
 getInitialState: function() {
  var ds = new ListView.DataSource({rowHasChanged:
(r1, r2) => r1 !== r2});
  return {
   dataSource: ds.cloneWithRows([])
  };
 },
```

```
componentDidMount: function() {
 this._refreshData();
},
_renderRow: function(rowData) {
 return <BookItem coverURL={rowData.book_image}
 title={rowData.title}
 author={rowData.author}/>;
},
_renderHeader: function() {
 return (<View style={styles.sectionDivider}>
  <Text style={styles.headingText}>
   Bestsellers in Hardcover Fiction
  </Text>
  </View>);
},
_renderFooter: function() {
 return(
  <View style={styles.sectionDivider}>
   <Text>Data from the New York Times Best Seller
list.</Text>
  </View>
  );
},
_refreshData: function() {
 fetch(ENDPOINT)
  .then((response) => response.json())
  .then((rjson) => {
   this.setState({
    dataSource: this.state.dataSource.cloneWithRow
s(rjson.results.books)
   });
  });
},
render: function() {
 return (
  <ListView
   style=
   dataSource={this.state.dataSource}
   renderRow={this._renderRow}
   renderHeader={this._renderHeader}
   renderFooter={this._renderFooter}
   />
```

```
    );
  }
});
var styles = StyleSheet.create({
 container: {
  flex: 1,
  justifyContent: 'center',
  alignItems: 'center',
  backgroundColor: '#FFFFFF',
  paddingTop: 24
 },
 list: {
  flex: 1,
  flexDirection: 'row'
 },
 listContent: {
  flex: 1,
  flexDirection: 'column'
 },
 row: {
  flex: 1,
  fontSize: 24,
  padding: 42,
  borderWidth: 1,
  borderColor: '#DDDDDD'
 },
 sectionDivider: {
  padding: 8,
  backgroundColor: '#EEEEEE',
  alignItems: 'center'
 },
 headingText: {
  flex: 1,
  fontSize: 24,
  alignSelf: 'center'
 }
});
module.exports = BookList;
```

The <BookItem> is a simple component that can also handle rendering each child view in the list

Bestsellers/BookItem.js

```
'use strict;
var React = require('react-native');
var {
 StyleSheet,
 Text,
 View,
 Image,
 ListView,
} = React;
var styles = StyleSheet.create({
 bookItem: {
  flex: 1,
  flexDirection: 'row',
  backgroundColor: '#FFFFFF',
  borderBottomColor: '#AAAAAA',
  borderBottomWidth: 2,
  padding: 5
 },
 cover: {
  flex: 1,
  height: 150,
  resizeMode: 'contain'
 },
 info: {
  flex: 3,
  alignItems: 'flex-end',
  flexDirection: 'column',
  alignSelf: 'center',
  padding: 20
 },
 author: {
  fontSize: 18
 },
 title: {
  fontSize: 18,
  fontWeight: 'bold'
 }
});
var BookItem = React.createClass({
 propTypes: {
```

```
    coverURL: React.PropTypes.string.isRequired,
    author: React.PropTypes.string.isRequired,
    title: React.PropTypes.string.isRequired
  },
  render: function() {
  return (
    <View style={styles.bookItem}>
     <Image style={styles.cover} source=/>
     <View style={styles.info}>
      <Text style={styles.author}>{this.props.aut
hor}</Text>
      <Text style={styles.title}>{this.props.title}</
Text>
     </View>
     </View>
     );
  }
});
module.exports = BookItem;
```

If you have complex data, or a very long list, you will need to pay attention to enabled functionality in some of the more complex <ListView> layouts of your choice. However, for most applications, this will suffice.

USING NAVIGATORS

<ListView> is a great example of combining multiple views together into a more usable collaboration. At the highest level, we can use features such as <Navigator> to present different application screens, just as we may have different pages on a website.

The Navigator is a hidden but key component and is used in many common applications. For example, the iOS Settings app can be used as a combination of <Navigator> and multiple <ListView> components. The Dropbox app also uses Navigator.

<Navigator> allows your application to switch between different screens (commonly referred to as "scenes"), while keeping "multiple" routes, so you can push, pop, or rotate regions. You can think as similar to the history API on the web. "Route" is the screen title, which corresponds to the index.

For example, in the Settings application, initially, the stack is empty. If you select one of the submenus, the first group is pushed into the stack. The "back" tap, in the upper left corner of the screen, will close it again.

If you are interested in how these play, UIExplorerapp has a good demo of a few ways to use the Navigator API. Note that there are two Navigator options: cross-platform <Navigator> component and <NavigatorIOS> component. In this book, we will choose to use <Navigator>.

OTHER ORGANIZATIONAL COMPONENTS

There are a lot of other parts of the organization, too. For example, a few ones include <TabBarIOS> and <SegmentedControlIOS> and <DrawerLayoutAndroid> and <ToolbarAndroid>.

You will notice that all of these are named with field-specific appendixes. That is because they are loading native APIs into field-specific UI elements.

These features are useful for setting up multiple screens within your app. <TabBarIOS> and <DrawerLayoutAndroid>, for example, give an easy way to switch between multiple functions. <SegmentedControlIOS> and <ToolbarAndroid> are suited for well-analyzed controls.

You will want to look at the field-specific design guidelines on how to best use these components:

- Android Interface Design Guide

- iOS Interface Design Guidelines

How do you make use of platform-specific components? Let us now take a look at how to handle platform-specific components in cross-platform applications.

PLATFORM-SPECIFIC COMPONENTS

Not every component is available on all platforms, and even not all interaction patterns are appropriate for all devices. It doesn't mean that you cannot use platform-specific code in your application, though! In this section, we will cover platform-specific components, as well as strategies for how to incorporate them in your cross-platform applications.

iOS- or Android-Only Components

Some components are available on a specific platform. It includes things like <TabBarIOS> or <SwitchAndroid>. They are usually platform specific because they wrap some kind of underlying platform-specific API. For some components, having a platform-agnostic version does not make sense. For example, the <ToolbarAndroid> component exposes an Android-specific API for a view type that does not exist on iOS anyway.

Platform-specific components are named after the appropriate appendix: IOS or Android. If you try to install one in the wrong place, your application will crash.

Components can also have field-specific resources. These are tagged in documents with a small badge indicating their use. For instance, <TextInput> has props that are platform-agnostic, others that are specific to iOS or Android

Components with Platform-Specific Versions

So, how can you handle platform-specific components or props in a cross-platform application? The good news is that you still use these components. Keep in mind how the app has both an index.ios.js and an index .android.js file. The naming convention can be used for any file to create a component that has different implementations on Android and iOS.

As an example, we will use the <SwitchIOS> and <SwitchAndroid> components. They reveal slightly different APIs, but what if we just want to use a simple switch? Let's create a wrap-up section, <Switch>, which provides a specific section for the forum.

We will start by implementing switch.ios.js. It's a quite simple wrapper around <SwitchIOS>, and allows us to provide a callback for when the switch value changes.

Switch.ios.js

```
var React = require('react-native');
var { SwitchIOS } = React;
var Switch = React.createClass({
 getInitialState() {
  return {value: false};
 },
 _onValueChange(value) {
  this.setState({value: value});
  if (this.props.onValueChange) {
   this.props.onValueChange(value);
  }
 },
 render() {
  return (
```

```
    <SwitchIOS
     onValueChange={this._onValueChange}
     value={this.state.value}/>
    );
  }
});
module.exports = Switch;
```

Next, let us implement switch.android.js

Switch.android.js

```
var React = require('react-native');
var { SwitchAndroid } = React;
var Switch = React.createClass({
 getInitialState() {
  return {value: false};
 },
 _onValueChange(value) {
  this.setState({value: value});
  if (this.props.onValueChange) {
   this.props.onValueChange(value);
  }
 },
 render() {
  return (
   <SwitchAndroid
    onValueChange={this._onValueChange}
    value={this.state.value}/>
   );
  }
});
module.exports = Switch;
```

Note that it looks almost identical to switch.ios.js, and it implements the same API. The difference is that it uses <SwitchAndroid> instead of <SwitchIOS>. We can now import our <Switch> component from another file with the syntax:

```
var Switch = require('./switch');
...
```

```
var switchComp = <Switch onValueChange={(val) =>
{console.log(val); }}/>;
```

Let us actually use the <Switch> component. Create a new file, CrossPlatform.js, and also include the code shown below. We have the background color change based on the current value of a <Switch>.

CrossPlatform.js Makes Use of the <Switch> Component

```
var React = require('react-native');
var {
Text,
 View,
 StyleSheet,
} = React;
var Switch = require('./switch');
var CrossPlatform = React.createClass({
 getInitialState() {
  return {val: false};
 },
 _onValueChange(val) {
  this.setState({val: val});
 },
 render: function() {
  var colorClass = this.state.val ? styles.
blueContainer : styles.redContainer;
  return (
   <View style={[styles.container, colorClass]}>
    <Text style={styles.welcome}>
     Make me blue!
    </Text>
    <Switch onValueChange={this._onValueChange}/>
   </View>
  );
 }
});
var styles = StyleSheet.create({
 container: {
  flex: 1,
  justifyContent: 'center',
  alignItems: 'center',
 },
```

```
blueContainer: {
  backgroundColor: '#5555FF'
},
redContainer: {
  backgroundColor: '#FF5555'
},
welcome: {
  fontSize: 20,
  textAlign: 'center',
  margin: 10,
}
});
module.exports = CrossPlatform;
```

Note that there is also a switch.jsfile, but we can callrequire (./ switch). The React Native package will automatically select the right application based on our platform, and use the appropriate eitherswitch.ios.jsorswitch.android.jsas. Lastly, return the contents of index.android.js and index .ios.jsso so that we can provide the <CrossPlatform> section. The files of index.ios.js and index.android.js should be identical, and they may simply import a crossplatform.js file.

```
var React = require('react-native');
var { AppRegistry } = React;
var CrossPlatform = require('./crossplatform');
AppRegistry.registerComponent('PlatformSpecific',
  () => CrossPlatform);
```

Now we can run application on both iOS and Android .

WHEN TO USE PLATFORM-SPECIFIC COMPONENTS

When is it appropriate to use the field-specific section? In most cases, you will want to do so when there is an interaction pattern specific to the platform to which you want your application to adhere. If you want the application to feel truly "traditional," it is worth paying attention to the UI-specific UI processes.

Apple and Google both provide guidelines for human interaction on their platforms, which should be discussed:

- IOS Human Interface Guidelines

- Android Design Reference

By creating field-specific versions only for specific sections, you can achieve a balance between reusing code and customizing field-based customization. In most cases, you should need a separate use of a few components to support both iOS and Android.

SUMMARY

In this chapter, we have covered various details of the most important aspects of React Native. We have discussed how to use low-level basic components, such as <Text> ,<Image>, as well as advanced order components such as <ListView>, <Navigator>, and <TabBarIOS>. We looked at how you can use different touch-focused APIs and components if you want to build your own custom touch handles. Finally, we saw how to use the field-specific components in our programs.

At this point, you should be able to build basic, functional apps using React Native! Now that you are familiar with the features discussed in this chapter, building on them and integrating them to make your own apps you should feel incredibly similar to working with React on the web.

Of course, building basic, functional applications is part of the battle. In the next chapter, we will focus on styling, as well as how to use React Native styles to get the look and feel you want on a mobile phone.

CONCLUSION

In this chapter, we learned about analogies between HTML elements and native components working with touch and gestures working with organizational components platform-specific components, and in the next chapter we are going to learn about styles in React Native.

Styles and Layouts

IN THIS CHAPTER

➤ Styles

➤ Declaring and manipulating styles

➤ Organization and inheritance

➤ Positioning and designing layouts

In the previous chapter, we learned about components for mobile, what they are and how they are used. In this chapter, we are going to learn about styles offered by React Native.

React Native projects adapt to the way in which they can be organized, especially when it comes to the use of style. We find many differences between the applications we run in the way they set up and organize styles. This leads to more overhead when new features of new projects are created and sometimes projects that reside in certain patterns make it difficult to duplicate in construction.

We have learned a few simple strategies that will lead us to more exciting activities as we work on React Native projects. Here are some of the ideas for using styles to enhance ergonomics and readability. This allows us to develop and replicate designs quickly, easily, and consistently.

If you would like to learn by looking directly at a particular code, we have included a small template application to show these ideas. You can find it here: RNStylingTemplate

DOI: 10.1201/9781003310440-5

1. STYLES ARE IMPORTANT: MAKE THEM EASY TO FIND

Keep styles in the root source folder.

Styling is a beginner class concern with as styles that can be accessible from a top folder in the application code.

```
MyReactNativeApp

  - src

      - assets

      - compontents

      - MyComponent.js

  - styles

      - colors.js

      - index.js

      - typography.js

      - ...

  ...
```

We refer to styles in almost every category and making them as accessible as possible will result in pure code.

Another way is to reduce the use of. / 's in our related systems. This not only reduces the amount of overhead in calculating the folders placed in the nest, but also allows for simplicity and understanding as the project progresses.

```
import { MyStyles } from "../styles"
```

is easier to work with than:
```
import { MyStyles } from "../../../../common/utils/
styles/my_styles"
```

2. GET ATOMIC!

Build complicated styles from simpler styles.

By using object construction in a style announcement, we get really short and readable styles that allow us to advertise in our sections.

```
// buttons.js
export const small = {
paddingHorizontal: 10,
paddingVertical: 12,
width: 75
};
export const rounded = {
borderRadius: 50
};
export const smallRounded = {
...base,
...small,
...rounded
};
// src/MyComponent/index.js
const styles = StyleSheet.create({
button: {
...Buttons.smallRounded,
},
})
```

It is easier to understand the intent and maintain than:

```
// src/MyComponent/index.js
const styles = StyleSheet.create({
button: {
paddingHorizontal: 10,
paddingVertical: 12,
width: 75,
borderRadius: 50
},
})
```

3. STYLES ARE IMPORTANT: MAKE THEM EASY TO USE

Group the same variables into modules and bundle them into an index .jsfile. The flexibility of the style is easy to find and understand when it is planned for work. Therefore, they must live with purposeful files. When we place an index.jsin in this folder, we can use JavaScript ES6 to import syntax for importing all styles at once.

- styles

- colors.js

- index.js

- spacing.js

- typography.js

- buttons.js

```
// src/styles/index.js
import * as Buttons from './buttons'
import * as Colors from './colors'
import * as Spacing from './spacing'
import * as Typography from './typography'
export { Typography, Spacing, Colors, Buttons }
```

This allows us to:

- import only what we need

- import from the same file every time

- give the variables descriptive, short names that are contained in a descriptive object.

- easily extend and modify the common styles

- write more concise and expressive code.

```
// src/MyComponent/index.js
import { Typography, Colors, Spacing } from '../
styles'
...
const styles = StyleSheet.create({
container: {
backgroundColor: Colors.background,
alignItems: 'center',
padding: Spacing.base,
},
header: {
flex: 1,
...Typography.mainHeader,
},
section: {
flex: 3,
...Typography.section,
```

```
}
})
```

is better than:

```
// src/MyComponent/index.js
import {
largePadding,
smallest,
small,
large,
base,
} from '../../../common/utils/styles/spacing'
import {
largeRadius,
baseTextColor,
headerFontSize,
smallFontSize,
} from '../../../common/utils/styles/common'
import { background, shuttleGray } from '../../../
common/utils/styles/colors'
const styles = StyleSheet.create({
container: {
backgroundColor: background,
padding: largePadding,
},
header: {
flex: 1,
alignItems: 'center',
backgroundColor: '#b7bdc5',
flexDirection: 'row',
justifyContent: 'center',
borderRadius: largeRadius,
color: shuttleGray,
fontSize: headerFontSize,
 paddingBottom: base,
},
section: {
flex: 3,
alignItems: 'center',
backgroundColor: background,
flexDirection: 'row',
```

```
justifyContent: 'center',
borderRadius: largeRadius,
color: baseTextColor,
fontSize: smallFontSize,
lineHeight: 19,
}
})
```

This summarizes the consensus of constantly pulling styles from the same place includes significant savings in the development period throughout the project life.

4. KEEP STYLES CLOSE

The simplicity of needing only to update a single file to improve one style change in part is fast and leads to fewer errors. Keep StyleSheets in line with sections. Defining StyleSheets in files similar to your part can help ensure that:

- styles of one section will not be written over another section in future repetitions;

- styles will be maintained as the segment grows;

- parts may change during design duplication;

- there is a small amount of mental overhead while using component designs as there is one area to look at styles than many.

One of the reasons you may want to not use online style sheets is to reduce the number of repetitions in code, but now that you are creating global style variables in files with active names, you can still remember to do D.R.Y. (Do not duplicate) coding, without reusing the style sheets themselves.

```
// src/MyNewComponent/index.js
import { Typography } from '../styles'
const MyNewComponent = () => (
<View style={styles.container}>
<View style={styles.header}>
<MyComponent />
</View>
 <View style={styles.body}>
<MyOtherComponent />
```

```
<View>
</View>
)
const styles = StyleSheet.create({
container: {
flex: 1,
},
header: {
...Typography.header
 },
 body: {
  ...Typography.body
},
})
```

is more self-contained than:

```
// src/MyNewComponent/index.js
import { styleSheetA, styleSheetB, styleSheetC }
from './stylesheets'
const MyNewComponent = () => (
<View style={styleSheetC.container}>
<View style={styleSheetA.header}>
<MyComponent />
</View>
 <View style={styleSheetB.body}>
<MyOtherComponent />
<View>
</View>
)
```

The simplicity of needing only to update a single file to improve one style change in part is fast and leads to fewer errors.

Caveats

What we have shown here works well as a start for us and our customers, but JavaScript and React Native are big and fast. There is no one-size-fits-all solution for projects, so distance may vary.

Larger projects with hundreds of components or projects with specific business needs may benefit from different patterns. Parts with themes and styles that are not in line, for example, some patterns may work better in your particular situation.

It is all a trade-off and here, we prepare for the speed and clarity of design implementation. Eventually you will need to replicate and find out what works for your project and team.

With React Native, you create the style for your application using JavaScript. All major components adopt a prop-styled prop style. The names and style are usually consistent with the way CSS works on the web, with the exception of words written using camel skin, e.g., backgrounder is the background color.

Styleprop can be an old JavaScript object. That is what we usually use as an example code. You can also skip many styles – the last style in the list is advanced, so you can use this to get styles as an asset.

As the segment grows more complex, it is often convenient to use the Style Sheet.create to define a few styles in one place. Here is an example:

One common pattern is accepting the styleprop which is used to style the lower parts. You can use this to make styling the way they do in CSS. There are many ways to customize the text style. See the References section of the text for a complete list.

Now you can make your text beautiful. The next step in becoming a stylist is learning how to control part size. There are a few ways to make your elements in React Native. You can use style property to add styles to the line. However, this is not a particularly good practice because it can be difficult to read the code.

In this chapter, we will use Stylesheet to create style.

Container Component

In this section, we will simplify the container component from our previous chapter.

App.js

```
import React from 'react';
import { StyleSheet, Text, View } from
'react-native';
import PresentationalComponent from './
PresentationalComponent'
export default class App extends React.Component {
state = {
myState: 'This is my state'
}
render() {
```

```
return (
<View>
<PresentationalComponent myState = {this.state.mySt
ate}/>
</View>
);
}
}
```

Presentational Component
In the following example, we shall import the *StyleSheet*. At the bottom of the file, you will create your stylesheet and assign it to the *style's* constant. Note that your styles are in *camelCase* and we do not use *px* or % for styling.

To apply styles to any text, we add *style = {styles.myText}* property to the *Text* element.

```
import React, { Component } from 'react';
import {StyleSheet , Text, View, } from
'react-native';
const PresentationalComponent = (props) => {
return (
<View>
<Text style = {styles.myState}>
{props.myState}
</Text>
</View>
)
}
export default PresentationalComponent
const styles = StyleSheet.create ({
myState: {
marginTop: 20,
textAlign: 'center',
color: 'blue',
 fontWeight: 'bold',
fontSize: 20
}
})
```

When we run this application, we will receive the following output.

REACT NATIVE STYLE METHOD

React Native gives us two powerful ways to automatically write our app:

Style Props

You can add style to your section using style props by simply adding style props to your element to accommodate the architectural object.

```
Import React,{Component}from 'react';
import {Platform, StyleSheet, Text, View} from
'react-native';
export default class App extends Component<Props> {
render() {
return (
<View style={{flex:1,justifyContent:"left",backgrou
ndColor:"#fff", alignItems:"center"}}>
<View style={{width:250,height:50,backgroundColor:"
red",padding:10}}>
<Text style={{fontSize:20, color:"#666"}}>Styled
with style props</Text>
</View>
</View>
);
}
}
```

If you look at our code using CSS-enabled features, note that some properties are not supported traditionally, an error will occur if you try to use any unsupported assets. CSS3 animations are not supported by React Native.

REACT NATIVE APPLICATION: THE FLEXBOX ARCHITECTURE

It is a great tool for defining the structure of your React Native application, elsewhere it doesn't work in the same way as CSS but is actually easier to use and more flexible.

```
import React, {Component} from 'react';
import { Text, View} from 'react-native';
export default class App extends Component<Props> {
render() {
return (
<View style={{flex:1,justifyContent:"center",backgr
oundColor:"#000", alignItems:"stretch"}}>
```

```
<View style={{flex:1,backgroundColor:"red"}}>
<Text style={{fontSize:20, color:"#fff"}}>Item
number 1</Text>
</View>
<View style={{flex:1,backgroundColor:"blue"}}>
<Text style={{fontSize:20, color:"#fff"}}>Item
number 1</Text>
</View>
<View style={{flex:1,backgroundColor:"purple"}}>
<Text style={{fontSize:20, color:"#fff"}}>Item
number 1</Text>
</View>
<View style={{flex:1,backgroundColor:"orange"}}>
<Text style={{fontSize:20, color:"#fff"}}>Item
number 1</Text>
</View>
</View>
);
}
}
```

React Native flexbox is a wonderful way to deal with the layout. Manipulation is so easy. You can design the layout but you need some basic understanding of flexbox.

Using StyleSheet

If you have a large codebase or want to set multiple layouts in your elements, writing our style rules directly within the styles will make our code more complex which is why React Native gives us another option that allows us to write a shortcode using StylesSheet.

Example:

```
import { View, StyleSheet } from 'react-native';
```

To assign some styling properties use the create () method that can take an object with properties.

```
const styles = StyleSheet.create({
container: {
flex:1,
justifyContent:"center",
```

```
backgroundColor:"#fff",
alignItems:"stretch"
},
title: {
fontSize:20,
color:"#fff"
},
item1: {
backgroundColor:"orange",
flex:1
},
item2: {
backgroundColor:"purple",
flex:1
},
item3: {
backgroundColor:"yellow",
flex:1
},
item4: {
backgroundColor:"red",
flex:1
},
});
```

And then we pass the styling object to the component via the style props:

```
<View style={styles.container}>
<View style={styles.item1}>
<Text style={{fontSize:20, color:"#fff"}}>Item
number 1</Text>
</View>
<View style={styles.item2}>
<Text style={{fontSize:20, color:"#fff"}}>Item
number 1</Text>
</View>
<View style={styles.item3}>
<Text style={{fontSize:20, color:"#fff"}}>Item
number 1</Text>
</View>
<View style={styles.item4}>
<Text style={{fontSize:20, color:"#fff"}}>Item
number 1</Text>
```

```
</View>
</View>
```

Our code looks so concise with StyleSheet and the result is still the same as flexbox.

The styling method that Reacts Native uses has excellent features that allow us to do some dynamic styling but it is limited especially when it comes to applying some CSS properties that are not supported by React Native, for example, applying box-shadow to your components you may have to do the following:

```
const Card=()=>( <View style={styles.ca
rd}> <Text>Hello!</Text>
</View>
)//our style const styles=StyleSheer.create({card:{
width:100,
height:120,
shadowColor: '#000000',
  shadowOffset: {
  width: 0,
  height: 3
  },
  shadowRadius: 5,
  shadowOpacity: 1.0}
})
```

Whereas if you have to do the same then add shadow in CSS:

```
.card{
width:100px,
height:120px,
box-shadow:0 0 5 #000000;
}
```

It is easier to do it with CSS, we all would love to do the same in React Native; unfortunately, we cannot write CSS directly in React Native.

Styled-Component in React Native

Yes, you can now use the style and native section to record your styles in React Native as you would type in a standard CSS. It is easy to install in your project and does not require any link. Just use the following command in the root directory of your application to install it:

```
>>> yarn add styled-components
```

And then simply start using it in components:

```
import React, {Component} from 'react';
import { StyleSheet,Text, View} from 'react-native';
import styled from 'styled-components'
const container=styled.View`
flex:1;
padding:20px 0;
 justify-content:center;
background-color:#f4f4f4;
align-items:center
`
const Title=styled.Text`
font-size:20px;
text-align:center;
 color:red;
`
const Item=styled.View`
flex:1;
border:1px solid #ccc;
margin:2px 0;
border-radius:10px;
box-shadow:0 0 10px #ccc;
background-color:#fff;
width:80%;
padding:10px;
`
export default class App extends Component {
 render() {
  return (
   <Container>
      <Item >
      <Title >Item number 1</Title>
      </Item>
      <Item >
      <Title >Item number 2</Title>
      </Item>
      <Item >
      <Title >Item number 3</Title>
      </Item>
      <Item >
```

```
    <Title >Item number 4</Title>
    </Item>
  </Container>
 );
 }
}
```

Even though you can completely write CSS with React Native and we provide those elements made in style, I prefer to use style elements to make my React Native style a day as I have found that it supports React Native gives me more freedom to style I easily and use better-parts- from now on and get the benefits of CSS to make a nice UI make your code cleaner, you can split your styles into one file away from your parts that will make your code more. it is organized. on the other hand, you can use the best features that give us style elements such as theming and passing props to create a flexible style as follows:

```
import React, {Component} from 'react';
import { StyleSheet,Text, View} from 'react-native';
import styled from 'styled-components'
const container=styled.View`
  flex:1;
  padding:50px 0;
  justify-content:center;
  background-color:#f4f4f4;
  align-items:center
`

const Title=styled.Text`
font-size:20px;
text-align:center;
 color:red;
const Item=styled.View`
flex:1;
border:1px solid #ccc;
margin:2px 0;
border-radius:10px;
box-shadow:0 0 10px #ccc;
height:200px;
// execute a specific style based on the props
background-color:${props=>props.transparent?"red":"b
lue"};
width:80%;
```

```
padding:10px;
`

const Shape=styled.View`
clip-path: polygon(50% 0%, 0% 100%, 100% 100%);
`

export default class App extends Component {
 render() {
  return (
   <Container>
      <Item transparent>{/*pass the props to the
components*/}
      <Title >Item number 1</Title>
      </Item>
      <Item primary>
      <Title >Item number 1</Title>
      </Item>
      <Item transparent>
      <Title >Item number 1</Title>
      </Item>
      <Item primary>
      <Title >Item number 1</Title>
      </Item>
   </Container>
  );
 }
}
```

Sometimes you may want to draw some complex shapes that include circles and a specific background style or gradient as an example (the background of a CSS gradient is not based on React Native). You might consider using other CSS methods that provide like clip-path or any other method that allows you to create complex situations in CSS, unfortunately, those methods are not supported in React Native at this time or using styled-components that allow you to use CSS to React Now in this case, we have to use other solutions such as using SVG.

Using React Native SVG to Draw Certain Conditions

React Native community brings react-native-sv that allows you to use SVG in React Native. You can add it to the project using yarn or NPM:

```
// using yarn
yarn add react-native
```

```
// npm
npm i react-native
```

Then make sure you connect it using the following command line:

```
react-native link react-native-SVG
```

And now let us start something with it:

```
/**
 * Sample React Native App
 * https://github.com/facebook/react-native
 *
 * @format
 * @flow
 * @lint-ignore-every XPLATJSCOPYRIGHT1
 */
import React, { Component } from "react";
import { StyleSheet, Text, View } from
"react-native";
import styled from "styled-components";
import Svg, {
 Circle,
 Ellipse,
 G,
 TSpan,
 TextPath,
 Path,
 Polygon,
 Polyline,
 Line,
 Rect,
 Use,
 Image,
 Symbol,
 Defs,
 LinearGradient,
 RadialGradient,
 Stop,
 ClipPath,
 Pattern,
 Mask
} from "react-native-svg";
```

```
const Container = styled.View`
 flex: 1;
 padding: 50px 0;
 justify-content: center;
 background-color: #f4f4f4;
 align-items: center;
`;
const Title = styled.Text`
 font-size: 20px;
 text-align: center;
 color: red;
`;
const Item = styled.View`
 flex: 1;
 border: 1px solid #ccc;
 margin: 2px 0;
 border-radius: 10px;
 box-shadow: 0 0 10px #ccc;
 height: 200px;
 background-color: ${props => (props.transparent ?
"red" : "blue")};
 width: 80%;
 padding: 10px;
`;
export default class App extends Component {
 render() {
  return (
   <Container>
    <Svg height="150" width="300">
     <Defs>
      <LinearGradient id="grad" x1="123" y1="0"
x2="170" y2="0">
       <Stop offset="0" stopColor="rgb(255,255,0)"
stopOpacity="0" />
        <Stop offset="1" stopColor="red"
stopOpacity="1" />
      </LinearGradient>
     </Defs>
     <Ellipse cx="150" cy="43" rx="85" ry="55"
fill="url(#grad)" />
    </Svg>
    <Svg height="100" width="100">
```

```
<Defs>
 <RadialGradient
  id="grad"
  cx="50%"
  cy="50%"
  rx="50%"
  ry="50%"
  fx="50%"
  fy="50%"
  gradientUnits="userSpaceOnUse"
 >
    <Stop offset="0%" stopColor="#ff0"
stopOpacity="1" />
    <Stop offset="100%" stopColor="#00f"
stopOpacity="1" />
 </RadialGradient>
 <ClipPath id="clip">
  <G scale="0.9" x="10">
   <Circle cx="40" cy="30" r="20" />
   <Ellipse cx="60" cy="70" rx="20" ry="10" />
   <Rect x="65" y="15" width="50" height="50" />
   <Polygon points="20,60 20,80 50,70" />
   <Text
    x="50"
    y="30"
    fontSize="32"
    fonWeight="bold"
    textAnchor="middle"
    scale="1.2"
   >
    Q
   </Text>
  </G>
 </ClipPath>
</Defs>
<Rect
 x="0"
 y="0"
 width="100"
 height="100"
 fill="url(#grad)"
 clipPath="url(#clip)"
```

```
     />
    </Svg>
    <Svg height="100" width="300">
     <Defs>
      <G id="shape">
       <G>
        <Circle cx="50" cy="50" r="50" />
        <Rect x="50" y="50" width="60" height="50" />
        <Circle cx="50" cy="50" r="5" fill="#c00" />
       </G>
      </G>
     </Defs>
     <Use href="#shape" x="20" y="0" />
     <Use href="#shape" x="170" y="0" />
    </Svg>
   </Container>
  );
 }
}
```

As you can see you can go so far with react-native-svgin, create a certain shape and gradient background and things you usually do with SVG. You can check the official documents to see the available options.

You can still use the React style method to do so, but it is always weird if we want to create complex styles, so you need to use other tools like react-native-SVG to do that to make the usual style we do. The stylish parts make things easier and we hope the React Native community will bring more support to other style options that will give us the freedom to make things easier.

ORGANIZATION AND INHERITANCE

Style Inheritance of React Native

In fact, React Native has a style heritage approach. In the official document, they show the following example:

```
<Text style={{fontWeight: 'bold'}}>
 I am bold
 <Text style={{color: 'red'}}>
  and red
 </Text>
</Text>
```

It works. Parts of the Nested text will be verified by an inherited system. But that is all a legacy of style so far. React Native still has the concept of a heritage asset, but is limited to subtitles.

Therefore, it is exceedingly difficult to use this machine in real development. Plus, I think we should not do and follow this way. Because it will create confusion in the future. Part of the React should behave in the same way everywhere and every time we use it.

Then, how do we achieve our expectation?

Realistic Way to Implement Custom Fonts to Your App

My recommendation is to create a custom section of your app. Usually, you can prepare your own piece of text as follows:

```
// shared/Typography.js
import React, { Component } from 'react';import {
View, Text, StyleSheet } from 'react-native';BASE_
FONT = 'YOUR_CUSTOM_FONTS_FAMILY';export class
AppText extends Component {
 render() {
  return (
   <Text {...this.props} style={[styles.myAppText,
this.props.style]}>{this.props.children}</Text>
  )
 }
}
const styles = StyleSheet.create({
 myAppText: {
  fontFamily: BASE_FONT,
  fontSize: 16,
 },
});
```

Then, you can use your AppText component in your view.

```
. . .
import { AppText } from 'PATH_TO_YOUR_COMPONENT/T
ypography';export default class MyView extends
Component {
. . .
render() {
```

```
return ( <AppText>Customized text is here</
AppText> )
}}
```

If you change the basic fonts, just change Typography.js. After a while, you will feel like you want to change a certain screen style or part from time to time. When you transfer the style tool to AppText, it will extract the default styles that you have defined. Some resources serve as part of the traditional text.

If you find that you are passing the same style on your particular screen or section many times, I highly recommend you specify another section wrapped by AppTextcomponent in Typography.js. For example, if you use the title text more than once, simply state this:

```
export class AppHeading extends Component {
 render() {
  return (
   <AppText {...this.props} style={[styles.
myAppHeading, this.props.style]}>
    {this.props.children}
   </AppText>
  )
 }
}
```

Inheritance is a concept that plays a key role in object-oriented programming. It is a technique that allows objects to have those structures that already exist in the past.

Two classes exist are:

1. Superclass(Parent Class)

2. Subclass(Child Class)

In React, the design model is used instead of the asset, so that the code can be reused between the components. In React the keywork "extend" uses the main function, i.e., the builder function. By using the extended keyword, you can make the current part have all the features of the component from the existing component. The design model uses a small class relationship by transcending status and resources. Part of the lower stage can achieve any further progression to another.

Creating React Application

Step 1: Create a React application by using the following command in the terminal/ command prompt:

create-react-app foldername

Step 2: After creating the folder, move it using the following command:

cd foldername.

Here, you have two components, i.e., *AppComponent* and a *ChildComponent*, and the child component takes over all the app properties.

Example: Now write the given following code in the App.js file. Here, the App is our default (parent) part where we write our code. In the below code, *this.state.message* is passed to ChildComponent.

- App.js

```
import logo from './logo.svg';
import React from 'react';
import './App.css';
import ChildComponent from "./ChildComponent";
 class App extends React.Component {
  constructor(props) {
    super(props);
    this.state = {
      message: " Message"
    };
  }
   render() {
    return (
      <div>
        <ChildComponent message={this.state.message}
/>
      </div>
    );
  }
}
export default App;
```

Now write below the following code in the ChildComponent.js file. The child component accepts all the app component properties.

- ChildComponent.js

```
import React from "react";
 class ChildComponent extends React.Component {
  render() {
    const { message } = this.props;
    return (
      <div>
        <p> Message from App component : {message} </
p>
      </div>
    );
  }
}
 export default ChildComponent;
```

Step to Run Application
Run the application by the command from the main (root) directory of the project:

npm start

Output: Positioning and Designing Layouts
Positioning
"When I reconcile things and excuse the content of the text or the visual elements never focus and go to random places."

Starting with the View
The View component is a tool that creates structure using FlexBox and is a considerably basic part of creating our UI. Views are divof React Native.

Positioning Basics
With React Native, we have Flexbox that works in the same way as CSS with a few differences in default.

Knowing your route through Flexbox will help set things up easily. Some of RN's Flexbox highlights are listed below.

Flex

All container features such as View in React Native are automatic Flex containers. To explain how container children will fill the available space near the main axis set flexproperty. The flexproperty for each element will be used to divide space.

```
<View style={{ flex: 1}}>
  <View style={{ flex: 1 }}>A</View>
  <View style={{ flex: 2 }}>B</View>
  <View style={{ flex: 3 }}>C</View>
</View>
```

Flex Direction

Defaults to column where the children of the container will be on top of each other on the y-axis.

```
<View style={{ flex: 1, flexDirection: 'column'}}>
 <View style={{ flex: one, borderWidth: 10,
borderColor: 'red'}}/>
 <View style={{ flex: two, borderWidth: 10,
borderColor: 'orange' }}/>
 <View style={{ flex: three, borderWidth: 10,
borderColor: 'green' }}/>
</View>
```

Changing the direction to row will arrange the children on the x-axis side by side (left to right).

```
<View style={{ flex: 1, flexDirection: 'row'}}>
 <View style={{ flex: 1, borderColor: 'red'}}/>
 <View style={{ flex: 2, borderColor: 'orange' }}/>
 <View style={{ flex: 3, borderColor: 'green' }}/>
</View>
```

Justify Content

To align children between x-axis (main axis) in a container set to justify-Contentproperty. The isflex-start default will align children at the beginning of the main axis of the containers.

Here is a quick look at the options available.

Align Items

To align children within the y-axis (cross axis) in the container, set the alignItems property. The default is stretch which corresponds to the length of the container crossing axis. One thing to note is that stretching will not have an effect if this is clarified for children.

Here is a quick look at the options available.

Let Us Position Things

Now let us see how to align that text input to the centre.

```
<View style={{ flex: 1, justifyContent: 'auto',
alignItems: 'center' }}>
  <TextInput
    style={{height: 40, borderWidth: 1}}
    value="Text Input"
  />
</View>
```

Positioning

Create a View section and place two TextInput and button features. Flexible View section replaces the full phone. TextInput and button objects are set to the default flex axis (like column).

```
import React, { Component } from "react";
import { StyleSheet, TextInput, View , Button } from
"react-native";
 export default class App extends Component {
state = {
placeName: "",
places: []
  };
  placeNameChangedHandler = val => {
    this.setState({
placeName: val
    });
  };
  placeSubmitHandler = () => {
alert("button clicked")
  };
  render() {
    return (
```

```
<View style={styles.container}>
      <TextInput
          placeholder="An awesome place"
onChangeText={this.placeNameChangedHandler}
          style={styles.placeInput}
      />
      <Button
          title="Button"
          onPress={this.placeSubmitHandler}
      />
    </View>
  );
 }
}
 const styles = StyleSheet.create({
  container: {
    flex: 1,
    padding: 26,
    backgroundColor: "#fff",
    justifyContent: "flex-start"
  }
});
```

Example 1:

In this example, we will place the Right Button in the TextInput element. Add child View section within parent View with flex: 1andflexDirtection: "row". Settingflex: 1Interior view takes place everywhere from top to bottom and left to right. TheflexDirtection: "line" sets the elements in the form of a line within the internal viewing component.

```
import React, { Component } from "react";
import { StyleSheet, View, TextInput, Button } from
"react-native";
 export default class App extends Component {
state = {
    placeName: "",
    places: []
 };
  placeNameChangedHandler = val => {
    this.setState({
      placeName: val
    });
```

```
};
placeSubmitHandler = () => {
 alert("button clicked")
};
 render() {
  return (
    <View style={styles.container}>
      <View style={styles.innerContainer}>
        <TextInput
          placeholder="An awesome place"
          onChangeText={this.placeNameChangedHandler}
        />
          title="Button"
          onPress={this.placeSubmitHandler}
        />
      </View>
    </View>
  );
 }
.}
const styles = StyleSheet.create({
  container: {
    flex: 1,
    padding: 26,
    backgroundColor: "#fff",
    justifyContent: "flex-start"
  },
  innerContainer:{
  }
});
```

The flex: 1Internal view takes up full space which does not look good as TextInput and button take up all the space from top to bottom.

Example 2:
In this example, we remove the flexible inner view and additional width: 100%. Extract the flexible internal form View. Set the default size of objects. Set width: "100%" Internal view takes the full width and default length of objects.

```
import React, { Component } from "react";
```

```
import { StyleSheet, View, TextInput, Button } from
"react-native";
 export default class App extends Component {
  state = {
    placeName: "",
    places: []
  };
   placeNameChangedHandler = val => {
    this.setState({
      placeName: val
    });
  };
  placeSubmitHandler = () => {
    alert("button clicked")
  };
   render() {
    return (
      <View style={styles.container}>
        <View style={styles.innerContainer}>
          <TextInput
              placeholder="An awesome place"
              onChangeText={this.placeNameChangedHan
                           dler}
              style={styles.textStyle}
          />
          <Button
              title="Button"
              onPress={this.placeSubmitHandler}
          />
        </View>
      </View>
    );
  }
}
const styles = StyleSheet.create({
  container: {
    flex: 1,
    padding: 26,
    backgroundColor: "#fff",
    justifyContent: "flex-start"
  },
  innerContainer:{
```

```
    // flex: 1,
    width: "100%",
flexDirection: "row",
    justifyContent: "space-between",
    alignItems: "center"
  },
  textStyle:{
    width: "70%",
    backgroundColor: "gray",
  },
  buttonStyle:{
    width: "30%",
  }
});
```

LAYOUT WITH FLEXBOX

The component can determine the layout of its children using the Flexbox algorithm. Flexbox is designed to provide a consistent format for a variety of screen sizes.

You will usually use a combination of flexDirection, Align Items, and edit Content to get the right layout.

Flexbox works in the same way in React Native as we do in CSS with the exception of a few exceptions. Default is different, there is flexDirection-defaulting to column instead of sorrow, alignDefault default variable-start instead of stretch, flexSomatically reduce to 0 instead of 1, the variable parameter supports only one number.

Flex

Flex will explain how your items will "fill" the space available next to your main axis. The space will be divided according to the layout of each element.

Flex Direction

flexionDirection controls how node children are positioned. This is also called the main axis. A cross axis is an axis facing the main axis, or axis on which the folding lines are placed.

- **column (default) Align from top to bottom**: If the wrap is enabled, the next row will start to the right of the first item at the top of the container.

- **row Align children from left to right**: If the wrap is enabled, the next row will start under the first item on the left side of the container.

- **column-reverse Arrange children from bottom to top**: If the wrap is enabled, the next row will start to the right of the first item under the container.

- **row-reverse Align the children from right to left**: If the wrap is enabled, the next row will start under the first item on the right of the container.

Layout Direction

Layout direction specifies the way in which children and section text should be placed. The structural guide also contributes to what the edge start and end refer to. By default, React Native sets the LTR architecture direction. In this mode, start refers to the left and then to the right.

- LTR (default value) text and children are displayed from left to right. The margin and pads used at the beginning of the item are used on the left side.

- RTLT text and children are spread from right to left. Margins and pads used at the beginning of the item are used on the right.

Justify Content

justifyContent describes how to align the given children within the axes of their container. For example, you can use this structure to place a child in the center horizontally inside a container with a flexDirectionset to row or straight inside a container with a flexDirectionset column.

- **flex-start (default value):** Align the children of the container at the beginning of the main container axis.

- **flex-end:** Align the container kids at the end of the main container axis.

- **Center:** Align the children of the container in the center of the main axis of the container.

- **Space-between:** Equerate space between children across the main axis of the container, distributing the remaining space between the children.

- **Space-around**: A equilibrium space for children within the main axis of the container, distributing the remaining space around the children. Compared to mid-space, using space-environment will result in space being distributed at the beginning of the first child and the end of the last child.

- **space-evenly distributed**: Children evenly within the directional container near the main axis. The space between each pair of adjacent objects, the edge of the main object and the first object, and the main edge and the end object, are exactly the same.

Align Items

alignItems describes a way to align children to the cross-section of their container. Same for giving one content instead of using it on the main axis, align the Tools on the cross axis.

- **stretch (fixed value)**: Stretch the children of the container to match the length of the opposite axis of the container.

- **flex-start**: Direct children container at the beginning of the container crossing axis.

- **flex-end**: Align the container children at the end of the axis of the container cross.

- **Center**: Align the children of the container in the center of the container axis.

- **Baseline**: Align children of a container at baseline then Individual children can be set to the reference baseline for their parents.

Children do not have a fixed dimension along the secondary axis for stretch to have an effect. For example, setting the alignItems: stretch; does nothing until the width: 50 is removed from the children.

Align Yourself

alignSelf has the same options and effects as alignItems. You can use this structure on a single child to change alignment within its parent instead of touching the children inside the container. It removes any parent-set option by aligning Items.

Align Content

It defines the distribution of lines along the cross axis. This only affects if the items are folded in multiple rows using flexWrap.

- **flex-start (the default value):** Align the folded lines at the beginning of the opposite axis of the container.

- **flex-end:** Direct the folded lines at the end of the container crossing axis.

- **stretch:** Extend the folded lines to match the length of the container crossing axis.

- **Center:** Align lines wrapped around the center of the container crossing axis.

- **Space-between:** The folded lines of equal space between the cross axis of the container, scatter the remaining space between the lines.

- **Space-around:** Refined lines of equal space between container cross axis, dispersing the remaining space in the rows. Compared to mid-range, using space-surroundings will result in space being distributed at the beginning of the line and the end of the last line.

Flex Wrap

The flexWrapproperty is set in containers and controls what happens when children overflow the container size near the main axis. By default, children are forced to form a single line (which can shrink the elements). If folding is allowed, items are folded in multiple rows with the main axis if needed.

When folding lines, alignContent can be used to determine how the rows are placed in a container.

Flex Basis, Grow, and Shrink

- FlexBasis is an independent axis method of providing a fixed size of an object associated with the main axis. Flex setting A child's foundation is the same as setting a child's width if his or her parent smokes flex. The flexBasos object is a fixed object size, object size before any flexGrowandflexShrinkcalculations calculations are performed.

- FlexGrow explains how any space inside a container should be distributed among its children near the main axis. After laying its young, the container will distribute any remaining space according to the ever-growing values specified by its offspring.

- FlexGrow Accept any floating-point value > = 0, 0 fixed value. The container will distribute any remaining space between its children loaded with childrenflexGrowvalues.

- FlexShrink describes how to reduce children to the main axis in a situation where the total size of the children exceeds the container size on the main axis. Flexofrrinks such as toflexTr growth can be viewed in the same way if any size is considered to be the wrong balance. The two structures also work well together to allow children to grow and shrink as needed.

- FlexShrink accepts any floating-point value > = 0, 0 fixed value (on the web, 1 default). The container will reduce its weight in children with flexShrinkvalues.

Width and Height

The width property specifies the spatial area of element content. Similarly, heightproperty specifies the spatial area of element content. Both the width and the length can take the following values:

- default (default value) React Native calculates the width/length of an element based on its content, whether other children, text, or image.

- pixelsDefine width/height in whole pixels. Depending on the styles set in the section, this may or may not be the final size of the node.

- percentDefines the width or height as a percentage of the width or height of its parent, respectively.

Absolute and Relative Layout

The type of object location describes how it is placed inside its parent.

- **relative (default value)**: By default, the element is similar. This means that the element is positioned according to the normal flow of the structure, and then the offset is compared to that area based on the values above, right, down, and left. Offset does not affect the location of any of your siblings or parental elements.

- **Absolute**: If it is completely placed; the elements do not participate in the flow of normal structure. Instead, it is set apart from their siblings. Location is determined based on the values of the top, right, bottom, and left.

CONCLUSION

In this chapter, we learned about styles offered by React Native. In the next chapter we are going to learn about Platform APIs.

Platform APIs

IN THIS CHAPTER

> ➢ Using gio-location

> ➢ Accessing the user's image and camera

> ➢ Storing persistent data with asynstore

In the previous chapter, we learned about styles of React Native used in mobile devices, in this chapter, we are going to learn about platform APIs .

PLATFORM APIS

The term "API Platform" has been used in a similar way by other vendors with API Management, Full Life API Management, and the API Gateway. Everyone likes to spice up a topic with the word platform, but loosening the word breaks the topic. What is an API Platform? The API Platform is all these things and more.

The purpose of the API Platform is to take advantage of new application development – building new skills, new knowledge, nurturing ecosystems, and more. The table anchors here are API Management, Full Life API Management, and API Gate. This brings the design and development of a health API, health cycle management, policy, and safety implementation, analysis, and growing development communities as users of these APIs. All critical.

API Platform is over. The API Platform becomes the ultimate destination for digital developers to innovate quickly and efficiently and as a

DOI: 10.1201/9781003310440-6

standard catalog of services and managed services. Learn five skills that every API Management Platform should have.

When you create mobile applications, you will naturally want to take advantage of certain forum APIs. React Native makes it easy to access things like a phone camera, location, and ongoing storage. These APIs are made available to React Native through the included modules, providing us with JavaScript links that are easy to use for these tasks.

React Native doesn't automatically threaten the performance of its hosting forum; most of the forum APIs will require to write own modules, or use modules written by others in the Native community. We will cover that process in Chapter 7. Documentation is the best place to test whether the API is supported.

This chapter covers some of the available APIs. For example, we will make some changes to the Weather system from the beginning. We will add geolocation to the app, so it can automatically detect the user's location. We'll also add "memory" to the app, so it can remember your previously searched locations. Finally, we will use the camera roll to transform the background image into one of the user's photos.

Although the appropriate code snippets will be introduced in each section, the full app code is included in the "Smart Weather Program."

Two things to look for:

1. The amount of services required to get a complete back-enddigital.

2. How to work with a standard catalog of services.

First look at the table stakes – the extension of the Full Life Cycle Management API. Businesses accept APIs. These are the very foundations of modern integration and the provision of innovations and remnants of new developments. The API Platform integrates background APIs, which are published for integration and the final APIs are discussed, protected, and published by developers with prior knowledge.

Meditation begins to play with various skills to integrate APIs to meet previous needs. Mediation also helps to protect the environment for safety and implementation policies, as well as to provide performance and performance analysis, threat monitoring, and SLA monitoring. A standard catalog of services provides one true source for all background and front-end APIs, with access and visibility controlled by groups including domain, dev groups, and sometimes even the community. This method goes beyond a simple API portfolio.

Let's take a look at the total number of services over the API Platform for managing API development teams currently working on this catalog. APIs and API management is important and develop teams that build good sense and need a solid set of background services to speed up their work. These include:

- MESHmicroservices management

- Developer tools and API Mediation

- Occupation time services

- Data as a service

- Streams/Event-Driven APIs

- Front-built rear services

- Application connectors

What Is an API Platform?
Adding to the Traditional Look in Managing the Full Life API

- **MESH and microservices management**: Any transformation step will go beyond a good app and requires background thinking and skills to be developed. Dev teams will be looking at modern microservice facilities. Packed maturity of small services, such as visibility and traffic management API within the mesh, with Ingres and Egress from the mesh key.

- **Developer and Mediation API Tools**: Developer tools include sub-code tools to build new APIs that work as microservices, to reduce or join APIs, to streamflow across all services. This allows development teams to build on background APIs and publish previous APIs specific to previous projects, mobile, IoT, or more.

- **Operating Time Services**: Quickly moving the back end without a server that can rotate up and down and scale alternately is required. This is important for creation from dev teams – containers and microservices, as well as APIs created by dev teams to launch critical infrastructure to support their previous projects. Learn more about how Axway provides, as part of its AMPLIFY platform, Runtime Services is an expandable infrastructure (Vessel As a Service) running your applications.

- **Data as a service:** The latter experience may require a custom data store that needs to be quickly deprecated and estimated, continuously. Pre-existing information can drive hundreds of millions of API calls to existing background information, and this requires protection from the load. Data as a service, as a layer between systems is often used as a protection between post-business systems and the front end.

  ○ Data as a service provides a scale to the asset limit at a lower cost (with the SQL line scale) and can work to reduce complexity and ensure the availability of any key information. LEARN MORE: Axway offers, as part of its AMPLIFY platform, Mobile Background Services, and cURL Firehose.

- **Streaming/Hosted API:** For applications where time is of the essence, event-driven properties are essential for getting real-time user information. The API Platform combines the capabilities of converting any application response API into an event-driven API to push data to successfully registered clients and to protect the conclusion of a common error in the previous voting. Learn more about how AMPLIFY Streams allows you to upgrade your API infrastructure with an event-based layout to publish data from your APIs.

- **Pre-built Background Services:** Usually referred to as mBaaS from its mobile roots, any new experience will need to be exploited by standard services, including user management preferences, Photos, Files, Locations, Logs, Posts, Events, Push Notifications, and more. We call these Backbound Services as this goes beyond mobile.

- **Application Connectors:** Controls API Platform is a complete set of mixed platform capabilities connected by a catalog feel. Verify from iPaaSone or more of over 200+ applications that expose the API endpoints that should be used in your launch.

Another map benefit to create a canonical API archive to update multiple recording systems in anAPI Call. Extra power comes from data opening with the API Platform part of the API enabled Hybrid Integration Platform Strategy!

API Platform is about managing the full life cycle of APIs and much more, bringing new applications and information. The API Platform must be built on the basis of providing teams of developers with skills through a rich catalog of accessibility and tools for teams to operate independently and successfully in their operations.

We have suggested this, but it is interesting to understand the crossroads with the Hybrid Integration Platform (HIP) and the development strategies to be developed. The API Platform can be part of a personal HIP or split – but the API Platform always comes up with a personal integration strategy.

In other words, the real power comes when the human integration strategy is aligned with and supports the API Platform for innovation and this remains the case with the well-used Hybrid Integration Platform (HIP).

This leads to the fact that these are not separate "objects" and when viewed properly, they are two sides of the same coin! When you look at one side, you have the idea of integration, you look at another creative concept. Both scenarios provide engineers and designers with an integrated multi-dimensional catalog where they can perform independently and quickly.

USING GEOLOCATION

Geolocation is more important now than ever. It's a great way to add a "program-like" feature to your ongoing web app. We like to know what businesses, attractions and destinations, where we are, and how we get to where we are going.

Browsers offer a standard JavaScript geolocation service that you can use to enrich your HTML-driven experience. Common uses of geolocation are to indicate where stores are located and possible driving directions. Geolocation is not just about selling. Delivery and driving services use location to let you and the drivers know where they are and how much time is left. I use it to find places of interest in relation to my location. Now that smartphones are everywhere, we want information right now, wherever we are. Popular apps like Google Maps, Yelp, and Facebook allow us to find businesses and friends near our locations right on our phone.

We have been amazed by geolocation-based data for a few years now and have watched the technology change. Prior to smartphones, specifying a user's location was the limit on mapping with a geo-coordinated IP site.

To access a geo-coordinated website, you need to sign up for a service that can translate an IP address into latitude and longitude, or you need to keep a local website with this information. This also had to be done on the server, which added a delay.

Any option was not cheap or completely reliable. To the others' knowledge, an IP address does not always associate with a device location. For example, we used to have Sprint 3G service for my laptop. The account that opened my service was in the Chicago, IL area. Whenever I visited sites using geolocated content, we found content related to the Chicago metro area.

Ironically the only time we were in the Chicago metropolitan area was changing planes at the airport! We've got a better way to identify user location thanks to http://www.w3.org/TR/geolocation-API/ "HTML Geolocation API. HTML Geolocation API. All browsers support and have supported native API geolocation support for nearly a decade. Therefore, the API is safe to use.

Using the geolocation API integrated with a map service such as Microsoft Bing, MapsGoogle, and MapsPlatforms provides detailed information about the end user. You can add a map service to the site to add more value and app-like information to expand your product.

Now you can pinpoint the visitor's location and add nearby locations to the map, provide driving directions, and more. You should be aware that these services charge for some features. You will need to consult the service pages to understand their price model, so you are not surprised.

Although every browser supports the geolocation API, it is still recommended to install it to see if the API is supported. The geolocation object must be a member of the navigator object, so you can check that it is in the navigator.

Detecting Geolocation Support

```
if ("geolocation" in navigator) {
    } else {
    }
```

The reason is that you should install a detector in case the user disables the app. You should also note that modern browsers now install the API after HTTPS and some need to get user permission before the API can run.

- Permission for ShapeGeolocation Prompt

- You can use HTTP if you are working locally, using the local host root. This helps to facilitate development. The geolocation object has three modes:

1. getCurrentPosition: a direct call to get the current location of the device;

2. WatchPosition: activates when device location changes;

3. clearWatch: stops or deletes a clock created by running the watchPosition mode.

Using getCurrentPosition

Easy use of geolocation object to locate the device with a single call using the getCurrentPosition method. The system has three parameters, a successful callback, a repeat call, and an optional item. The last two parameters are voluntary. Rewinding success will have one transfer parameter, a Local object. Similarly, the back drive error gets one parameter, the PositionError object. The options parameter is a PositionOptions item.

Position Error Timeout

- **maximum:** the total number (milliseconds) indicating how much archive storage is valid;

- **expiration time:** how many milliseconds before the error holder is requested, default is not closing time;

- **enableHighAccuracy:** true or false, false automatically. Empowerment results in more energy consumption and more time to accumulate position.

All PositionOptions structures are selected. If the value is not specified, the geolocation system uses the default. The successful Callback object feature has two properties, codes (the coordinates item), and a timestamp. Links have all the (read-only) values we follow:

- **latitude:** double

- **length:** double

- **height:** twice, meters above sea level

- **accuracy:** it is also called as radius of accuracy in meters

- **altitudeAc accuracy:** accuracy or radius of accuracy in meters

- **subject:** how many degrees from the true North mobile device

- **speed:** speed in meters/second the device is moving

You should be aware that not all prices will be provided. You will always find the least latitude and length. I will update the accuracy after a while. The height depends on the power of the device, so you should consider the prices not given. Create a positive enhancement experience when height adds value to the app's feel. The timestamp value is a data item that determines when a location was determined.

```
if ( navigator.geolocation ) {
    navigator.geolocation.getCurrentPosition(
setCurrentPosition, positionError, {
    enableHighAccuracy: false,
    timeout: 15000,
    maximumAge: 0
    } );
}
    function setCurrentPosition( position ) {
        document.querySelector( '.accuracy' ).innerHTML
= position.coords.accuracy;
        document.querySelector( '.altitude' ).innerHTML
= position.coords.altitude;
        document.querySelector( '.altitudeAccuracy'
).innerHTML = position.coords.altitudeAccuracy;
        document.querySelector( '.heading' ).innerHTML =
position.coords.heading;
        document.querySelector( '.latitude' ).innerHTML
= position.coords.latitude;
        document.querySelector( '.longitude' ).innerHTML
= position.coords.longitude;
        document.querySelector( '.speed' ).innerHTML =
position.coords.speed;
    }
```

Managing Position Errors

If there is a problem recording the location of the user's device the error dialing function will be started. The PositionError item contains a numerical code feature, as well as a message. The code feature is an unsigned shortcut that you can compare from the error item value.

- **UNKNOWN_ERROR**: Code 0, The most common error because the location could not be determined and the browser does not know why.

- **PERMISSION_DENIED**: Code 1, User denied permission to use geolocation API from permission.

- **POSITION_UNAVAILABLE**: Code 2, Device location was not found.

- **LIFESTYLE**: Code 3, Location could not be collected during closing time

This is an example of how an error handling callback might work.

```
function positionError( error ) {
    switch ( error.code ) {
    case error.PERMISSION_DENIED:
            console.error( "User denied the
request." );
        break;
    case error.POSITION_UNAVAILABLE:
        console.error( "Location is unavailable."
);
        break;
    case error.TIMEOUT:
        console.error( "The request to get location
timed out." );
        break;
    case error.UNKNOWN_ERROR:
        console.error( "An unknown error occurred."
);
        break;
    }
}
```

Tracking Position Changes
GetCurrentPosition is good for finding the current user's location. But if your app needs to track user status changes, consider switching by changing driving directions or tracking speed, for the device to provide updated links that work best.

Thanks to the position of the Position Clock that starts re-dialing when the device location is updated. If this is not the case, you would probably need to use the setInterval or applicationAnimationFrame to get getCurrentPosition repeatedly.

Enabling the device to trigger an update when the device update is at its best. This saves battery and excessive CPU usage. The Watch Position method has the same signature as the getCurrentPosition, so you can easily update using the watchPosition method. The method returns a number id, similar to setInterval. You can use this id to stop the clock later.

```
var geoWatch;
function startWatch() {
    if ( !geoWatch ) {
        if ( "geolocation" in navigator &&
"watchPosition" in navigator.geolocation ) {
            geoWatch = navigator.geolocation.
watchPosition( setCurrentPosition, positionError, {
                enableHighAccuracy: false, timeout:
15000, maximumAge: 0
            } );
        }
    }
}
```

The geolocation clearWatch method accepts the clock id and clears the clock back. In this example, I forward the geoWatch id to the clearWatch path to stop calling again. I also set the unspecified variable because I check if it is in use before calling the watch Position method.

```
function stopWatch() {
    navigator.geolocation.clearWatch( geoWatch );
    geoWatch = undefined;
}
```

Now you can also turn your phone into an expensive counter!

Just for fun you can also create an ongoing web version of Pokemon Go. The geolocation watchPosition method can use to track where a player is found to show small monsters. We will leave it now on you to find out how to use monsters to get used to pointing.

Setting Links Using Chromium Developer Tools

In Chrome, the new Edge and other Chromium-based browsers have developer tools with a "sensor" tab. In this panel, you can set the latitude and longitude of the device. You can also adjust the shape of the device, but that is in line with the gyroscope API.

Geolocation sensor simulation comes with many of the world's largest cities already set. You can add more locations as needed.

To select a location, simply click on the "Geolocation" right input field. It looks like a text entry, but it will show a list of available locations.

By pressing the button "Manage" will display a list of locations and the ability to add a new location.

This is a great feature you can use when developing geolocation-based applications. The only result is that you can't mimic a moving device. But since watchPosition has the same signature as the getCurrentPosition method, you can at least ensure that the flow of your work processes the object of the position correctly.

How the Position Is Determined

There are three ways devices determine location.

1. Wi-Fi

2. Satellite

3. Cell Tower Triangulation

When using Wi-Fi network router, it is usually in a fixed location and turns out to be very popular. There are several very accurate services that track that type of item, and all major retailers use one or more of these kinds of services to determine the location of the device.

Remember in the old days you needed access to an IP site and a more accurate website or service was more expensive? Well, Apple, Google, Microsoft, etc., take care of this, as long as you use the geolocation API.

As far as I know, these numbers usually have my pinned area within 100 feet or about 30 meters. Browsers are not a deciding factor when determining the location and accuracy. They simply asked for the visual interface of the GPS hardware operating system.

The next step is to connect to a geolocation satellite. These figures are often extremely accurate, within ten meters. The problem is to have an unobstructed view of one of the satellites, usually when you are outside.

This means that when you are inside the building, you cannot use this method, but the Wi-Fi method should be replaced. However, if one of these methods is not available and you have a mobile device, the last option is to triangle the cell tower areas.

The accuracy of this process is not very good, usually between 1000 and 3500 meters. Because these methods may vary, it is a good idea to always check the accuracy to see if you need to adjust your application response properly. Remember that you do not control how the user device receives its links, but you can determine how you use the location value based on accuracy.

Nearby iOS Location

Apple has introduced a new setting for iOS 14, almost locally. The purpose is to protect user privacy by providing a wide range of locations. Since devices can provide the most accurate locations, this can lead to bad people finding you.

Limited location adjustment adds some obfuscation to your location. My interpretation is that it will report your location, such as if removed by a triangle from cell towers, or approximately within 1 km distance.

The problem with this is that your app needs specific locations. An example is a request to share a ride. The driver needs to know where the rider stands so that he can pick him up. Because Apple did not disclose the user's option to control this in-app level, it is an all-or-nothing configuration. When a user chooses almost the location of his iPhone it affects all apps.

There is no flag or value the app can check to see if the location is accurate or approximate. You can use the accuracy feature to determine how true a reported situation is. Even setting the high precision feature to reality does not change the value.

Price is reported on the 15-minute rise. So there are no updates when the user leaves. You will not know for 15 minutes.

Find User Location

The geolocation API of HTML is used to locate the user's location. As this may reduce privacy, the position is not available unless the user authorizes it.

Using the Geolocation API

The ThegetCurrentPosition () method is used to retrieve user location. The example below returns the latitude and length of the user's location:

Example:

```
<script>
const x = document.getElementById("demo");
```

```
function getLocation() {
 if (navigator.geolocation) {
 navigator.geolocation.getCurrentPosition(showPos
ition);
 } else {
 x.innerHTML = "Geolocation is does not supported
by this browser.";
 }
}
function showPosition(position) {
 x.innerHTML = "Latitude: " + position.coords.latit
ude +
 "<br>Longitude: " + position.coords.longitude;
}
</script>
```

An example is explained:

- Check that geolocation is supported.

- If supported, use the getCurrentPosition () method. If not, show a message to the user.

- If the getCurrentPosition () method returns the link object to the function specified in the parameter (showPosition) when it succeeds.

- The ShowPosition () function determines Latitude and Longitude.

The example above is a basic geolocation script, with no error handling.

Handling Errors and Rejections

The second parameter of thegetCurrentPosition () method is used to manage errors. Specifies the function to start if it fails to locate the user's location:

Example:

```
function showError(error) {
 switch(error.code) {
 case error.PERMISSION_DENIED:
 x.innerHTML = "User denied the request."
 break;
 case error.POSITION_UNAVAILABLE:
```

```
    x.innerHTML = "Location information is not
aviabable."
      break;
    case error.TIMEOUT:
    x.innerHTML = "The request to user location timed
out."
      case error.UNKNOWN_ERROR:
      x.innerHTML = "An unknown error."
      break;
    }
  }
```

Showing the Result in the Map

To show the result on the map, you need to access a map service, such as Google Maps. In the example below, the restored latitude and longitude are used to show the location in Google Map (using still image).

Example:

```
function showPosition(position) {
  let latlon = position.coord.latitude + "," +
position.coord.longitude;
  let imgUrl = "https://maps.googleapix.com/maps/api/
staticmap?center=
  "+lat-lon+"&zoom=14&size=420x320&sensor=false&key
=YOUR_KEY";
//console.log("IMG")
  document.getElementById("mapholder").innerHTML =
"<img src='"+imgUrl+"'>";
}
```

Location-Specific Information

This page has shown how to display the user's position on the map. Geolocation is also very useful for geographical information, such as:

- Latest local information.

- Displays points of interest near the user.

- Turn-by-turn navigation (GPS).

THE GETCURRENTPOSITION() METHOD – RETURN DATA

The getCurrentPosition() returns an object on success. The latitude, longitude, and accuracy properties are returned. The other properties are returned if available:

Property	Returns
coords.latitude	It is a decimal number (always returned).
coords.longitude	It is a decimal number (always returned).
coords.accuracy	It is accuracy of position (always returned).
coords.altitude	It is altitude in meters above the mean sea level (returned if available).
coords.altitudeAccuracy	It is altitude accuracy of position (returned if available)
coords.heading	It is heading as degrees clockwise from North (returned if available).
coords.speed	It is speed in meters per second (returned if available).
timestamp	It is date/time of the response (returned if available).

GEOLOCATION OBJECT – OTHER INTERESTING METHODS

The geolocation object has other methods:

- **watchPosition()**: It returns the exact position of the user and then continues to return updated position as the user moves it (like the GPS in a car).

- **clearWatch()**: It stops the watchPosition() method.

The below example shows the watchPosition() method. You will need an accurate GPS device to test this like smartphone:

Example:

```
<script>
const x = document.getElementById("demo");
function showPosition(position) {
 x.innerHTML = "Latitude: " + position.coords.latit
ude +
 "<br>Longitude is : " + position.coords.longitude;
}
```

```
function getLocation() {
 if (navigator.geolocation) {
  navigator.geolocation.watchPosition(showPosition);
 } else {
  x.innerHTML = "Geolocation is not supported.";
 }
}
 }
</script>
```

@capacitor/geolocation

The geolocation API provides methods for getting and tracking the exact position of the device by using GPS with altitude, heading, and speed information if available.

Install

- npm install @capacitor/geolocation

- npx cap sync

iOS

It requires privacy descriptions to be specified in Info.plist for location information:

- NSLocationAlwaysUsageDescription (Privacy for Location Always Usage)

- NSLocationWhenInUseUsageDescription (Privacy for Location When In Use Usage)

Read about configuring from the Info.plist in the iOS Guide for further information on setting iOS permissions in Xcode.

Android

It is an API that requires the following permissions to be added to your AndroidManifest.xml:

```
<!-- Geolocation API -->
<uses-permission android:name="android.permissi
on.ACCESS_COARSE_LOCATION" />
```

```
<uses-permission android:name="android.permissi
on.ACCESS_FINE_LOCATION" />
<uses-feature android:name="android.hardware.locati
on.gps" />
```

The first two permissions will be location data, both for fine and coarse, and the last line is so optional but necessary if the app *requires* GPS to function. You can leave it out, though keep with you that this may mean the app is installed on devices lacking GPS hardware.

Read about permissions (Setting) in the Android Guide for further information on setting Android permissions.

Variables

Is plugin will use the following project variables (it will define in your app's variables.gradle file):

- $playServicesLocationVersion version of com.google.android.gms:play-services-location (default: 17.1.0)

Example:

```
import { Geolocation } from '@capacitor/
geolocation';
const printCurrentPosition = async () => {
 const coordinates = await Geolocation.
getCurrentPosition();
 console.log('Current position:', coordinates);
};
```

API

- getCurrentPosition(...)

- watchPosition(...)

- clearWatch(...)

- checkPermissions()

- requestPermissions(...)

- Interfaces

- Type Aliases

getCurrentPosition(…)

getCurrentPosition(options?: PositionOptions | undefined) => Promise <Position>

It gets the current GPS location of the device.

Arguments	Type
options	*PositionOptions*

Returns: Promise<*Position*>
Since: 1.0.0

watchPosition(…)

```
watchPosition(options: PositionOptions, callback:
WatchPositionCallback) => Promise<CallbackID>
```

It sets up a watch for location changes that consumes a large amount of energy, then be smart only when you need to.

Param	Type
options	*PositionOptions*
callback	*WatchPositionCallback*

Returns: Promise<string>
Since: 1.0.0

clearWatch(…)

```
clearWatch(options: ClearWatchOptions) =>
Promise<void>
```

Clear a given watch.

Param	Type
options	*ClearWatchOptions*

Since: 1.0.0

checkPermissions()

```
checkPermissions() => Promise<PermissionStatus>
```

Check location permissions.
Returns: Promise<*PermissionStatus*>
Since: 1.0.0

requestPermissions(...)

```
requestPermissions(permissions?:
GeolocationPluginPermissions | undefined) =>
Promise<PermissionStatus>
```

Request location permissions.

Arguments	Type
permissions	*GeolocationPluginPermissions*

Returns: Promise<*PermissionStatus*>

Interfaces
Position

Prop	Type	Description
timestamp	Number	Creation timestamp for coords
coords	{ latitude: num; longitude: number; accuracy: num; altitudeAccuracy: num | null; altitude: num | null; speed: num | null; heading: num | null; }	The GPS coordinates with the accuracy of the data

PositionOptions

Prop	Type	Description	Default	
enableHighAccuracy	boolean	It is high accuracy mode (such as GPS). On Android 12+ devices it will be ignored if users didn't grant ACCESS_FINE_ LOCATION permissions (can also be checked with location alias).	false	
timeout	number	The maximum waiting time in milliseconds for location updates.	10000	
maximumAge	number	The maximum age in milliseconds of a possible cached position that is acceptable to return.	0	1.0.0

ClearWatchOptions

Prop	Type
id	*CallbackID*

PermissionStatus

Prop	Type	Description	Since
location	*PermissionState*	Permission state for location alias. On Android it requests/checks both ACCESS_ COARSE_LOCATION and ACCESS_ FINE_LOCATION permissions. On iOS and web it requests/checks location permission.	1.0.0
coarseLocation	*PermissionState*	Permission state for coarseLocation alias. On Android it requests/checks ACCESS_ COARSE_LOCATION. On Android 12+, users can choose between Approximate location (ACCESS_COARSE_ LOCATION) or Precise location (ACCESS_FINE_LOCATION), so this alias can be used if the app doesn't need high accuracy. On iOS and web, it will have the same value as the location alias.	1.2.0

GeolocationPluginPermissions

Prop	Type
permissions	GeolocationPermissionType[]

Type Aliases
WatchPositionCallback

```
(position: Position | null, err?: any): void
```

CallbackID

```
string
```

PermissionState

```
'prompt' | 'prompt-with-rationale' | 'granted' |
'denied'
```

GeolocationPermissionType

```
'location' | 'coarseLocation'
```

Accessing the User's Images and Camera

Among the many developing utilities in HTML5 are various methods for accessing user pictures from mobile devices and webcams. In this tutorial, we will use the Camera API to import a user photo into a web page, displaying it in a canvas element. The Camera API is primarily aimed at browsers on mobile devices running systems such as Android and iOS. The process involves a little JavaScript, but you should be able to complete it as long as you have basic scripting experience.

CREATE THE PAGE

Start by creating a new HTML5 page – use the following outline:

```
<!DOCTYPE html>
<html>
<head>
<style type="text/css">
</style>
<script type="text/javascript">
</script>
</head>
<body>
<div>
</div>
</body>
</html>
```

We will be adding to the HTML body and the script section in the page head throughout the tutorial.

ADD FILE INPUT

With the Camera API, you can use a file input element set to accept images. Add a little explanatory text to the body section of your page first:

```
1      <p>
2      Choose a picture from device or capture one
       with any of your camera now:
3      </p>
```

Next add the input element:

```
1    <input type="file" accept="image/*" onchange=
     "picChange(event)"/>
```

The element is set to accept any type of image. We also set a function to execute when the onchange event occurs, which will be whenever the user either chooses an image file from their device or takes one with the device camera.

Notice that the input element is much the same as the standard file input element you will have seen on other pages. As well as accepting images from a mobile device camera, the input element will also accept image files selected from the device, for example, via a gallery app or file explorer.

ADD A CANVAS

To demonstrate what you can do with the photo taken by the user, we will write the image into an HTML5 canvas element. Add one after the input element, along with some more explanatory information:

```
<p>
Photo:
</p>
<canvas id="capturedPhoto" width="500"
height="400">
</canvas>
```

We give the canvas an ID attribute so that we can refer to it in JavaScript and set dimensions – feel free to change these if you like.

You can optionally add the following CSS declarations to the page style section:

RESPOND TO CHANGE

Now let's add the function we specified as onchange event listener for the input element – in the script section:

```
function picChange(evt){
//bring selected photo in
}
```

The remainder of the code for the tutorial should be placed in this function. Remember that we passed the event as a parameter when calling the function – we will be able to retrieve the input data from it. Inside the function, do that now:

```
//get files captured through input
var fileInput = evt.target.files;
```

The input file is retrieved as an array, so we will need to access the first element in it. First make sure we have a minimum of one element:

```
if(fileInput.length>0){
//get the file
}
```

The rest of the function code will sit inside this conditional block. Start by getting a reference to the window URL:

```
//window url
var windowURL = window.URL || window.webkitURL;
```

Now attempt to get the URL representing the location of the file we are trying to import into the page:

```
//picture url
var picURL = windowURL.
createObjectURL(fileInput[0]);
```

The file may be one the user selected from their device gallery or one they have just taken using their device camera. Either way, we need its location to bring it into the page. The createObjectURL call lets us do that.

If the createObjectURL method is not supported by the user's browser, this code will fail. You can take steps to use the FileReader object instead if that happens – see this tutorial for an example of how you could do that.

DRAW INTO THE CANVAS

Now let's draw the user photo into the canvas. After calling createObjectURL, get a reference to the canvas element we added to the page earlier:

```
//get canvas
var photoCanvas = document.getElementById("captu
redPhoto");
```

We use the ID value we gave the element to retrieve it. Now get the context:

```
var ctx = photoCanvas.getContext("2d");
```

Now let's create an Image object for the photo:

```
//create image
var photo = new Image();
```

We won't attempt to draw the photo into the page until it has loaded, so add an onload function next:

```
photo.onload = function(){
//draw photo into canvas when ready
ctx.drawImage(photo, 0, 0, 500, 400);
};
```

We draw the image using the context object, setting X and Y coordinates followed by width and height – adjust these any way you like. After the onload function, load the image by setting it as source for the Image element we created:

```
//load photo into canvas
photo.src = picture;
```

When the image has loaded, the onload function will execute, writing it into the canvas element on the page. Finally, revoke the ObjectURL:

```
//release object URL
windowURL.revokeObjectURL(picURL);
```

You should be able to test your page on a mobile device. When you click the input button, your device may prompt you with a pop-up dialog asking which application you want to use to select a picture, including the camera application and your gallery or file explorer. When you select the camera, what happens next will depend on your device's operating system. For example, on Android, you are taken to the camera and asked whether you want to save/accept any image you capture – if you choose to save, the file is returned to the page where the code we added writes it into the canvas element.

The code we used in this tutorial demonstrates writing the user-captured photo into a canvas element so that you could then manipulate it. However, another option is to simply write the image into an img element, by setting its URL as the src attribute in your JavaScript function, instead of loading it into the Image object.

OPTIONS

The above coding approach is aimed at capturing photos on mobile devices – a range of other utilities are currently under development for capturing images from webcams, including the getUserMedia method. You may also wish to consider using utilities such as Modernizr to handle feature detection on the user device and browser.

Storing Persistent Data with asyncstore

AsyncStorage is an unencrypted, persistent, key-value system storage that is global to the app. It should be used instead of LocalStorage.

It is recommended that you use abstraction on AsyncStorage instead of AsyncStorage directly on anything other than light consumption as it operates worldwide.

For iOS, AsyncStorage is supported by native code that stores small amounts in a fixed dictionary and large amounts in separate files. For Android, AsyncStorage will use RocksDB or SQLite based on what is available.

TheAsyncStorage JavaScript code is a facade that provides a clear JavaScript API, realErrorobjects, and not many functions. Each path to the API returns a Promiseobject.

Importing AsyncStorage Library

```
import { AsyncStorage } from 'react-native';
```

Persisting Data

```
_storeData = async () => {
  try {
    await AsyncStorage.setItem(
      '@MySuperStore:key',
      'I like to save it.'
    );
```

```
} catch (error) {
// Error saving data
}
};
```

Fetching Data

```
_retrieveData = async () => {
try {
  const value = await AsyncStorage.getItem('TASKS');
  if (value !== null) {
  // We have data!!
  console.log(value);
  }
} catch (error) {
// Error retrieving data
}
};
```

Methods
getItem()

```
static getItem(key: string, [clbk]: ?(error: ?err,
result: ?string) => void)
```

It fetches an item for a key and invokes a callback upon completion. Returns a Promise object.

Arguments

Name	Data Type	Description
key	string	It is a key of the item to fetch.
callback	?(error: ?err, result: ?string) => void	Function that will call with a result if found or any error.

setItem()

```
static setItem(key: str, value: str, [clbk]:
?(error: ?Error) => void)
```

It sets the value for a key and also invokes a callback upon completion. Returns a Promise as object.

Arguments

NAME	TYPE		DESCRIPTION
key	string		Key of the item to set.
value	string	Yes	Value to set for the key.
callback	?(error: ?Error) => void	No	Function that called with an error.

removeItem()

```
static removeItem(key: string, [clbk]: ?(error:
?err) => void)
```

It removes an item for a key and invokes a callback upon completion and also returns a Promise object.

Parameters

NAME	TYPE	DESCRIPTION
key	string	Key of the item to remove.
callback	?(error: ?Error) => void	Function that called with an error.

mergeItem()

```
static mergeItem(key: str, value: str, [clbk]:
?(error: ?Error) => void)
```

Merges an existing key-value with an input value, assuming both values are stringified JSON. It also returns a Promise object.

Note: It is not supported by all native implementations.

Arguments

Name	Type	Description
key	string	Key of the item to modify.
value	string	New value to merge for the key.
callback	?(error: ?Error) => void	This function that will be called with an error.

Example:

```
let UID223_object = {
 name: 'ABC',
 age: 50,
 traits: { hair: 'red', eyes: 'grey' }
};
// You need to define what will be added or updated
let UID223_delta = {
 age: 50,
 traits: { eyes: 'green', shoe_size: 20 }
};
AsyncStorage.setItem(
 'UID124',
 JSON.stringify(UID124_object),
 () => {
  AsyncStorage.mergeItem(
   'UID124',
   JSON.stringify(UID123_delta),
   () => {
    AsyncStorage.getItem('UID124', (err, result) =>
{
    console.log(result);
   });
  }
 );
 }
);
// Console result:
// => {'name':'ABC','age':14,'traits':
//  {'shoe_size':10,'hair':'red ','eyes':'blue'}}
```

clear()

```
static clear([clback]: ?(error: ?Error) => void)
```

It can erase *all* AsyncStorage for all clients, libraries, etc. You don't want to use this; use removeItem or multiRemove to clear only your app's keys. Returns a Promise object.

Parameters

NAME	TYPE	REQUIRED	DESCRIPTION
callback	?(error: ?Error) => void	No	Function that called with an error.

getAllKeys()

```
static getAllKeys([clbk]: ?(error: ?Error, keys:
?Array<string>) => void)
```

Gets *all* keys known to your app; for all callers, libraries, etc. Returns a Promise object.

Arguments

NAME	TYPE	DESCRIPTION
callback	?(error: ?Error, keys: ?Array<string>) => void	Function that will with all keys found and any error.

flushGetRequests()

```
static flushGetRequests(): [object Object]
```

Flushes are pending requests using a single batch call to get the data.
//

multiGet()

```
static multiGet(keys: Array<string>, [clbk]:
?(errors: ?Array<err>, result: ?Array<Array<str>>)
=> void)
```

This allows to batch the fetching of given an array items of key inputs. Then your callback will be invoked with an array of key-value pairs found:

```
multiGet(['aa1', 'k2'], cb) -> cb([['aa1', 'val1'],
['k2', 'val2']])
```

The method returns a Promise object.

Parameters

NAME	TYPE	DESCRIPTION
keys	Array<string>	Array of key for the getting the items.
callback	?(err: ?Array<err>, result: ?Array<arr<string>>) => void	Function that will call with a key-value array of the results, then an array of key-specific errors found.

Example:

```
AsyncStorage.getAllKeys((err, keys) => {
AsyncStorage.multiGet(keys, (err, stores) => {
  stores.map((result, value , store) => {
  // get at each store's key/value,you can work
with it
    let key = store[i][0];
    let value = store[i][1];
  });
 });
});
```

multiSet()

```
static multiSet(keyValPairs: Array<Array<string>>,
[callback]: ?(errors: ?Array<Error>) => void)
```

Use this as a operation for storing multiple key-value pairs. When the operation get completed you'll get a single callback with any errors:

```
multiSet([['aa1', 'val1'], ['bb2', 'val2']], cb);
```

The method returns a Promise object.

Arguments

NAME	TYPE	DESCRIPTION
keyValuePairs	Array<Array<string>>	It is an array of key-value array for the items to set.
callback	?(errors: ?Array<Error>) => void	Function that will call the an array of key-specific errors found.

multiRemove()

```
static multiRemove(keys: Array<str>, [clbk]:
?(errors: ?Array<Error>) => void)
```

It calls this to batch the deletion of all keys in the keys array. Returns a Promise object.

Arguments

NAME	TYPE	DESCRIPTION
keys	Array<string>	Array of keys for the deleting the items.
callback	?(errors: ?Array<Error>) => void	Function that will call an array of key-specific errors found.

Example:

```
let keys = ['k1', 'k2'];
AsyncStorage.multiRemove(keys, (err) => {
  // keys k1 & k2 removed, if they existed
  // most stuff after removal
});
});
//multimerge function
```

multiMerge()

```
static multiMerge(keyValuePairs:
Array<arr<string>>, [callback]: ?(errors:
?Array<err>) => void)
```

Batch operation to merge in existing and then new values for a set of keys. Its values are stringified JSON and returns a Promise object.

Note: It is not supported by all native implementations.

Arguments

NAME	TYPE	DESCRIPTION
keyValuePairs	Array<Array<string>>	Array of key-values for merging the items.
callback	?(errors: ?Array<Error>) => void	Function that will be called with an array of key-specific errors found.

Example:

```
// first user, initial values
let UID134_object = {
 name: 'ABC',
 age: 15,
 traits: { hair: 'brown', eyes: 'brown' }
};
// first user, delta values
let UID134_delta = {
 age: 31,
 traits: { eyes: 'blue', shoe_size: 10 }
};
// second user, initial values
let UID145_object = {
 name: 'Marge',
 age: 25,
 traits: { hair: 'blonde', eyes: 'blue' }
};
// second user, delta values
let UID345_delta = {
 age: 26,
 traits: { eyes: 'green', shoe_size: 6 }
};
let multi_set_pairs = [
 ['UID234', JSON.stringify(UID234_object)],
 ['UID345', JSON.stringify(UID345_object)]
];
let multi_merge_pairs = [
 ['UID234', JSON.stringify(UID234_delta)],
 ['UID345', JSON.stringify(UID345_delta)]
];
AsyncStorage.multiSet(multi_set_pairs, (err) => {
 AsyncStorage.multiMerge(multi_merge_pairs, (err) =>
{
  AsyncStorage.multiGet(['UID234', 'UID345'], (err,
stores) => {
   stores.map((result, i, store) => {
    let key = store[i][0];
    let val = store[i][1];
    console.log(key, val);
    });
```

```
    });
   });
  });
  // Console log results:
  // => UID234 {"name":"Chris","age":31,"traits":{
  "shoe_size":10,"hair":"brown","eyes":"blue"}}
  // => UID345 {"name":"Marge","age":26,"traits":{
  "shoe_size":6,"hair":"blonde","eyes":"green"}}
```

In this chapter, we will see you how to persist your data using *AsyncStorage.*

Step 1: Presentation: In this step, we will create the *our file named App.js* file.

```
    import React from 'react';
    import AsyncStorageExample from './async_storage
    _example.js'
    const App = () => {
      return (
       <AsyncStorageExample />
      )
    }
    export default App
```

Step 2: Logic:

- Name from the initial state is an empty string. We will update it from storage when the component is mounted.

- *setName* function will take the text from our input field, save it by using the *AsyncStorage* and update the state.

async_storage_example.js

```
import React, { Component } from 'react'
import { StatusBar } from 'react-native'
import { AsyncStorage, Text, View, TextInput,
StyleSheet } from 'react-native'
class AsyncStorageExample extends Component {
  state = {
    'name': ''
  }
```

```
  componentDidMount = () => AsyncStorage.getItem
('name').then((value) => this.setState({ 'name':
value }))
   setName = (value) => {
   AsyncStorage.setItem('name', value);
   this.setState({ 'name': value });
   }
  render() {
  return (
    <View style = {styles.container}>
    <TextInput style = {styles.textInput}
autoCapitalize = 'none'
    onChangeText = {this.setName}/>
    <Text>
      {this.state.name}
    </Text>
    </View>
  )
  }
}
export default AsyncStorageExample
const styles = StyleSheet.create ({
  container: {
  flex: 1,
  alignItems: 'center',
  marginTop: 50
  },
  textInput: {
  margin: 5,
  height: 100,
  borderWidth: 1,
  backgroundColor: '#7685ed'
  }
})
```

CONCLUSION

In this chapter, we learned about platform APIs. In the next chapter we are going to learn about modules of React Native.

React Native Modules

IN THIS CHAPTER

➤ Installing JavaScript libraries with NMP

➤ Native modules for iOS

➤ Native modules for Android

➤ Cross-platform native modules

In the previous chapter, we learned about platform APIs in React Native; in this chapter, we will learn about React Native modules.

MODULES

Native Modules Intro

A React Native app may require access to a native platform API that is not available by default in JavaScript, such as the native APIs for Apple or Google Pay. You want to leverage some existing Objective-C, Swift, Java, or C++ libraries without having to reimplement them in JavaScript or build some high-performance, multi-threaded code for image processing.

The NativeModule system exposes instances of Java/Objective-C/C++ (native) classes as JS objects to JavaScript (JS), allowing you to run arbitrary native code from within JS. While we do not anticipate this functionality to be part of the standard development process, its existence is critical. If React Native does not expose a native API that your JS project requires, you should be able to create one. If React Native does not expose a native API that your JS project requires, you should be able to create one!

DOI: 10.1201/9781003310440-7

INSTALLING JAVASCRIPT LIBRARIES WITH NPM

Libraries include pre-written codes that a developer may combine with their own code to do various activities that would otherwise need considerable, difficult coding.

Libraries, sub-packages, and other files can be included in packages. Libraries and packages are synonymous in several languages.

What Exactly Is NPM?

NPM is a package manager for the Node.js packages that is used to obtain and integrate packages into JavaScript scripts. These packages include all the files necessary for a module (library).

NPM is an essential component of the JavaScript ecosystem, including a plethora of open-source software, libraries, modules, and packages. It makes developing code much easier since developers may rely on already created code to do various operations.

How to Download NPM?

NPM is included with node.js and is installed automatically when you install node.js. So, first, we must download and install node.js from their official website: https://nodejs.org/en/download/.

Download the LTS (Recommended) version of node.js from the above-mentioned URL. Install node.js in your system after the download is complete. NPM will be installed immediately after node.js has been successfully installed on your machine.

You may use the command prompt (cmd) to check whether node.js and NPM have been correctly installed on your system.

```
> Node -v
> Npm -v
```

How to Download Packages Using NPM?

Now we will use NPM to get a package, which is a simple operation. To download any package using NPM, start a terminal and use the following syntax:

```
> npm install [package_name]
```

Now we will use NPM to get a package, which is a simple operation. To download any package using NPM, start a terminal and use the following syntax:

```
> npm install chalk
```

To store the package, NPM generates a new subdirectory called "node_ modules" (if it does not already exist). This folder will now include all your downloaded packages.

Run the following command to confirm that package was successfully installed:

```
> ls node_modules
```

How to Download Packages Globally with NPM

The technique described above only installs the NPM package locally, which implies that the package can only be accessed by the current project. If you wish to install an NPM package that can be accessed by any project on your system, use the following syntax:

```
> npm install -g [package_name]
> npm install -g upper-case
```

How to Use the package

The following is how an NPM package may be inserted into JavaScript source code:

```
const upper_case = require('upper-case');
console.log(upper_case.upperCase("Hello Linux
Hint!"));
```

Node.js, as most of you are undoubtedly aware, is a server-side technology. So, when we execute the above-mentioned code in a browser, we get the following error:

This issue may be avoided by installing a utility that handles all the requirements of the need() method in a browser. Browserify will be used in this case. Run the following command to install Browserify:

```
npm install -g browserify
```

Use the following command to generate a file containing all your source code's dependencies:

```
> browserify source-code_file-name.js -o bundle.js
```

If you get an error when performing the above-mentioned command, open the Windows Power Shell and run the following instructions before running the above-mentioned command:

```
> Set-ExecutionPolicy -Scope CurrentUser
-ExecutionPolicy Unrestricted
> Set-ExecutionPolicy RemoteSigned
```

Run the above-mentioned command again; it should work this time. Now, in the HTML file's header, replace the script source from your source-code file's name with bundle.js and execute the code again. This time, the code will execute correctly and will not generate any errors.

IOS NATIVE MODULES

Welcome to Native Modules for iOS. Please begin by reading the Native Modules Intro for an overview of what native modules are.

Create a Calendar Native Module

The following session will walk you through the process of creating a native module, CalendarModule, that will allow you to use Apple's calendar APIs from JavaScript. In conclusion, you should be able to invoke CalendarModule. createCalendarEvent('Dinner Party,' 'My House'); is a JavaScript method that invokes a native function that creates a calendar event.

The React Native team is presently re-architecting the Native Module framework. TurboModules is a new mechanism that will allow for more efficient type-safe communication between JavaScript and native code without relying on the React Native bridge. It will also allow for new expansions that were not previously available with the Native Module framework. More information may be found here. We've added notes throughout this documentation concerning Native Modules characteristics that will change in the TurboModules release, as well as how to best prepare for a smooth transition to TurboModules.

Setup

To begin, launch Xcode and navigate to the iOS project within your React Native application. Within a React Native app, you can access your iOS project here:

We recommend writing your native code with Xcode. Xcode is designed for iOS programming, and utilizing it will assist you in swiftly resolving minor issues such as code syntax.

Create Custom Native Module Files
The first step is to design our primary custom native module header and implementation files. Make a new file with the name RCTCalendarModule.h. and then add the following:

```
// RCTCalendarModule.h
#import <React/RCTBridgeModule.h>
@interface RCTCalendarModule : NSObject
<RCTBridgeModule>
@end
```

You may choose any name that corresponds to the native module you are creating. Because you are constructing a calendar native module, name the class RCTCalendarModule. Because ObjC does not have language-level support for namespaces like Java or C++, the class name is prefixed with a substring. This might be an abbreviation for your application or infra name. In this case, RCT stands for React.

The CalendarModule class implements the RCTBridgeModule protocol, as illustrated below. An Objective-C class that implements RCTBridgeModule protocol is referred to as a native module.

Next, let us get started on developing the native module. In the same folder, create the related implementation file, RCTCalendarModule.m, and contain the following content:

```
// RCTCalendarModule.m
#import "RCTCalendarModule.h"
@implementation RCTCalendarModule
// To export a module named RCTCalendarModule
RCT_EXPORT_MODULE();
@end
```

Module Name
For the time being, the only macro in your RCTCalendarModule.m native module is RCT EXPORT MODULE, which exports and registers the native module class with React Native. The RCT EXPORT MODULE

macro accepts an extra parameter that defines the module name in your JavaScript code.

This is not a string literal parameter. In the following example, RCT EXPORT MODULE(CalendarModuleFoo) is used instead of RCT EXPORT MODULE ("CalendarModuleFoo").

```
// To export a module named CalendarModuleFoo
RCT_EXPORT_MODULE(CalendarModuleFoo);
```

The native module may then be accessed in JS as follows:

```
const { CalendarModuleFoo } = ReactNative.
NativeModules;
```

If no name is specified, the JavaScript module name will be the same as the Objective-C class name, with "RCT" or "RK" prefixes removed.

Let us use the following example to use RCT EXPORT MODULE without any parameters. Therefore, because CalendarModule is the Objective-C class name, the module will provide to React Native with the RCT removed.

```
// Without passing in a name this will export native
module name as the Objective-C class name with "RCT"
removed
RCT_EXPORT_MODULE();
```

In JS, the native module may then be accessed as follows:
```
const { CalendarModule } = ReactNative.
NativeModules;
```

Export a Native Method to JavaScript
Unless expressly instructed, React Native will not expose any methods in a native module to JavaScript. The RCT_EXPORT_METHOD macro can be used to do this. Because methods written in the RCT_EXPORT_ METHOD macro are asynchronous, the return type is always void. You can utilize callbacks or emit events to transmit a result from an RCT_ EXPORT_METHOD function to JavaScript (covered below). Let us use the RCT_EXPORT_METHOD macro to create a native method for our CalendarModule native module. Call it createCalendarEvent() for the

time being, and accept name and location inputs as strings. The various argument types will be discussed.

```
RCT_EXPORT_METHOD(createCalendarEvent:(NSString *)
name location:(NSString *)location)
{
}
```

Keep in mind that the RCT_EXPORT_METHOD macro is not required when using TurboModules unless the method relies on RCT argument conversion. We discourage users from using RCTConvert since React Native will eventually delete RCT_EXPORT_MACRO. Alternatively, you may do the parameter conversion within the method body.

Before you extend the functionality of the createCalendarEvent() method, include a console log in the method to ensure that it was invoked from JavaScript in your React Native application. Make use of React's RCTLog APIs. Let us add the log call after importing that header at the start of your code.

```
#import <React/RCTLog.h>
RCT_EXPORT_METHOD(createCalendarEvent:(NSString *)
name location:(NSString *)location)
{
RCTLogInfo(@"Pretending to create event %@ at %@",
name, location);
}
```

Synchronous Methods

To construct a synchronous native method, utilize the RCT_EXPORT_ BLOCKING SYNCHRONOUS METHOD.

```
RCT_EXPORT_BLOCKING_SYNCHRONOUS_METHOD(getName)
{
return [[UIDevice currentDevice] name];
}
```

This method's return type must be of object type (id) and serializable to JSON. As a result, the hook may only return nil or JSON data (e.g., NSNumber, NSString, NSArray, NSDictionary).

At the time, we do not encourage utilizing synchronous methods because they might have significant performance implications and bring threading-related issues into your native modules. Keep in mind that if you utilize RCT_EXPORT_BLOCKING_SYNCHRONOUS_METHOD, your app will no longer be able to use the Google Chrome debugger. This is since synchronous methods need the JS VM to share memory with the app. React Native operates inside the JS VM in Google Chrome and connects asynchronously with mobile devices using WebSockets for the Google Chrome debugger.

Test What You Have Built

You have now completed the fundamental scaffolding for your native iOS module. Access native module and invoke its exported method in JavaScript to test this.

Locate a location in your application where you want to include a call to the native module's createCalendarEvent() function. An example of a component, NewModuleButton, that you may use in your app is shown below. Within the onPress() method of NewModuleButton, you may call the native module.

```
import React from 'react';
import { NativeModules, Button } from
'react-native';
const NewModuleButton = () => {
 const onPress = () => {
  console.log('We will invoke native module here!');
 };
 return (
  <Button
   title="Click to invoke native module!"
   color="#841584"
   onPress={onPress}
  />
 );
};
export default NewModuleButton;
```

To access native module from JavaScript, you must first import NativeModules from React Native:

```
import { NativeModules } from 'react-native';
```

The CalendarModule native module may then be accessed using NativeModules.

```
const { CalendarModule } = NativeModules;
```

Now that you have the CalendarModule native module, you may call your native function createCalendarEvent(). It is added to the onPress() procedure of NewModuleButton like follows:

```
const onPress = () => {
CalendarModule.createCalendarEvent('testName',
'testLocation');
};
```

The last step is to rebuild the React Native app so that you have access to the most recent native code (including your new native module!). Execute the following commands from the command line where you discovered the React Native application:

```
npx react-native run-ios
```

Building as You Iterate

As you go through these steps and iterate on your native module, you will need to execute a native rebuild of your application to access your most recent JavaScript modifications. This is since the code you are developing is contained within the native portion of your program. While React Native's metro bundler can listen for changes in JavaScript and rebuild the JS bundle on the fly, it cannot do the same for native code. If you wish to test your most recent native modifications, you must rebuild with the npx react-native run-ios command.

Recap

In JavaScript, you should now be able to call your native module's create-CalendarEvent() function. Because you are using RCTLog in the function, you can verify that your native method is being called by setting debug mode in your app and inspecting the JS console in Chrome or the mobile app debugger Flipper. Each time you use the native module function, you should see your RCTLogInfo(@"Pretending to create an event %@ at %@", name, location); message.

At this point, you have generated an iOS native module and used JavaScript to call a function on it in your React Native application.

Continue reading to learn more about what argument types your native module function accepts and how to configure callbacks and promises within your native module.

Beyond a Calendar Native Module

Better Native Module Export

Importing your native module by fetching it from NativeModules is a little clumsy.

You may develop a JavaScript wrapper for your native module to avoid customers from having to do this each time they want to access your native module. Make a new JavaScript file called NativeCalendarModule .js and fill it with the following code:

```
/**
* This exposes native CalendarModule module as a JS
module. This has a
* function 'createCalendarEvent' which takes
following arguments:
* 1. String name: A string representing name of the
event
* 2. String location: A string representing location
of the event
*/
import { NativeModules } from 'react-native';
const { CalendarModule } = NativeModules;
export default CalendarModule;
```

This JavaScript file is also a lovely place to implement any JavaScript side functionality. If you use a type system, such as TypeScript, you may add type annotations for your native module here. While React Native does not yet enable Native to JS type safety, these type annotations will ensure that all your JS code is type-safe. These annotations will also make it easier to transition to type-safe native modules in the future. Here is an example of how to provide type safety to the Calendar Module:

```
/**
* This exposes native CalendarModule module as a JS
module. This has a
* function 'createCalendarEvent' which takes
following parameters:
*
* 1. String name: A string representing name of the
event
```

```
* 2. String location: A string representing location
of the event
*/
import { NativeModules } from 'react-native';
const { CalendarModule } = NativeModules
interface CalendarInterface {
  createCalendarEvent(name: string, location:
string): void;
}
export default CalendarModule as CalendarInterface;
```

You may access the native module and invoke its function in other JavaScript files by doing the following:

```
import NativeCalendarModule from './
NativeCalendarModule';
NativeCalendarModule.createCalendarEvent('foo',
'bar');
```

It should be noted that this implies the place where you are importing CalendarModule is in the same hierarchy as CalendarModule.js. Please keep the relative import up to date as needed.

Argument Types
When a JavaScript native module method is called, React Native translates the parameters from JS objects to Objective-C/Swift object analogs. For example, if your Objective-C Native Module method takes an NSNumber, you must call it with a number in JS. The conversion will be handled by React Native. The following is a list of the parameter types supported by native module methods, as well as the JavaScript equivalents.

OBJECTIVE-C	JAVASCRIPT
NSString	string, ?string
BOOL	boolean
NSNumber	?boolean
double	number
NSNumber	?number
NSArray	Array, ?Array
NSDictionary	Object, ?Object
RCTResponseSenderBlock	Function (success)
RCTResponseSenderBlock, RCTResponseErrorBlock	Function (failure)
RCTPromiseResolveBlock, RCTPromiseRejectBlock	Promise

The kinds listed below are presently supported but will not be in TurboModules. Please refrain from using them.

- Function (failure) -> RCTResponseErrorBlock

- Number -> NSInteger

- Number -> CGFloat

- Number -> float

You can also create native iOS module methods that accept any argument type supported by the RCTConvert class (see RCTConvert for details about what is supported). All the RCTConvert helper functions take a JSON value as input and convert it to a native Objective-C type or class.

Exporting Constants

By overriding the native function constantsToExport, a native module can export constants(). ConstantsToExport() is overridden below and returns a Dictionary with a default event name property that you may access in JavaScript as follows:

```
- (NSDictionary *)constantsToExport
{
return @{ @"DEFAULT_EVENT_NAME": @"New Event" };
}
```

The constant may then be accessible in JS by using getConstants() on the native module as follows:

```
const { DEFAULT_EVENT_NAME } = CalendarModule.
getConstants();
console.log(DEFAULT_EVENT_NAME);
```

Technically, constants exported via constantsToExport() can be accessed straight from the NativeModule object. This will no longer be supported by TurboModules, thus we recommend the community to use the above solution to avoid future migration.

Because constants are only exported at startup time, changing constantsToExport() values during runtime has no effect on the JavaScript environment.

If you override constantsToExport() on iOS, you need also implement + requiresMainQueueSetup to notify React Native that your module must be initialized on the main thread before any JavaScript code runs. Otherwise, unless you explicitly opt-out with + requiresMain-QueueSetup, you will get a warning that your module may be started on a background thread in the future. If your module does not require UIKit access, answer to + requiresMainQueueSetup with NO.

Callbacks

A callback is a special type of argument that is only supported by native modules. For asynchronous methods, callbacks are utilized to transmit data from Objective-C to JavaScript. They may also be used to run JS asynchronously from the native side.

Callbacks are implemented in iOS using the type RCTResponseSenderBlock. The callback argument myCallBack is introduced to the createCalendarEventMethod() just below the callback parameter:

```
RCT_EXPORT_METHOD(createCalendarEvent:(NSString *)
title
        location:(NSString *)location
        myCallback:(RCTResponseSenderBlock)callback)
```

The callback may then be invoked in your native code, with any result you want to give to JavaScript as an array. It is worth noting that RCTResponseSenderBlock only takes one argument: an array of arguments to give to the JavaScript callback. You will return the ID of an event produced in a previous call in the section below.

It is crucial to note that the callback is not immediately executed when the native function completes – remember, the communication is asynchronous.

```
RCT_EXPORT_METHOD(createCalendarEvent:(NSString *)
title location:(NSString *)location callback:
(RCTResponseSenderBlock)callback)
{
NSInteger eventId = ...
callback(@[@(eventId)]);
RCTLogInfo(@"Pretending to create an event %@ at
%@", title, location);
}
```

This method could then be accessed in JavaScript by typing:

```
const onSubmit = () => {
 CalendarModule.createCalendarEvent(
  'Party',
  '04-12-2020',
  (eventId) => {
   console.log(`Created a new event with id
${eventId}`);
  }
 );
};
```

A native module should only call its callback once. It can, however, cache the callback and subsequently activate it. This method is frequently used to cover iOS APIs that need delegates; for example, see RCTAlertManager. Some memory is leaked if the callback is never triggered.

There are two techniques for managing errors using callbacks. The first method is to adhere to Node's practice and consider the first input supplied to the callback array as an error object.

```
RCT_EXPORT_METHOD(createCalendarEventCallback:(NSS
tring *)title location:(NSString *)location
callback: (RCTResponseSenderBlock)callback)
{
 NSNumber *eventId = [NSNumber numberWithInt:123];
 callback(@[[NSNull null], eventId]);
}
The first parameter may then be checked in
JavaScript to verify if an error was sent through:
const onPress = () => {
 CalendarModule.createCalendarEventCallback(
  'testName',
  'testLocation',
  (error, eventId) => {
   if (error) {
    console.error(`Error found! ${error}`);
   }
   console.log(`event id ${eventId} returned`);
  }
 );
};
```

Another possibility is to utilize two distinct callbacks: onFailure and onSuccess.

```
RCT_EXPORT_METHOD(createCalendarEventCallback:(NSS
tring *)title
         location:(NSString *)location
         errorCallback: (RCTResponseSenderBlock)
errorCallback
         successCallback: (RCTResponseSenderBlock)
successCallback)
{
 @try {
  NSNumber *eventId = [NSNumber numberWithInt:123];
  successCallback(@[eventId]);
 }
 @catch ( NSException *e ) {
  errorCallback(@[e]);
 }
}
```

Then, in JavaScript, you can add a callback for both error and success responses:

```
const onPress = () => {
 CalendarModule.createCalendarEventCallback(
  'testName',
  'testLocation',
  (error) => {
   console.error(`Error found! ${error}`);
  },
  (eventId) => {
   console.log(`event id ${eventId} returned`);
  }
 );
};
```

Use RCTMakeError from RCTUtils.h to provide error-like objects to JavaScript. For the time being, this merely sends an Error-shaped dictionary to JavaScript, but React Native intends to build true JavaScript Error objects in the future. You may additionally include an RCTResponseErrorBlock parameter, which is used for error callbacks and takes an NSError * object. Please keep in mind that TurboModules will not accept this argument type.

Promises

Native modules may also fulfill a promise, which can help to simplify your JavaScript, especially when utilizing the async/await syntax of ES2016. When the last parameter of a native module function is an RCTPromiseResolveBlock or RCTPromiseRejectBlock, the equivalent JS method returns a JS Promise object.

The following is the result of refactoring the above code to use promise instead of callbacks:

```
RCT_EXPORT_METHOD(createCalendarEvent:(NSString *)
title
        location:(NSString *)location
        resolver:(RCTPromiseResolveBlock)resolve
        rejecter:(RCTPromiseRejectBlock)reject)
{
NSInteger eventId = createCalendarEvent();
if (eventId) {
  resolve(@(eventId));
 } else {
  reject(@"event_failure", @"no event id returned",
nil);
 }
}
```

This method's JavaScript equivalent returns a Promise. This implies that within an async function, you may use the await keyword to call it and wait for result:

```
const onSubmit = async () => {
 try {
  const eventId = await CalendarModule.
createCalendarEvent(
   'Party',
   'my house'
  );
  console.log(`Created a new event with id
${eventId}`);
 } catch (e) {
```

```
  console.error(e);
  }
};
```

Sending Events to JavaScript
Native modules can send events to JavaScript without being directly called. For example, you could want to notify JavaScript that a calendar event from the native iOS calendar app is approaching. The ideal method is to subclass RCTEventEmitter, implement supportedEvents, and then call self sendEventWithName:

Import RCTEventEmitter and subclass RCTEventEmitter in your header class:

```
// CalendarModule.h
#import <React/RCTBridgeModule.h>
#import <React/RCTEventEmitter.h>
@interface CalendarModule : RCTEventEmitter
<RCTBridgeModule>
@end
```

JavaScript code may subscribe to these events by enclosing your module in a new NativeEventEmitter class.

If you waste resources by sending an event when there are no listeners, you will receive a warning. You can override startObserving and stopObserving in your RCTEventEmitter subclass to avoid this and improve your module's burden (for example, by unsubscribing from upstream notifications or suspending background processes).

```
@implementation CalendarManager
{
 bool hasListeners;
}
// Will be called when this module's first listener
is added.
-(void)startObserving {
  hasListeners = YES;
  // Set up any upstream listeners or background
tasks as necessary
}
// Will be called when this module's last listener
is dealloc or removed.
```

```
- (void) stopObserving {
  hasListeners = NO;
  // Remove upstream listeners, stop unnecessary
background tasks
}
- (void) calendarEventReminderReceived: (NSNotificatio
n *) notification
{
  NSString *eventName = notification.
userInfo[@"name"];
  if (hasListeners) { // Only send events if anyone
is listening
    [self sendEventWithName:@"EventReminder" body:@
{@"name" : eventName}];
  }
}
```

Threading

Unless the native module offers its own method queue, it should not make any assumptions about the thread on which it is called. Currently, if a native module lacks a method queue, React Native will build a separate GCD queue for it and execute its methods from there. Keep in mind that this is an implementation detail that may change. Override (dispatch_queue_t) methodQueue method in the native module if you want to explicitly specify a method queue for it. If it wants to utilize a main-thread-only iOS API, for example, it should express this via:

```
- (dispatch_queue_t) methodQueue
{
  return dispatch_get_main_queue();
}
```

Similarly, if an operation is likely to take a long time to complete, the native module can define its own queue on which to conduct operations. Again, React Native will now offer a distinct method queue for your native module, but this is an implementation detail on which you should not rely. If you do not offer your own method queue, your native module's long-running activities may wind up blocking async calls being done on unrelated native modules in the future. The RCTAsyncLocalStorage module, for example, generates its own queue to avoid blocking the React queue while waiting on slow disk access.

```
- (dispatch_queue_t)methodQueue
{
return dispatch_queue_create("com.facebook.React.Asy
ncLocalStorageQueue", DISPATCH_QUEUE_SERIAL);
}
```

The method specified in the queue will be shared by all your module's methods. If only one of our methods is long-running (or must run on a separate queue than the others for any reason), you may use dispatch_async inside the method to execute that method's code on a different queue without impacting the others:

```
RCT_EXPORT_METHOD(doSomethingExpensive:(NSString *)
param callback:(RCTResponseSenderBlock)callback)
{
dispatch_async(dispatch_get_global_queue(DISPATCH_
QUEUE_PRIORITY_DEFAULT, 0), ^{
  // Call long-running code on the background thread
  ...
  // we can invoke callback from any thread/queue
  callback(@[...]);
});
}
```

Modules can share dispatch queues.

The methodQueue function will be called once when the module is initialized and then maintained by React Native, so you do not need to hold a reference to the queue unless you want to utilize it within your module. However, if you want to share the same queue between many modules, you must keep and return the same queue object for each of them.

Dependency Injection

Any registered native modules will be created and initialized automatically by React Native. However, you may want to create and initialize your own module instances to inject dependencies, for example.

Create a class that implements the RCTBridgeDelegate Protocol, then initialize an RCTBridge with the delegate as an argument and an RCTRootView with the initialized bridge.

```
id<RCTBridgeDelegate> moduleInitialiser =
[[classThatImplementsRCTBridgeDelegate alloc] init];
```

```
RCTBridge *bridge = [[RCTBridge alloc] initWithDeleg
ate:moduleInitialiser launchOptions:nil];
RCTRootView *rootView = [[RCTRootView alloc]
        initWithBridge:bridge
          moduleName:kModuleName
        initialProperties:nil];
("ios - Dependency Injection in React Native modules
- Stack Overflow")
```

Exporting Swift

Because Swift does not allow macros, exposing native modules and their functions to JavaScript within React Native needs a little more setup. However, it functions in a comparable manner. Assume you have the same CalendarModule but in Swift:

```
// CalendarManager.swift
@objc(CalendarManager)
class CalendarManager: NSObject {
@objc(addEvent:location:date:)
func addEvent(_ name: String, location: String,
date: NSNumber) -> Void {
  // Date is ready to use!
}
@objc
func constantsToExport() -> [String: Any]! ("Swift
Native Module export하기 - Tistory") {
  return ["someKey": "someValue"]
}
}
```

It is critical to utilize the @objc modifications to guarantee that the class and functions are correctly exported to the Objective-C runtime.

Then, build a private implementation file in which you will register the necessary information with React Native:

```
// CalendarManagerBridge.m
#import <React/RCTBridgeModule.h>
@interface RCT_EXTERN_MODULE(CalendarManager,
NSObject)
RCT_EXTERN_METHOD(addEvent:(NSString *)name
location:(NSString *)location date:(nonnull
NSNumber *)date)
@end
```

If you are new to Swift and Objective-C, combining the two languages in an iOS project will also necessitate the use of an additional bridging file, known as a bridging header, to expose the Objective-C files to Swift. If you use the Xcode File>New File menu option to add your Swift file to your application, Xcode will offer to construct this header file for you. In this header file, you must include RCTBridgeModule.h.

```
// CalendarManager-Bridging-Header.h
#import <React/RCTBridgeModule.h>
```

Reserved Method Names
invalidate()
On iOS, native modules can comply with the RCTInvalidating protocol by implementing the invalidate() function. When the native bridge is invalidated, this function can be called (i.e., on devmode reload). Please utilize this technique when needed to provide the appropriate cleaning for your native module.

NATIVE MODULES FOR ANDROID

Welcome to Native Modules for Android. Please begin by reading the Native Modules Intro to learn more about native modules.

Create a Calendar Native Module

The following tutorial will explain the process of creating a native module, CalendarModule, that will allow you to use Android's calendar APIs from JavaScript. You will be able to call CalendarModule toward the end. In JavaScript, call createCalendarEvent('Dinner Party,' 'My House'); to invoke a Java function that generates a calendar event.

The React Native team is presently re-architecting the Native Module framework. TurboModules is a new mechanism that will allow for more efficient type-safe communication between JavaScript and native code without relying on the React Native bridge. It will also allow for new expansions that were not previously available with the Native Module framework. More information may be found here. We've included comments throughout this documentation regarding Native Modules features that will change in the TurboModules release, as well as how to best prepare for a seamless transition to TurboModules.

Setup

To begin, launch Android Studio and navigate to the Android project within your React Native application. Within a React Native app, you may access your Android project here:

- We recommend writing your native code in Android Studio. Android Studio is an IDE designed for Android programming that can assist you in swiftly resolving small issues such as code syntax mistakes.

- We also recommend that you use Gradle Daemon to accelerate builds while you iterate on Java code.

Create Custom Native Module File

The first step is to create CalendarModule.java Java file in the folder andro id/app/src/main/java/com/your-app-name/. This Java file will include the Java class for your native module.

Then add the following information:

```
package com.your-app-name; // replace com.your-app
-name with app's name
import com.facebook.react.bridge.NativeModule;
import com.facebook.react.bridge.ReactApplicationCon
text;
import com.facebook.react.bridge.ReactContext;
import com.facebook.react.bridge.ReactContextBaseJav
aModule;
import com.facebook.react.bridge.ReactMethod;
import java.util.Map;
import java.util.HashMap;
public class CalendarModule extends
ReactContextBaseJavaModule {
  CalendarModule(ReactApplicationContext context) {
    super(context);
  }
}
```

Your CalendarModule class, as you can see, extends the ReactContextBaseJavaModule class. Java native modules for Android are built as classes that extend ReactContextBaseJavaModule and implement the JavaScript functionality.

It is worth noting that for a Java class to be considered a Native Module by React Native, it only must extend the BaseJavaModule class or implement the NativeModule interface.

However, as stated, we recommend that you utilize ReactContextBaseJavaModule. ReactContextBaseJavaModule grants Native Modules access to the ReactApplicationContext (RAC), which is handy for hooking into activity lifecycle functions.

Using ReactContextBaseJavaModule will also make future type safety of your native module easy. For native module type safety, which will be available in future versions, React Native examines the JavaScript spec for each native module and constructs an abstract base class that extends ReactContextBaseJavaModule.

Module Name
The getName() function must be implemented by all Java native modules in Android. This function returns a string that reflects the native module's name. The name of the native module may then be used to access it in JavaScript. In the code below, for example, getName() yields "CalendarModule."

```
// add to CalendarModule.java
@Override
public String getName() {
  return "CalendarModule";
}
```

In JS, the native module may then be accessed as follows:
```
const { CalendarModule } = ReactNative.
NativeModules;
```

Export a Native Method to JavaScript
Then, in your native module, add a function that will generate calendar events that may be triggered in JavaScript. All native module methods that are intended to be called from JavaScript must be annotated with @ ReactMethod.

Create a function for CalendarModule called createCalendarEvent() that can be called in JS through CalendarModule.

createCalendarEvent(). For the time being, the method will accept strings for a name and a location. The various argument types will be discussed shortly.

```
@ReactMethod
public void createCalendarEvent(String name, String
location) {
}
```

When you call the method from your application, add a debug log to validate that it was invoked. The code demonstrates how to import and utilize the Log class from Android util package:

```
import android.util.Log;
@ReactMethod
public void createCalendarEvent(String name, String
location) {
  Log.d("CalendarModule", "Create event called with
the name: " + name
  + " and location: " + location);
}
```

Once you have finished creating the native module and connecting it to JavaScript, you may use the following steps to examine your app's logs.

Synchronous Methods
You may mark a native method as synchronous by passing it isBlocking-SynchronousMethod = true.

```
@ReactMethod(isBlockingSynchronousMethod = true)
```

We do not currently suggest this since invoking methods synchronously might have significant performance penalties and introduce threading-related issues into your native modules. Keep in mind that if you enable isBlockingSynchronousMethod, your app will no longer be able to use the Google Chrome debugger. This is since synchronous methods need the JS VM to share memory with the app. React Native operates inside the JS VM in Google Chrome and connects asynchronously with mobile devices using WebSockets for the Google Chrome debugger.

Register the Module (Android Specific)
After creating a native module, it must be registered with React Native. To accomplish this, put your native module to a ReactPackage and register the ReactPackage with React Native. During startup, React Native will loop through all packages, registering each native module within each ReactPackage.

To obtain a list of native modules to register, React Native calls the function createNativeModules() on a ReactPackage. If a module is not built and returned by createNativeModules for Android, it will not be accessible from JavaScript..

To add Native Module to ReactPackage, first build a new Java Class named MyAppPackage.java in android/app/src/main/java/com/app-name/ folder that implements ReactPackage:

Then provide the following information:

```
package com.your-app-name; // replace app-name with
your app's name
import com.facebook.react.ReactPackage;
import com.facebook.react.bridge.NativeModule;
import com.facebook.react.bridge.ReactApplicationCon
text;
import com.facebook.react.uimanager.ViewManager;
import java.util.ArrayList;
import java.util.Collections;
import java.util.List;
public class MyAppPackage implements ReactPackage {
  @Override
  public List<ViewManager> createViewManagers(R
eactApplicationContext reactContext) {
    return Collections.emptyList();
  }
  @Override
  public List<NativeModule> createNativeModules(
    ReactApplicationContext reactContext) {
    List<NativeModule> modules = new ArrayList<>();
    modules.add(new CalendarModule(reactContext));
    return modules;
  }
}
```

This file imports the native module CalendarModule that you wrote. The CalendarModule is then instantiated within the createNativeModules() method and returned as a list of NativeModules to register. If you subsequently add more native modules, you may instantiate them and add them to the list returned here.

It is worth mentioning that this method of registering native modules immediately initializes all native modules when the program starts, which increases the application's starting time. As an alternative, you may utilize TurboReactPackage. TurboReactPackage offers a getModule(String name, ReactApplicationContext rac) function that produces the native module object as necessary, rather than createNativeModules, which returns a list of instantiated native module objects. TurboReactPackage is now more difficult to implement. In addition to implementing getModule() method, you must also implement a getReactModuleInfoProvider() method, which returns a list of all the native modules that the package may instantiate as well as a function to do so, as seen below. Again, utilizing TurboReactPackage will help your application to start faster, but it is currently a bit difficult to develop. So, if you decide to utilize TurboReactPackages, proceed with caution.

To register the CalendarModule package, add MyAppPackage to the list of packages provided by the getPackages() function of ReactNativeHost. Open the MainApplication.java file, which is in the following path: android/app/src/main/java/com/your-app-name/MainApplication.java

Locate ReactNativeHost's getPackages() function and add your package to the list of packages returned by getPackages():

```
@Override
 protected List<ReactPackage> getPackages() {
 @SuppressWarnings("UnnecessaryLocalVariable")
 List<ReactPackage> packages = new
PackageList(this).getPackages();
 // below MyAppPackage is add to the list of
packages returned
 packages.add(new MyAppPackage());
 return packages;
 }
```

You have now successfully registered your native Android module.

Test What You Have Built

You have now completed the fundamental framework for your native module on Android. To test this, access the native module and call its exported function in JavaScript.

Locate a location in your application where you want to include a call to the native module's createCalendarEvent() function. An example of a component, NewModuleButton, that you may use in your app is shown below. Within the onPress() method of NewModuleButton, you may call the native module.

```
import React from 'react';
import { NativeModules, Button } from
'react-native';
const NewModuleButton = () => {
 const onPress = () => {
  console.log('We will invoke native module here!');
 };
 return (
  <Button
   title="Click to invoke your native module!"
   color="#841594"
   onPress={onPress}
  />
 );
};
export default NewModuleButton;
```

To access native modules from JavaScript, you must first import NativeModules from React Native:

```
import { NativeModules } from 'react-native';
```

The CalendarModule native module may then be accessed using NativeModules.

```
const { CalendarModule } = NativeModules;
```

Now that you have CalendarModule native module, you may call your native function createCalendarEvent (). It is added to the onPress() procedure of NewModuleButton as follows:

```
const onPress = () => {
CalendarModule.createCalendarEvent('testName',
'testLocation');
};
```

The ultimate step is to rebuild the React Native app so that you have access to the most recent native code (including your new native module!). Run the following commands from the command line where you find the React Native application:

```
npx react-native run-android
```

Building as You Iterate

As you go through these steps and iterate on your native module, you will need to execute a native rebuild of your application to access your most recent JavaScript modifications. This is because the code you are developing is contained within the native portion of your program. While the React Native metro bundler can listen for changes in JavaScript and recompile on the fly, it will not do so for native code. To test your newest native modifications, you must rebuild using the npx React Native run-android command.

Recap

You should now able to call your native module's createCalendarEvent() function from within the app. In our case, this is accomplished by pressing the NewModuleButton. You may verify this by inspecting the log you provide in your createCalendarEvent() function. You may access ADB logs in your app by following these instructions. You should now be able to search for your Log.d message (in our illustration, "Create event called with the name: testName and location: testLocation") and see it logged each time you execute your native module function.

You have now generated an Android native module and called its native function from JavaScript in your React Native app. Continue reading to discover more about the parameter types accessible to a native module method, as well as how to set up callbacks and promises.

Beyond a Calendar Native Module

Better Native Module Export

Importing your native module by pulling it from NativeModules is a little clumsy.

You may develop a JavaScript wrapper for your native module to avoid customers from having to do this each time they wish to access your native module. Make a new JavaScript file called CalendarModule.js and fill it with the following code:

```
/**
* This exposes native CalendarModule module as a JS
module. This has a
* function `createCalendarEvent` which takes the
following parameters:
* 1. String name: String representing name of event
* 2. String location: String representing the
location of event
*/
import { NativeModules } from 'react-native';
const { CalendarModule } = NativeModules;
export default CalendarModule;
```

This JavaScript file is also a delightful place to implement any JavaScript side functionality. If you use a type system, such as Typescript, you may add type annotations for your native module here. While React Native does not yet provide type safety from Native to JS, all your JS code will be. This will also make it easier to transition to type-safe native modules in the future. Here is an example of how to apply type safety to the CalendarModule:

```
/**
* This exposes native CalendarModule module as a JS
module. This has a
* function `createCalendarEvent` which takes
following parameters:
*
* 1. String name: A string representing name of the
event
* 2. String location: A string representing location
of the event
*/
import { NativeModules } from 'react-native';
const { CalendarModule } = NativeModules
interface CalendarInterface {
```

```
  createCalendarEvent(name: string, location:
string): void;
}
export default CalendarModule as CalendarInterface;
```

You may access the native module and invoke its function in other JavaScript files by doing the following:

```
import CalendarModule from './CalendarModule';
CalendarModule.createCalendarEvent('foo', 'bar');
```

This implies that the location from which you are importing CalendarModule is in the same directory as CalendarModule.js. Please keep the relative import up to date as needed.

Argument Types

When a JavaScript native module method is called, React Native translates the parameters from JS objects to Java object counterparts. For example, if your Java Native Module method supports a double, you must call it with a number in JS. The conversion will be handled by React Native. The following is a list of the parameter types supported by native module methods, as well as the JavaScript equivalents.

JAVA	JAVASCRIPT
Boolean	?boolean
boolean	boolean
Double	?number
double	number
String	string
Callback	Function
ReadableMap	Object
ReadableArray	Array

The kinds listed below are presently supported but will not be in TurboModules. Please refrain from using them:

- Integer -> ?number

- int -> number

- Float -> ?number

- float -> number

You must handle the conversion for argument kinds that are not stated above. Date conversion, for example, is not supported out of the box on Android. You may handle the conversion to the Date type yourself within the native method by doing the following:

```
String dateFormat = "yyyy-MM-dd";
SimpleDateFormat sdf = new
SimpleDateFormat(dateFormat);
  Calendar eStartDate = Calendar.getInstance();
  try {
    eStartDate.setTime(sdf.parse(startDate));
  }
```

Exporting Constants

A native module can export constants by implementing the native method getConstants(), which is accessible in JS. In the following code, you will implement getConstants() and return a Map containing a DEFAULT_ EVENT_NAME constant that you can access in JavaScript:

```
@Override
public Map<String, Object> getConstants() {
    final Map<String, Object> constants = new
HashMap<>();
    constants.put("DEFAULT_EVENT_NAME", "New Event");
    return constants;
}
("[RN] React Native Docs #10 : Native Modules ::
leejiwonn.log")
```

The constant may then be retrieved by calling the native module's get-Constants method in JS:

```
const { DEFAULT_EVENT_NAME } = CalendarModule.
getConstants();
console.log(DEFAULT_EVENT_NAME);
```

Technically, constants exported in getConstants() can be accessed straight from the native module object. This will no longer be supported by TurboModules thus, we recommend the community use the above solution to avoid future migration.

Constants are presently exposed solely at startup time, therefore changing getConstants values during runtime has no effect on the JavaScript environment. This will change with the introduction of TurboModules. With TurboModules, getConstants() is transformed into a standard native module function, and each invocation is sent to the native side.

Callbacks

A callback is an argument that is only supported by native modules. For asynchronous methods, callbacks are utilized to transmit data from Java to JavaScript. They can also be used to run JavaScript asynchronously from the native side.

To add a callback to a native module method, first import the Callback interface, and then add a new argument of type Callback to your native module function. There are a few quirks with callback parameters that will be eliminated with TurboModules. To begin, your function parameters can only include two callbacks: a successCallback and a failureCallback.

```
import com.facebook.react.bridge.Callback;
@ReactMethod
public void createCalendarEvent(String name, String
location, Callback callBack) {
}
```

You may call the callback from your Java method, passing any data you wish to JavaScript. Please keep in mind that only serializable data may be sent from native code to JavaScript. If you need to return a native object, use WriteableMaps; if you need to return a collection, use WritableArrays. It is also worth noting that the callback is not called right after the native function finishes. The ID of an event produced in a previous call is supplied to the callback below.

```
@ReactMethod
  public void createCalendarEvent(String name,
String location, Callback callBack) {
    Integer eventId = ...
    callback.invoke(eventId);
  }
("[RN] React Native Docs #10 : Native Modules ::
leejiwonn.log")
```

In JavaScript, this function might then be accessed as follows:

```
const onPress = () => {
 CalendarModule.createCalendarEvent(
  'Party',
  'My House',
  (eventId) => {
   console.log(`Created new event with id
${eventId}`);
  }
 );
};
```

Keep in mind that a native module method may only call one callback at a time. This means that you can only call a success or failure callback, not both, and each callback can only be called once. A native module, on the other hand, can save the callback and call it later.

There are two techniques for managing errors using callbacks. The first is to follow Node's approach and treat the callback's first parameter as error object.

```
@ReactMethod
public void createCalendarEvent(String name, String
location, Callback callBack) {
  Integer eventId = ....
  callBack.invoke(null, eventId);
}
```

The first parameter may then be checked in JavaScript to verify if an error was sent through:

```
const onPress = () => {
 CalendarModule.createCalendarEventCallback(
  'testName',
  'testLocation',
  (error, eventId) => {
   if (error) {
    console.error(`Error found! ${error}`);
   }
   console.log(`event id ${eventId} returned`);
  }
 );
};
```

Another possibility is to utilize onSuccess and onFailure callbacks:

```
@ReactMethod
public void createCalendarEvent(String name, String
location, Callback myFailureCallback, Callback
mySuccessCallback) {
}
```

Then, in JavaScript, you can add callback for both success and error responses:

```
const onPress = () => {
 CalendarModule.createCalendarEventCallback(
  'testName',
  'testLocation',
  (error) => {
   console.error(`Error found! ${error}`);
  },
  (eventId) => {
   console.log(`event id ${eventId} returned`);
  }
 );
};
```

Promises

Native modules may also fulfill a Promise, which can help to simplify your JavaScript, especially when utilizing the async/await syntax of ES2016. When the last parameter of a native module Java function is a Promise, the corresponding JS method will return a JS Promise object.

The following is the effect of rewriting the preceding code to utilize promises rather than callbacks:

```
import com.facebook.react.bridge.Promise;
@ReactMethod
public void createCalendarEvent(String name, String
location, Promise promise) {
  try {
    Integer eventId = ...
    promise.resolve(eventId);
  } catch(Exception e) {
    promise.reject("Create Event Error", e);
  }
}
```

A native module method, like callbacks, can reject or resolve a promise (but not both) but only once. This means that you can only call a success or failure callback, not both, and each callback can only be called once. A native module, on the other hand, can save the callback and call it later.

This method's JavaScript equivalent returns a Promise. This implies that within an async function, you may use the await keyword to call it and wait for its result:

```
const onSubmit = async () => {
 try {
  const eventId = await CalendarModule.
createCalendarEvent(
    'Party',
    'My House'
   );
   console.log(`Created new event with id
${eventId}`);
 } catch (e) {
  console.error(e);
 }
};
```

The reject approach can be used with a variety of arguments, including:

```
String code, String message, Throwable throwable,
WritableMap userInfo
```

The Promise.java interface may be found here for further information. React Native will set userInfo to null if it is not given. React Native will use a default value for the remaining arguments. The message parameter specifies the error message that appears at the top of the error call stack. The following is an example of a JavaScript error message caused by the following Java reject call.

Java reject call:

```
promise.reject("Create the Event error", "Error
parsing date", e);
```

When a promise is refused, the error me

Sending Events to JavaScript

Native modules can send events to JavaScript without being directly called. For example, you could want to notify JavaScript that a calendar event from the native Android calendar app is approaching. The RCTDeviceEventEmitter, which can be retrieved from the ReactContext.

```java
. . .
import com.facebook.react.modules.core.DeviceEventMa
nagerModule;
import com.facebook.react.bridge.WritableMap;
import com.facebook.react.bridge.Arguments;
. . .
private void sendEvent(ReactContext reactContext,
        String eventName,
        @Nullable WritableMap params) {
reactContext
    .getJSModule(DeviceEventManagerModule.RCTDevi
ceEventEmitter.class)
    .emit(eventName, params);
}
@ReactMethod
public void addListener(String eventName) {
// Setup any upstream listeners or background tasks
as necessary
}
@ReactMethod
public void removeListeners(Integer count) {
// Remove the upstream listeners, stop unnecessary
background tasks
}
. . .
WritableMap params = Arguments.createMap();
params.putString("eventProperty", "someValue");
. . .
sendEvent(reactContext, "EventReminder", params);
```

After that, JavaScript modules can register to accept events by using addListener on the NativeEventEmitter class.

```javascript
import { NativeEventEmitter, NativeModules } from
'react-native';
. . .
componentDidMount() {
    . . .
```

```
  const eventEmitter = new NativeEventEmitter(Native
Modules.ToastExample);
  this.eventListener = eventEmitter.addListener(
'EventReminder', (event) => {
   console.log(event.eventProperty) // "someValue"
  });
  ...
}
componentWillUnmount() {
  this.eventListener.remove(); //Removes the
listener
}
```

Getting Activity Result from startActivityForResult
If you want to retrieve results from an activity you began using startActivityForResult, you will need to listen to onActivityResult. You must extend BaseActivityEventListener or implement ActivityEventListener to do this. The former is chosen since it is less susceptible to API changes. Then, in the module's constructor, register the listener as follows:

```
reactContext.addActivityEventListener(mActivityRes
ultListener);
```

You can now listen for onActivityResult events by implementing the following method:

```
@Override
public void onActivityResult(
final Activity activity,
final int requestCode,
final int resultCode,
final Intent intent) {
// logic here
}
```

To show this, lets create a simple image picker. When invoked, the image picker will expose the function pickImage to JavaScript, which will return the path to the picture.

```
public class ImagePickerModule extends
ReactContextBaseJavaModule {
 private static final int IMAGE_PICKER_REQUEST = 1;
 private static final String E_ACTIVITY_DOES_NOT_
EXIST = "E_ACTIVITY_DOES_NOT_EXIST";
```

```java
 private static final String E_PICKER_CANCELLED =
"E_PICKER_CANCELLED";
 private static final String E_FAILED_TO_SHOW_PICKER
= "E_FAILED_TO_SHOW_PICKER";
 private static final String E_NO_IMAGE_DATA_FOUND =
"E_NO_IMAGE_DATA_FOUND";
 private Promise mPickerPromise;
 private final ActivityEventListener
mActivityEventListener = new
BaseActivityEventListener() {
  @Override
  public void onActivityResult(Activity activity,
int requestCode, int resultCode, Intent intent) {
    if (requestCode == IMAGE_PICKER_REQUEST) {
     if (mPickerPromise != null) {
      if (resultCode == Activity.RESULT_CANCELED) {
       mPickerPromise.reject(E_PICKER_CANCELLED,
       "Image picker was cancelled");
      } else if (resultCode == Activity.RESULT_OK) {
       Uri uri = intent.getData();
       if (uri == null) {
        mPickerPromise.reject(E_NO_IMAGE_DATA_FOUND,
        "No image data found");
       } else {
        mPickerPromise.resolve(uri.toString());
       }
      }
      mPickerPromise = null;
     }
    }
  }
 };
 ImagePickerModule(ReactApplicationContext
reactContext) {
  super(reactContext);
  // Add listener for the `onActivityResult`
  reactContext.addActivityEventListener(mActivityE
ventListener);
 }
 @Override
 public String getName() {
  return "ImagePickerModule";
```

```
}
@ReactMethod
public void pickImage(final Promise promise) {
 Activity currentActivity = getCurrentActivity();
 if (currentActivity == null) {
  promise.reject(E_ACTIVITY_DOES_NOT_EXIST,
  "Activity doesn't exist");
  return;
 }
 // Store promise to resolve or reject when picker
    returns the content
 mPickerPromise = promise;
 try {
  final Intent galleryIntent = new Intent(Intent.
  ACTION_PICK);
  galleryIntent.setType("image/*");
  final Intent chooserIntent = Intent.
createChooser(galleryIntent, "Pick an image");
  currentActivity.startActivityForResult(chooserI
  ntent, IMAGE_PICKER_REQUEST);
 } catch (Exception e) {
  mPickerPromise.reject(E_FAILED_TO_SHOW_
  PICKER, e);
  mPickerPromise = null;
 }
}
}
```

Listening to Lifecycle Events

Listening to LifeCycle events of the activity, such as onResume, onPause, and so on, is quite like how ActivityEventListener was built. LifecycleEventListener must be implemented in the module. Then, in the constructor of the module, register a listener as follows:

```
reactContext.addLifecycleEventListener(this);
```

You may now listen to the activity's LifeCycle events using the following methods:

```
@Override
public void onHostResume() {
```

```
    // Activity `onResume`
}
@Override
public void onHostPause() {
    // Activity `onPause`
}
@Override
public void onHostDestroy() {
    // Activity `onDestroy`
}
```

Threading

On Android, all native module async functions are currently executed on a single thread. Native modules should not make any assumptions about the thread on which they are being called, as the present assignment is susceptible to change in the future. If a blocking call is necessary, the hard lifting should be delegated to an internally controlled worker thread, from which any callbacks should be distributed.

CROSS-PLATFORM NATIVE MODULES

A cross-platform app development framework is a collection of technologies that enables you to create native or native-like apps for several platforms, including Android, iOS, Windows, and Web, from a single codebase.

This enables you to reach a significantly larger target audience across many platforms at a cheaper cost and in less time.

Based on programming languages, below are some of the top opensource cross-platform app development frameworks:

Programming Language	Framework
Java	Codename One
JavaScript	React Native, Cordova, Ionic, NativeScript, Appcelerator
Python	Kivy, BeeWare
C#	Xamarin
C++	Qt
Ruby	RubyMotion
Dart	Flutter
Basic	B4A

WHAT ARE THE ADVANTAGES OF CROSS-PLATFORM APPLICATION DEVELOPMENT FRAMEWORKS?

Here are a few advantages of cross-platform app development frameworks.

Code Reusability

The ability to reuse code is the most significant advantage of cross-platform app development frameworks. Developers just need to write code once, and that codebase can then be utilized to deliver the program across numerous platforms. This is known colloquially as "Write Once Run Anywhere," or WORA.

WORA eliminates repetition, resulting in lower operational expenses. A unified codebase also enables you to easily add another platform in the future.

Reduced Costs and Resources

Cross-platform app development frameworks enable you to be agile while employing a smaller team with a single skill set and codebase for several platforms, allowing you to strike a solid balance between quality and cost.

It is as easy as this: Lower expenses are related to less time, money, and efforts spent on app development.

Easy Deployment and Maintenance

Developers just need to produce and maintain an only source code because there is a single codebase for many platforms. This means that deployment, maintenance, upgrades, and bug fixes are simple and quick.

Changes to the code are instantly synced across several platforms and devices, saving time and effort.

Wider Market Reach

Cross-platform frameworks provide you with the most exposure to your target audience by allowing you to launch your program on numerous platforms, such as Android, iOS, Windows, MacOS, and web. These guarantee that potential consumers have a broader market reach.

Uniform Design

Cross-platform frameworks make it possible to share a consistent UI/UX across several platforms while adhering to platform-specific standards.

Users will be able to recognize and interact with the app on every platform if they have a consistent experience.

CONCLUSION

Installing JavaScript Libraries with NPM, Native Modules for iOS, Native Modules for Android, and Cross-Platform Native Modules were all covered in this chapter. In the following chapter, we will learn about debugging and developer tools.

Debugging and Developer Tools

IN THIS CHAPTER

➤ Debugging and developer tools

➤ JavaScript debugging practices, translated

➤ React Native debugging tools

➤ Debugging beyond JavaScript

In the previous chapter, we learned about modules in React Native, in this chapter, we are going to learn about debugging and developer tools.

DEBUGGING AND DEVELOPER TOOLS

Shaking your smartphone or heading to the Hardware menu in the iOS Simulator and selecting "Shake Gesture" will take you to the Developer Menu. Use the D keyboard shortcut while your app is running in the iOS Simulator, M when running in an Android emulator on the Mac OS, and Ctrl+M on Windows and Linux. To reach the Dev Menu on Android, execute the command adb shell input keyevent 82. (82 being the Menu key code.)

DOI: 10.1201/9781003310440-8

Enabling Fast Refresh

React Native's Fast Refresh functionality gives near-instant feedback for modifications to React components. It may be beneficial to have Fast Refresh activated while troubleshooting. Fast Refresh is enabled by default and may be turned off by toggling the "Enable Fast Refresh" option in the React Native Developer Menu. Many of your changes should be apparent in a second or two if enabled.

Enabling Keyboard Shortcuts

In iOS Simulator, React Native supports a few keyboard shortcuts. They are detailed further down. To activate them, go to the Hardware menu, choose Keyboard, and tick the "Connect Hardware Keyboard" box.

LogBox

In development builds, errors and warnings are presented in LogBox within your program.

LogBox is disabled by default in release (production) versions.

Console Errors and Warnings

Console faults and warnings are presented on-screen as on-screen alerts with a red or yellow badge, as well as the number of errors or warnings in the console. To view a console problem or warning, press the notice to get full-screen details about the log and to paginate through all the console's logs.

These alerts can be hidden by using LogBox.ignoreAllLogs(). This is useful for product demos, for example. LogBox.ignoreLogs() may also be used to hide notifications on a per-log basis. This is handy when a loud warning cannot be corrected, such as those in a third-party reliance.

As a last option, ignore logs and set a task to fix any ignored logs.

```
import { LogBox } from 'react-native';
// Ignore log notification by message:
LogBox.ignoreLogs(['Warning: ...']);
// Ignore all log notifications:
LogBox.ignoreAllLogs();
```

Copy

Unhandled Errors

Unhandled JavaScript errors, like undefined, are not a function and will result in a full-screen LogBox error displaying the fault source. When these problems occur, they are dismissible and minimized so you can monitor the state of your app, but they should always be fixed.

Syntax Errors

When syntax errors occur, the full-screen LogBox error will appear, displaying the stack trace and the location of the syntax problem. This error cannot be ignored since it signifies faulty JavaScript execution, which must be corrected before proceeding with your program. Fix the syntax problem and either save to automatically dismiss or cmd+r to reload to dismiss these errors.

Chrome Developer Tools

To debug the JavaScript code in Chrome, go to the Developer Menu and select "Debug JS Remotely." This will launch a new tab with the address http://localhost:8081/debugger-ui.

To launch the Developer Tools, go to the Chrome Menu and select Tools Developer Tools. You may also use keyboard shortcuts to access the DevTools. For a better debugging experience, you may also wish to activate Pause On Caught Exceptions.

On Android, if the times between the debugger and the device have shifted, features like animation, event behavior, and so on may not operate correctly, or the results may be inaccurate. Please fix this by executing adb shell "date +%m%d%H%M%Y.%S%3N on your debugger computer. For usage on a genuine device, root access is necessary.

Please keep in mind that the React Developer Tools Chrome extension does not support React Native, but you may use its standalone version instead.

Debugging Using a Custom JavaScript Debugger

To use a custom JavaScript debugger instead of Chrome Developer Tools, set the REACT DEBUGGER environment variable to a command that will run your own debugger instead of Chrome Developer Tools. Then, from the Developer Menu, click "Debug JS Remotely" to begin debugging.

The debugger will get a list of all project roots, separated by a space. If you set REACT_DEBUGGER="node/path/to/launchDebugger.js --port 2345 --type ReactNative", the command node /path/to/launchDebugger. js —port 2345 --type ReactNative /path/to/reactNative/app will be used to launch your debugger.

Custom debugger commands run in this manner should be short-lived processes that emit no more than 200 kilobytes of output.

Safari Developer Tools

You may use Safari to debug your iOS app without having to activate "Debug JS Remotely."

- Enable Develop menu in the Safari: Preferences → Advanced → Select "Show Develop menu in menu bar"
- Select your app's JSContext: Develop → Simulator → JSContext
- Safari's Web Inspector should open which has Console and a Debugger

While sourcemaps are not enabled by default, they may be enabled by following these steps or viewing this video and adding breakpoints at the appropriate places in the source code.

However, every time the app is restarted (either via live reload or manually), a new JSContext is produced. You may avoid having to manually choose the most current JSContext by selecting "Automatically Show Web Inspectors for JSContexts."

React Developer Tools

To debug the React component hierarchy, you may utilize the standalone version of React Developer Tools. Install the react-devtools package globally to utilize it:

React-devtools version 4 requires react-native version 0.62 or higher to function properly.

- npm
- Yarn

```
npm install -g react-devtools
```

Now, from the terminal, run react-devtools to launch the standalone DevTools app:

```
react-devtools
```

It should connect to your simulator in a matter of seconds.

Add react-devtools as a project dependency to avoid global installations. Add react-devtools package to your project using npm install --save-dev react-devtools, then add "react-devtools": "react-devtools" to your package.json's scripts section, and then activate the DevTools with npm run react-devtools from your project folder.

Integration with React Native Inspector

Select "Toggle Inspector" from the in-app Developer Menu. It will provide an overlay that allows you to tap on any UI element to get information about it.

When react-devtools is running, Inspector will collapse and instead use the DevTools as the primary UI. In this mode, clicking on something in the simulator will bring up the relevant components in the DevTools:

To escape this mode, select "Toggle Inspector" from the same menu.

Inspecting Component Instances

When debugging JavaScript in Chrome, you may view the React components' properties and state in the browser console.

To begin, open the Chrome console by following the steps for debugging in Chrome.

Check that the debuggerWorker.js option in the top left corner of the Chrome console is selected. This is a critical stage.

Then, in React DevTools, choose a React component. A search bar at the top allows you to find one by name. When you pick it, it will appear in the Chrome console as $r, allowing you to explore its props, state, and instance attributes.

Performance Monitor

By selecting "Perf Monitor" from the Developer Menu, you may activate a performance overlay to assist you in debugging performance issues.

Debugging Application State

Reactotron is an open-source desktop program for inspecting Redux or MobX-State-Tree application state, as well as seeing custom logs, running custom commands like resetting state, storing, and restoring state snapshots, and other useful debugging capabilities for React Native apps.

The README file contains installation instructions. If you are using Expo, here is an article that will walk you through the installation process.

Native Debugging

Projects with Native Code Only

The next section only applies to projects that have exposed native code. If you are using the managed expo-cli process, check the ejecting tutorial to learn how to utilize this API.

Accessing Console Logs

You may see an iOS or Android app's console logs by executing the following commands in a terminal while the program is running:

```
npx react-native log-ios
npx react-native log-android
```

These may also be viewed using the iOS Simulator's Debug Open System Log option or by running adb logcat *:S. ReactNative:V When an Android app is running on a device or emulator, type ReactNativeJS:V in a terminal.

Console logs display in the same terminal output as the bundler whether you are using Create React Native App or Expo CLI.

Debugging on a Device with the Chrome Developer Tools

If you are using Create React Native App or Expo CLI, this is already set up for you.

On iOS, open the file RCTWebSocketExecutor.mm and replace "localhost" with your computer's IP address, then choose "Debug JS Remotely" from the Developer Menu.

You may use the adb command line tool on Android 5.0+ devices connected via USB to configure port forwarding from the device to your computer:

```
adb reverse tcp:8081 tcp:8081
```

Alternatively, under the Developer Menu, click "Dev Settings," then adjust the "Debug server host for device" setting to match your computer's IP address.

If you encounter any problems, it is conceivable that one of your Chrome extensions is interfering with the debugger in unexpected ways. Disable all extensions and then re-enable them one by one until you find the defective one.

Debugging Native Code

When working with the native code, such as when developing native modules, you may launch the app from Android Studio or Xcode and utilize native debugging tools (for example, setting breakpoints) exactly as you would when building a standard native app.

JAVASCRIPT DEBUGGING PRACTICES TRANSLATED

Debugging is a challenging task. It is a talent that every developer should be able to master. When developing code, developers are constantly prone to making mistakes. We cannot completely eradicate bugs, but we can learn how to deal with them intelligently.

We will look at numerous approaches for debugging JavaScript code in this section. The good news is that all current browsers provide a built-in JavaScript debugger.

Best Practices

It is preferable to keep our code from being prone to bugs. A single piece of code/logic can be written in a variety of ways. The quality with which programmers and beginners write their code is important here. We also need well-structured code that will aid in debugging later.

Beautify to Debug

We might have to debug in production. However, if our code has been minified or unindented, we may un-minify it into a more legible style.

The code will not be as useful as our actual code, but at least we will know what is going on. Below is a button accessible in Chrome for beautifying our code and making it more readable.

Debugging Methods

Console Method

To debug the JavaScript code, we may utilize a console API. For the console API, there are several possibilities.

- **console.log()**: We may use console.log() to output any string or object value in the browser's debugger window.

  function add(num1, num2) {return num1 + num2}let num1 = 5, num2 = 6;let result = add(num1, num2);console.log("%d + %d = %d", num1, num2, result);console.info("%d + %d = %d", num1, num2, result);console.warn("%d + %d = %d", num1, num2, result); console.error("%d + %d = %d", num1, num2, result);

- **console.table(data, obj)**: This method accepts one necessary argument data, which must be an array or an object, and one optional parameter columns, which is an array of strings. It outputs data in the form of a table.

  function Band(firstName, lastName, roll) {this.firstName = firstName;this.lastName = lastName;this.roll = roll;}var Zack = new Band("Zack", "Wyld", 1);var Ozzy = new Band("Ozzy", "Osbourne", 2);var Ronie = new Band("Ronie", "Dio", 3);console .table([zack,ozzy,ronie]);

  We may use the optional columns argument to display only a subset of the columns:

  console.table([Zack,Ozzy,Ronie],["firstName","lastName"]);

- **console.trace()**: This will display the call path used to get to the point where you called console.trace ()
  ```
  function func1() {func2();}function func2()
  {func3();}function func3() {console.trace();}
  func1();
  ```

- **console.assert(expression,object)**: If the assertion is false, this method prints an error message to the console. Nothing happens if the statement is true.
  ```
  function isOddNumber(num1) {let result = num1 % 2
  !== 0console.assert(result,{ number: num1, errorMsg:
  "this number is even" });return result;}
  isOddNumber(6)
  ```

Using a Debugger

Since ES5, the keyword debugger has been reserved in EcmaScript. When we insert the debugger into our code, the Javascript execution is halted.

When we launch our inspector tool, it can only take effect and we may begin debugging.

Breakpoints

There are several approaches we may use to debug our code. At each breakpoint, JavaScript will pause its execution and allow us to inspect the values within our code.

Unconditional Breakpoints

The unconditional breakpoint is used when we wish to interrupt the execution of the code when we reach its line. By clicking on the line number on the left, we may establish an unconditional breakpoint.

The line number is shown by a red dot.

Here is the simple code sample above, with our unconditional breakpoint set at line number 5. And from there, we can delve deeper into our debugging process.

Using a Breakpoint List

The unconditional breakpoint is used when we wish to interrupt the execution of the code when we reach its line. By clicking on the line number on the left, we may establish an unconditional breakpoint.

The line number is shown by a red dot.

Here is the simple code sample above, with our unconditional breakpoint set at line number 5. And from there, we can delve deeper into our debugging process.

Adding Logpoints

Sometimes we want to see the value of a variable but do not want to interrupt execution. We can utilize logpoints for this method.

Logpoints assist us by printing a message to the Console without halting the code's execution. When we set a logpoint, a red bubble with a little caret appears.

We may also examine our log point in the right panel of breakpoints. When we hit a logpoint, the message we defined is written directly into the console.

Unsetting Breakpoints

If we already have it set, we may unset it again. That is, we can just delete the breakpoint as well.

We may delete breakpoints by right-clicking on the number.

This is a huge time saver since we will be able to readily retrieve the information we want to identify until that point of execution.

Using Watches

Watch is the same as witnessing any expression in our code that we want to observe. To discover problems, we may utilize a watch expression in conjunction with the inspector tool.

We may watch the variables by clicking on the watch icon in the watch panel and entering the variable name.

In this instance, we are looking at two variables, one minute and one second. Using watches, we can evaluate any expression we want into our code.

Using Call Stack

It is a bottom-up method. If we used a breakpoint to enable call stack in the browser, it would provide us with the function calls one after the other. The function that was performed first would remain at the bottom, while the function that came before it would remain at the top.

Peek at the code, for example. Three primary calls are stacked on top of each other in this case. The one at the bottom is the first to execute.

Debugging Tools

Rookout

Rookout is a debugging platform that lets developers define when and how a breakpoint is triggered. You may test their sandbox environment to see it in action.

This remote debugging tool provides us with detailed information about our program without requiring us to restart, redeploy, or create code. It is simple to debug at every step, whether cloud, local, development, or production, monolithic or Microservices architecture, including Serverless architecture.

NodeJS Inspector

Backend developers that use JS have access to a GUI-based debugger for Node as well. It may also be triggered by entering the following command into our terminal:

```
npm install -g node-inspectorpath:\>node-inspector
--web-port=5500
```

Using a Code Editor

There are many wonderful text editors available, and we can locate several addons that can help us debug our code. Sublime, Visual Studio, Webstorm, Vim, and more well-known editors are available.

Framework Debugging Tools (Angular, React, Vue)
There are browser addons/extensions for debugging frameworks for framework enthusiasts. The main and popular frameworks, such as React, Vue, and Angular, each have their own extensions that may be installed for debugging.

JSON Formatter and Validator
JSON might be tough to interpret at times. To work with JSON data, we offer a JSON formatter and a validator. The first assists us in formatting it into a human-readable format, while the validator assists us in determining if our JSON is legitimate or not.

"use strict" Mode
This is the method for restricting specific variants in our JavaScript code that was introduced in ECMAScript5. Browsers that don't support strict mode will run the code in a different manner.

Strict mode modifies both runtime behavior and syntax. We normally use strict mode for the entire script as well as individual functions, but it does not apply to a block of statements enclosed by braces.

REACT NATIVE DEBUGGING TOOLS

Top 6 Debugging Tools for React Native Developers
Many people have contributed numerous tools to the ecosystem that will benefit other React Native developers. Here is a list of the best six debugging tools for React Native developers to debug rapidly to increase productivity and handle any problems.

Chrome's DevTools
It is the first tool that springs to mind when a developer thinks of debugging React Native. We may use it to debug web apps developed on React Native.within since it is driven by JavaScript.

Requirements
Connect both devices to the same Wi-Fi network to utilize this tool for React Native debugging.

Previously, the simplest method to debug any code was to use Chrome's DevTools. In MacOS, use Ctrl+D to launch the iOS simulator and Ctrl+M to launch the Android emulator in Chrome. Use Ctrl + M if you are using

Windows (like iOS). Remote debugging is also possible by shaking the mobile device to reveal in-app developer choices. Select Debug JS remotely, and then open Chrome to the URL http://localhost:8081/debugger-ui/ to launch the basic debugger with the fundamental functionality.

This tool's configuration can be a bit difficult. For answers to your query, you can look at GitHub demonstrations or Stack Overflow. You can quickly toggle the Chrome inspector after it is linked. It should be noted that it does not debug styles or alter their properties. When investigating React's component hierarchy, things become much more difficult.

Other high-level debugging tools for professionals are listed below.

React Developer Tools

This tool may be used to debug React Native using the desktop app. The setup is quite straightforward. Simply add the following command, either locally or globally.

```
yarn add react-devtools
```

Use the command below to install NPM.

```
npm install react-devtools --save
```

You can now run yarn react-devtools to launch the app. Using this tool, you may inspect the React component hierarchy. In addition, you can debug styles in React Native, implement style properties, and see the direct reflection of changes made without reloading.

React Native Debugger

It is a desktop program that is available for macOS, Windows, and Linux. This is the most recommended debugging tool, especially if you are creating your React Native application with Redux. Other debugging tools, such as Redux's DevTools and React's Developer Tools, can be integrated. As a result, you may mix all these tools to get the most out of them. Furthermore, unlike the React Developer Tools, no installation is necessary.

Every developer would advocate this combo since it has all the fundamental pieces and functionalities necessary for React Native mobile development. You may analyze and debug React elements by inspecting and debugging the redux logs and actions using an interface and another interface for React Developer Tools. Its setup is extremely simple and quick. The installation process may be found here. In addition, the toggling inspector from the Dev Menu allows you to examine and alter the React elements. Some of the top features available in this combo are listed below.

1. **Elements**: Inspect the element's styles, edit, and view the results instantly in the simulator.

2. **Profiler**: Get a flamegraph with components render duration to detect performance issues.

3. **Console**: Inspect errors and warnings.

4. **Sources**: Debugg javascript, set breakpoints and step through the code.

5. **Network**: Inspect and record network requests (enable it with MacBook touch bar button).

6. Memory – Check memory leaks.

Redux DevTools

Redux, as you may know, is a standalone framework for common state management that is widely used in both React JS and React Native. As a result, you cannot simply ignore this critical function when troubleshooting. Redux Devtools is regarded as the greatest debugging tool for that specific function. You can easily explore the relationships between activities and their repercussions on your data store.

Redux DevTools allows you to seamlessly dock redux debugging components into your application. However, this will add to the complexities. However, Redux DevTools has some of the most helpful functionalities, like as

1. Inspector showing real-time actions

2. Action tab

3. State tab

4. Diff tab

5. Test tab

6. Log Monitor

7. Dispatcher

8. Chart

9. Slider

10. Export/import

Redux Devtools Extension may also install in your Chrome or Firefox browser. This addon uses a pre-built debugging UI that is kept independent from your application code.

Nuclide – Atom's Plug-in

It is an open-source React Native tool that is installed as a plug-in on top of Atom, a popular IDE created by Facebook.

This debugger's strong community support allows you to get the help you need to do anything with Nuclide. It is regarded as the finest because of its built-in support for the React Native framework. It also includes an extra set of components and extensions that allow you to develop in the Flow and JavaScript programming languages, as well as the React UI framework.

Inline errors, auto-complete, jump-to-definition features, and additional services such as Remote and JavaScript development, Hack development, built-in debugging, working sets, mercurial support, task runner, and so on are among the expressive features of Nuclide.

Reactotron

It is a 2016 open-source desktop program developed by Infinite Red that is accessible for several platforms such as Windows, MacOS, and Linux. It is the best substitute for React Native Debugger, which offers just identical functionality.

The same application may be used to debug both React JS and React Native projects. In addition, developers may watch the console and follow the status of the program, record messages, make API requests, examine, and do additional operations. It is simple and quick to install, as is the installation method. Set up various extensions quickly and easily to conduct activities more flexibly. The most useful feature of this React Native debugging tool is that it mixes redux actions with console answers.

Some of Reactotron's finest features are listed below.

1. **Connections**: Run multiple devices and quickly switch debugging.

2. **Timeline tab**: track app events and redux actions.

3. State tab.

4. React Native tab.

Furthermore, there are several tools available for debugging React Native. Other prominent tools include Expo, Flow, Visual Studio Code, ESLint, Ignite, and others. Choose the proper React Native Debugging tool by considering the project's unique demands as well as the developer's convenience. Choose the one that will save you time and money eventually.

DEBUGGING BEYOND JAVASCRIPT

The Basics of Console Logging

Let us start with the fundamentals of console debugging. I am sure most of you have used these, but if you are new to JavaScript, here are some of the common techniques for console logging to aid in debugging your application.

- **console.log:** Logs a message or object to the console.

- **console.info:** Logs a message or object to the console, which is informational.

- **console.warn:** Logs the console log message as a warning, to indicate a potential problem.

- **console.error:** Logs the console log message as an error, to indicate an error has occurred.

```
console.log('Hello Everyone');
console.info('Informational Logging');
console.warn('Warning to indicate something weird');
console.error('This is bad, here is error');
```

The above list includes the most frequent console logs found in various codebases. These are quite useful for troubleshooting a program, but that is not all.

Beyond the Basics of Console Logging

To see all the examples, right-click -> inspect and open the console in any browser. And, while reading this text, follow along and write the instructions on the console to better comprehend them.

console.table()

I only recently learned about console.table() and wish I had known about it sooner for easier debugging. Let us define an object called myShopping-Cart below:

```
const myShoppingCart = [{
  id: "1",
  name: "Banana",
  price: 10,
},
{
  id: "2",
  name: "Apple",
  price: 20,
},
{
  id: "3",
  name: "Orange",
  price: 30,
}];
```

If I used the standard console.log() function to log the myShopping-Cart, the output would be as follows:

Assume you have a large object that would seem cleaner and be easier to debug if it were in the form of a table. Look no further. To gain a better look, use console.table() to output your object in the form of a lovely table.

Isn't this beautiful?

One thing to remember is that console.table() can only handle up to 1000 rows.

console.assert()

You may conduct conditional logging without using an if-else condition by using console.assert(). console.assert(condition, message) is the syntax. When a condition is falsely passed, the assertion can be recorded. See the examples below to better understand them.

console.trace()

This is another another important console feature. The console.trace() function is used to print a stack trace to the console. This is handy if you are debugging and get stuck at a given point in the code and want to look at the stack trace in more detail. This is incredibly important for confirming that your code is operating as it should and for navigating the stack trace.

console.count()

This is handy if you have the same piece of code running numerous times and want to keep track of it for whatever reason. See the sample below to see how it is used.

It is worth noting that the console.count() function returns the current count each time the same piece of code is performed.

console.memory

If you need a fast snapshot of your memory use, you may access the JavaScript heap size using the console.memory property.

This can come in useful if you suspect a performance leak while the code is running and want to get a brief snapshot of the memory usage on the console.

console.time()

The control.time() function launches a timer on the console.

```
var i;
console.time("test1");
for (i = 0; i < 1000000000; i++) {
  // some code
}
console.timeEnd("test1");
VM732:6 test1: 2624.0439453125ms
```

It may be used to determine how long a piece of code takes to execute. The console.timEnd() function can be used to stop the timer. As illustrated in the sample above, you may pass a label to these methods to keep track of the console logging.

CONCLUSION

In this chapter, we learned about React Native debugging and developer tools; in the following chapter, we will learn about bringing it all together in React Native.

Putting It All Together

Let's put it all together now that we've covered many of the components you'll need to create your own React Native applications. We have worked with minor cases up to this point. We will look at the structure of a bigger application in this chapter. We will go through how to utilize Reflux, a Flux-based framework for unidirectional dataflow. We'll also look at how to resize text to match different screen sizes using the Dimensions API. Finally, we will go through some homework: assignments that you can do to get a sense of what it is like to add new features to an existing React Native codebase.

Here are some stages to assist you synthesize everything you have learned from this book to answer the two key questions: should I create a legal company for my firm, and if so, what kind? At this point, it is good setting aside several of this book's issues that are not related to these basic questions. Choosing a name for your company is enjoyable, but it can wait. Also, it is good to take a break from all the technical intricacies about how LLCs and companies work that this book has thrown at you. If the answers to the truly key issues indicate a certain company structure, it will

DOI: 10.1201/9781003310440-9

be worth the time and effort to master the little administrative nuances, no matter how opaque they appear today.

Step 1: Evaluate Your Business Risk: Why shouldn't I run my business the right way? is another approach to frame the question regarding whether to create a legal structure for your firm. The major reason for founding an LLC or company, as we discussed in Chapter 1, is to control your personal risk. Risk management in corporate organizations is concerned with two issues: taxation and legal responsibility. Recognizing your risk tolerance and desire for risk are important considerations in the decision you face.

Consider the kind of risks you encounter in your firm. Do you have any litigious clients? Do you work with high-value, delicate materials? Do you frequently travel for business? Consider how your company will grow in the future. If your ambitions lead you into riskier ground than you have previously explored, you should consider this while making your decisions. When you begin a large, dangerous project, it is much simpler to hold your system to identify if it is already organized.

Consider your risk tolerance. Do you possess property that you want to shield from potential corporate creditors, such as a home or a retirement account? How willing are you to subject your own assets to the hazards that you anticipate encountering?

Step 2: What Business Form Best Manages Your Risk? We examined three forms of freelancing businesses: sole proprietorships, limited liability companies (LLCs), and corporations. Because the state in which you reside may have such a significant impact on which of these forms is best for you, this book is unlikely to provide a conclusive answer as to which is best for your case. However, if we set aside the insignificant details, such as how these entities are generated and handled, we may gain a feel of them in a larger context. Compare the major characteristics of the various company kinds using the provided.

Step 3: Think about Your Existing Business: If you have been running your firm as a single proprietor for a time, chances are you have amassed some assets (hard assets like a computer and soft assets like customer testimonials) and administrative details (accounting records, websites, service contracts). Many freelancers' most valuable company assets will be their own brand and a network of existing clients. How will you handle rebranding under a new legal entity so that your current and future clients are aware that the professional behind your single proprietorship will be working under a new name? Do you have any long-term contracts that you would like to transfer to a new entity? What do they say about transferability if you do?

Consider how you now operate your business and how that may need to alter if you create a legal organization. Is there anything you will need to do to be organized, such as choosing a new bank for business purposes, that will take some time? Do you require a new website or e-mail address?

Step 4: Map Out Costs and Consider Taxes: Before deciding on a business structure, it is a promising idea to conduct an approximate estimate of your projected revenue and costs. Consider how much money you intend to make each year. Then, write a list of all your expected normal business costs. This can begin with your state's expenses for founding and maintaining a legal company. Typically, this information is easily available on the website of a state's Secretary of State. Will you be purchasing health insurance via your employer? What about liability coverage? What kind of service contracts and other business costs do you expect your organization to accrue?

Once you have estimated your revenue and expenses, assess if your predicted income is sufficient to cover the costs of having a business. Then consider whether your firm might benefit from becoming a tax-regarded entity. If a high cost is tax deductible for a C corporation but not for an S corporation, having your firm pay separate taxes may turn out to be advantageous. If you are having trouble figuring these things out, get a tax specialist and run your circumstances by them. Making wise decisions from the outset may save you a lot of money in taxes overall, so hiring an expert is money well spent.

After going through these processes, ideally, you will have learned more than enough to make the best decision for your company. The good news is that after you have selected a decision and become organized, the time-consuming task of establishing your company will be over. You can enjoy the fun of running your business knowing that your risks are under control and that your bottom line is not smaller than it should be.

THE FLASHCARD APPLICATION

React Native Flashcards

Allows you to create your own flashcards and continue studying daily.

How to Install

In your Terminal(mac)/Command Line(Windows), enter the commands below ("React Native Flashcard App Tutorial - 01/2021")

$ git clone https://github.com/amazeIvy/react-native-flashcards.git

$ cd react-native-flashcards

$ yarn install

$ yarn start OR $ expo start

How to Run

This app requires a simulator or a mobile device to run. The simplest method is to install the Expo App on your mobile device and then connect to the app.

- Expo on App Store: iOS

- Expo on Google Play: Android

MODELING AND STORING DATA

Every major app requires local storage to save part of the user's information locally even after the user is offline; this aids in gathering all the information once again when you log in and provides the user with a smooth experience. For this reason, it also enables local storage. We should not mix up the stored data with the state data because it is not a replacement for it. When the app is closed, all state data is removed. Async Storage can also be used for local storage. AsyncStorage can also be utilized in place of Local Storage since it is more efficient in terms of data storage techniques such as database systems.

STORING DATA IN THE REACT NATIVE LOCAL STORAGE WITH EXAMPLES

Examples of data storage are provided below:

1. **Simple React Native Local Storage:** Components inside the src folder:

Components inside the src folder:

- index.js

- styles.css

    a. index.js

```
import React from "react";
import ReactDOM from "react-dom";
import "./styles.css";
const initialState = { color: "green", showEmoji:
false };
class App extends React.Component { state = {
...initialState };
componentDidMount() { try {
const deserialisedState = JSON.parse( window.
localStorage.getItem("state")
);
this.setState({ ...deserialisedState });
} catch (err) {}
}
componentDidUpdate() {
const serialisedState = JSON.stringify(this.state);
window.localStorage.setItem("state",
serialisedState);
}
toggleShowEmoji = () => {
this.setState({ showEmoji: !this.state.showEmoji });
};
handleChangeColor = e => {
this.setState({ color: e.target.value });
};
```

```
handleClearLocalStorage = () => { window
.localStorage.clear();
};
render() { return (
<div className={`App ${this.state.color}`}>
<div className="flex">
<button className="flex-child" onClick={() => this.
toggleShowEmoji()}>
{`ClickHere to ${this.state.showEmoji ? "Hide" :
"Display"}
Emoji`}{" "}
</button>
<div className="emoji">{`${this.state.showEmoji ?
"" : ""}`}</div>
<label> Drop-down Menu Helps in Selecting
Background Colors</label>
<select onChange={e => this.handleChangeColor(e)}>
<option value="red">GREEN</option>
<option value="yellow">BLACK</option>
<option value="purple">BLUE</option>
</select>
<button
className="flex-child"
onClick={() => this.handleClearLocalStorage()}
>
For the Clearing Local Storage, Click Here.
</button>
</div>
</div>
);
}
}
const rootElement = document.getElementById("root");
ReactDOM.render(<App />, rootElement);
```

b. styles.css

```
.App {
font-family: sans-serif; text-align: center; height:
90vh;
width: 90%;
}
```

```
.App.black {
background-image: linear-gradient(
to right bottom, #ffef0a, #f5ee3f, #def297, #f7f391,
#fcfaa8
);
}.App.green {
background-image: linear-gradient( to top,
#f50f17, #f20b17, #e64b59,
#f29c8b, #ffd0c8
);
}.App.purple {
background-image: linear-gradient( to top,
#9000ff,
#de58ed, #be7ae6, #bc8de0, #f6b8fc
);
}
.App.black {
background-image: linear-gradient( to right bottom,
#ffef0a, #f5ee2f, #def297, #f7f382,
#fcfaa9
);
}
.flex {
display: flex;
flex-direction: column; width: fit-content; margin:
auto;
}
.flex-child {
margin: 3vh auto 7px auto; background-color:
#b9fa8e; border-radius: 6px;
}
.emoji {
font-size: 42pt;
}
button {
font-size: 18px; padding: 7px 11px 6px;
}
button:hover {
background-color: #fc84aa; color: #fcf7f8;
transition: color 201ms ease-in, background-color
301ms ease-in;
```

2. **React Native Counter with the Local Storage:** Components inside the src folder:

- index.js

- styles.css

  a. index.js

```
import React from "react";
import ReactDOM from "react-dom";
import "./styles.css";
console.log("new counter-example");
class Counter extends React.Component {
constructor(props) {
super(props);
this.handleAddOne = this.handleAddOne.bind(this);
this.handleMinusOne = this.handleMinusOne.b
ind(this); this.handleReset = this.handleReset.b
ind(this); this.state = {
count: 0
};
}
componentDidMount() {
const stringCount = localStorage.getItem("count");
const count = parseInt(stringCount, 12);
if (!isNaN(count)) { this.setState(() => ({ count
})));
}
}
componentDidUpdate(prevProps, prevState) {
if (prevState.count !== this.state.count) {
localStorage.setItem("count", this.state.count);}
}
handleAddOne() { this.setState(prevState => {
return {
count: prevState.count + 1
};
});
}
handleMinusOne() { this.setState(prevState => {
return {
count: prevState.count - 1
```

```
};
});
}
handleReset() { this.setState(() => {
return { count: 0
};
});
}
render() {
return (
<div class="container">
<h1>Count Value: {this.state.count}</h1>
<button onClick={this.handleMinusOne}>-1</button>
<button onClick={this.handleAddOne}>+1</button>
<button onClick={this.handleReset}>reset</button>
<p>Count start from Last Number you entered.</p>
<p>This is done, by storing the data in Local
Storage.</p>
</div>
);
}
}
const rootElement = document.getElementById("root");
ReactDOM.render(<Counter />, rootElement);
```

b. styles.css

```
.container {
margin-top: 42px; margin-left: auto; margin-right:
auto; width: 59%;
border: 17px solid#c4f782; padding: 10px;
text-align: center; background-color: #fff186;
}
```

3. Movie List with React Native Local Storage: Main files

- main folder

- header folder

- App.js

- index.html

- index.js
- movie folder
- NotFound.js
- index.css
- index.js

Components inside header folder:

- Header.css
- Header.js

Components inside main folder:

- movies folder
- navigation folder
- Main.css
- Main.js

Components inside movies folder:

- MovieListItem.css
- MovieListItem.js
- Movies.css
- Movies.js

Components inside navigation folder:

- Button.css
- Button.js
- Navigation.css
- Navigation.js

- Selection.css

- Selection.js

- Slider.css

- Slider.js

Components inside movie folder:

- LoadingMovie.js

- Movie.css

- Movie.js

    a. Header.css

```css
header { display: flex; height: 81px;
justify-content: center; align-items: center;
border-bottom: 3px solid #98bad4;
}
header h1 {
font-size: 3rem; color: #d4f23d;
}
```

b. Header.js

```js
import React from "react"; import "./Header.css";
const Header = () => (
<header>
<h1>Movie Mannia</h1>
</header>
);
export default Header;
```

c. Main.css

```css
.main {
display: flex;
}
```

d. Main.js

```
import React from "react";
import "./Main.css"
import Navigation from "./navigation/Navigation";
import Movies from "./movies/Movies";
class Main extends React.Component { state = {
movies: [], total_pages: 1,
page: 1,
url:
`https://api.themoviedb.org/3/genre/movie/list?api
_key=651925d45022d1ae6580
63b443c99784&language=en-US`,
moviesUrl:
`https://api.themoviedb.org/3/discover/movie?api_key
=651925d45022d1ae658063 b443c99784&language=en-
US&sort_by=popularity.desc&include_adult=false&inc
lude_video=false&page=1`,
genre: "Comedy", genres: [], year: {
label: "year", min: 1992,
max: 2022,
step: 1,
value: { min: 2001, max: 2022 }
},
rating: {
label: "rating", max: 10,
min: 0,
step: 1,
value: { min: 7, max: 10 }
},
runtime: {
label: "runtime", max: 300,
min: 0,
step: 20,
value: { min: 59, max: 119 }
}
}
componentDidMount(){
const savedState = this.getStateFromLocalStorage();
if ( !savedState || (savedState && !savedState
.movies.length)) { this.fetchMovies(this.state
.moviesUrl);
```

```
} else {
this.setState({ ...savedState }); this.
generateUrl(savedState);
}
}
componentWillUpdate(nextProps, nextState) { this.
saveStateToLocalStorage();
if (this.state.moviesUrl !== nextState.moviesUrl) {
this.fetchMovies(nextState.moviesUrl);
}
if (this.state.page !== nextState.page) { this.
generateUrl(nextState);
}
}
onGenreChange = event => {
this.setState({ genre: event.target.value });
}
setGenres = genres => { this.setState({genres});
}
onChange = data => { this.setState({
[data.type]: {
...this.state[data.type], value: data.value
}
});
};
generateUrl = params => {
const {genres, year, rating, runtime, page } =
params; const selectedGenre = genres.find( genre =>
genre.name ===
params.genre);
const genreId = selectedGenre.id;
const moviesUrl = `https://api.themoviedb.org/3/
discover/movie?` +
`api_key=651925d45022d1ae658063b443c99784&` +
`language=en-US&sort_by=popularity.desc&` +
`with_genres=${genreId}&` +
`primary_release_date.gte=${year.value.min}-01-01&` +
`primary_release_date.lte=${year.value.max}-12-31&` +
`vote_average.gte=${rating.value.min}&` +
`vote_average.lte=${rating.value.max}&` +
`with_runtime.gte=${runtime.value.min}&` +
`with_runtime.lte=${runtime.value.max}&` +
```

```
`page=${page}`;
this.setState({ moviesUrl });
}
onSearchButtonClick = () => { this.setState({page:
1}); this.generateUrl(this.state);
}
saveStateToLocalStorage = params => { localStora
ge.setItem("sweetpumpkins.params",
JSON.stringify(this.state));
}
getStateFromLocalStorage = () => {
return JSON.parse(localStorage.getItem("sweetpumpkin
s.params"));
}
fetchMovies = (url) => { fetch(url)
.then(response => response.json())
.then(data => this.storeMovies(data))
.catch(error => console.log(error));
}
storeMovies = data => {
const movies = data.results.map(result => {
const {
vote_count, id, genre_ids, poster_path, title, vote_
average, release_date
} = result;
return { vote_count, id, genre_ids, poster_path,
title, vote_average, release_date };
});
this.setState({ movies, total_pages: data.total_
pages });
};
onPageIncrease = () => {
const { page, total_pages } = this.state const
nextPage = page + 1;
if (nextPage <= total_pages) { this.setState({
page: nextPage })
}
}
onPageDecrease = () => {
const nextPage = this.state.page - 1; if (
nextPage
> 0 ) {
```

```
this.setState({ page: nextPage })
}
}
render() { return (
<section className="main">
<Navigation onChange={this.onChange}
onGenreChange={this.onGenreChange} setGenres={this.
setGenres} onSearchButtonClick={this.onSearchButton
Click}
{...this.state} />
<Movies movies={this.state.movies} page={this.state
.page}
onPageIncrease={this.onPageIncrease}
onPageDecrease={this.onPageDecrease}
/>
</section>
)
}
}
export default Main;
```

e. MovieListItem.css

```
.movie-item {
flex-basis: 23%; display: flex;
flex-direction: column; list-style: none;
box-sizing: border-box;
margin: 1.6%;
border: 1px solid #ffffff;
box-shadow: 0 11px 27px -6px #050505;
}
.movie-item img {
width: 90%;
}
.thumbnail {
display: flex;
flex-direction: column; flex-grow: 1;
cursor: pointer;
text-decoration: none;
}
.movie-description {
display: flex; flex: 1 0 99%;
```

```css
flex-direction: column; justify-content:
space-between;
padding: 12px;
}
.movie-description h2 { color: #63bdc8; font-weight:
bold;
margin-bottom: 22px;
}
.movie-details {
display: flex; margin-top: auto;
justify-content: space-between;
}
.movie-details span { color: #75d1ff; font-size:
0.8rem; font-weight: bold;
}
.movie-year, .movie-rating { display: flex;
flex-direction: column;
}
.movie-year .title, .movie-rating .title { color:
#70a8c4;
margin-bottom: 7px; font-size: 0.69rem; font-weight:
normal;
}
.movie-rating {
align-items: flex-end;
```

f. MovieListItem.js

```javascript
import React from "react";
import "./MovieListItem.css";
import { Link } from "react-router-dom";
const MovieListItem = ({ movie }) => {
const { id, title, poster_path, release_date, vote_
average } = movie; const imgUrl = `https://image
.tmdb.org/t/p/w342/${poster_path}`; const year =
release_date.substring(0, 4);
return (
<li className="movie-item">
<Link to={`/movie/${id}`} className="thumbnail">
<img src={imgUrl} alt={title} />
<div className="movie-description">
<h2>{title}</h2>
```

```
<section className="movie-details">
<div cassName="movie-year">
<span className="title">YEAR</span>
<span>{year}</span>
</div>
<div className="movie-rating">
<span className="title">RATING</span>
<span>{vote_average}</span>
</div>
</section>
</div>
</Link>
</li>
);
};
export default MovieListItem;
```

g. Movies.css

```
.movies {
flex-basis: 83%; display: flex; flex-wrap: wrap;
margin: 0;
padding: 22px 0;
}
.pagination { display: flex;
justify-content: space-between; padding: 42px 23px;
```

h. Movies.js

```
import React from "react"; import "./Movies.css";
import MovieListItem from "./MovieListItem"; import
Button from "../navigation/Button";
const Movies = ({ movies,
page, onPageIncrease, onPageDecrease
}) => (
<section>
<ul className="movies">
{movies.map( movie => (
<MovieListItem key={movie.id} movie={movie} />
))}
</ul>
<div className="pagination">
```

```
<Button onClick={onPageDecrease}>PREVIOUS</Button>
<span>{`Page ${page}`}</span>
<Button onClick={onPageIncrease}>NEXT</Button>
</div>
</section>
)
export default Movies;
```

i. Button.css

```css
.search-button { display: flex;
justify-content: center;
}
.search-button button { padding: 13px 22px;
background: #c4708a; color: #fcfafb;
font-size: 1.2rem; cursor: pointer;
transition: color 0.22s ease-out; outline: 0;
border: 0;
}
.search-button button:hover { color:#ffffff;
}
```

j. Button.js

```javascript
import React from "react"; import "./Button.css"
const Button = ({ onClick
, children }) => (
<div className="search-button">
<button onClick={onClick}>
{children}
</button>
</div>
)
export default Button;
```

k. Navigation.css

```css
.navigation {
flex-basis: 22%; min-width: 302px; padding: 42px;
}
```

l. Navigation.js

```
import React from "react"; import "./Navigation.c
ss";
import Selection from "./Selection"; import Slider
from './Slider'; import Button from './Button'
class Navigation extends React.Component {
componentDidMount() { fetch(this.props.url)
.then(response => response.json())
.then(data => this.props.setGenres(data.genres))
.catch(error => console.log(error));
}
render() {
"const { genre, genres, onGenreChange, onChange,
year, rating, runtime, onSearchButtonClick } = this
.props;" ("React Native Local Storage | Examples of
React Native Local Storage - EDUCBA")
return (
<section className="navigation">
<Selection genre={genre} genres={genres}
onGenreChange={onGenreChange}
/>
<Slider data={year} onChange={onChange} />
<Slider data={rating} onChange={onChange} />
<Slider data={runtime} onChange={onChange} />
<Button onClick={onSearchButtonClick}> Search
</Button>
</section>
)
}
}
export default Navigation;
```

m. Selection.css

```
.selection { display: flex;
flex-direction: column; margin-bottom: 62px;
}
.selection label { font-size: 1.2rem; margin-bottom:
12px; color: #bda4a4;
}
```

```css
.selection select { max-width: 153px;
}
```

n. Selection.js

```jsx
import React from "react"; import "./Selection.css";
const Selection = ({genre, genres, onGenreChange })
=> (
<div className="selection">
<label>Genre</label>
<select value={genre} onChange={onGenreChange}>
{ genres.map( genre => (
<option value={genre.name} key={genre.id}>{genre.na
me}</option>
))}
</select>
</div>
);
export default Selection;
```

15. Slider.css

```css
.slider {
margin-bottom: 42px;
}
.slider label { color: #948890; font-size: 1.2rem;
margin-bottom: 22px; display: block;
text-transform: capitalize;
}
.input-range slider { background: #c466a2; border:
none;
}
.input-range track { background: #f0e9e9;
}
.input-range track--active { background: #c466a2;
}
.input-range label--value .input-range label-
container { background: #c466a2;
color: #ffffff; font-size: 0.68rem; padding: 4px
7px; border-radius: 3px;
}
.input-range label--min .input-range
label-container,
```

```
.input-range label--max .input-range label-container
{
font-size: 0.68rem; color: #ada5ab; left: 0;
}
.input-range label--max .input-range label-container
{ left: 27%;
```

o. Slider.js

```
import React from "react";
import InputRange from "react-input-range";
import 'react-input-range/lib/css/index.css'; import
"./Slider.css"
class Slider extends React.Component { onChange =
range => {
this.props.onChange({
type: this.props.data.label, value: range
});
}
render() {
const { min, max, step, value, label } = this.props
.data; return (
<div className="slider">
<label>{label}</label>
<InputRange minValue={min} maxValue={max}
step={step}
onChange={this.onChange} value={value}
/>
</div>
)
}
}
export default Slider;
```

p. LoadingMovie.js

```
import React from "react";
const LoadingMovie = () => <h2>Movie Loading</h2>
export default LoadingMovie;
```

q. Movie.css

```
.movie-page {
```

```css
display: flex;
flex-direction: column;
}
.movie-page h5 { color: #888;
font-weight: normal; line-height: 1.27rem;
}
.movie-page h5 span { font-size: inherit; font-
weight: normal; color: #000001; padding-left:
1.2rem;
}
.movie-page h4 { margin: 0;
font-size: 1.27rem; line-height: 4;
}
.movie-page p { color: #bdb3b3; line-height: 1.59;
}
.movie-page .movie-image {
flex-basis: 90%;
height: 579px; background-size: cover;
background-position: center center;
}
.movie-page .movie-details { display: flex;
flex-direction: column; max-width: 804px;
margin: 23px auto 62px auto;
}
.movie-page .movie-details h1 { line-height: 1.56em;
}
.movie-page .movie-details h1 span { font-size:
inherit;
font-weight: normal; padding-left: 1.2rem; color:
#d9cece;
line-height: inherit;
}
.movie-page .genres { display: flex;
margin-bottom: 1.2rem;
}.movie-page .genres span { font-weight: normal;
}.movie-page .separator { color: #e8dfdf; padding: 0
12px;
}
```

r. Movie.js

```javascript
import React from "react";
import LoadingMovie from "./LoadingMovie"; import
"./Movie.css";
```

```
class Movie extends React.Component { state = {
isLoading: true, movie: {}}
}
componentDidMount() {
const { movieId } = this.props.match.params; const
movieUrl =
`https://api.themoviedb.org/3/movie/${movieId}?api_
key=651925d45022d1ae6580
63b443c99784&language=en-US`;
fetch(movieUrl)
.then(response => response.json())
.then(data => {
this.setState({ movie: data, isLoading: false })
})
.catch(error => console.log("Error:", error));
}
render() {
const { isLoading } = this.state; const {
title, backdrop_path, release_date, genres,
overview, vote_average, runtime
} = this.state.movie;
const year = release_date ? release_date.
substring(0, 4) : null;
const backgroundStyle = { backgroundImage:
`url(http://image.tmdb.org/t/p/
w128/${backdrop_path})`
}
return (
<div className="movie-page">
{
isLoading
? <LoadingMovie />
: <div>
<div className="movie-image" style={backgroundStyle} />
<div className="movie-details">
<h1>
{title}
<span>({year})</span>
</h1>
<section className="genres">
{genres.map((genre, index) => (
<div key={genre.id}>
<span>{genre.name}</span>
{index < genres.length - 1 && (
```

```
<span className="separator">|</span>
)}
</div>
))}
</section>
<h5>
Ratings of the Movie:
<span>{vote_average}</span>
</h5>
<h5>
Runtime of the Movie:
<span>{`${runtime} min`}</span>
</h5>
<h4>Overview of Movie</h4>
<p>{overview}</p>
</div>
</div>
}
</div>
)
}
export default Movie;
```

s. App.js

```
import React from "react"; import { BrowserRouter
, Switch
, Route } from "react-router-dom" import Header from
"./header/Header"; import Main from "./main/Main";
import Movie from "./movie/Movie"; import NotFound
from "./NotFound";
const App = () => { return (
<BrowserRouter>
<div>
<Header />
<Switch>
<Route exact path='/' component={Main} />
<Route path="/movie/:movieId" component={Movie} />
<Route component={Not-Found} />
</ Switch>
</div>
```

```
</BrowserRouter>
);
};
export default App;
```

t. NotFound.js

```
import React from "react";
import { Link } from "react-router-dom";
const NotFound = () => (
<div>
<h3>Unable to find Movie that you are looking for
:(</h3>
<Link to="/">Below is List of Movies that can
browse</Link>
</div>
);
export default NotFound;
```

u. index.css

```
body {
margin: 1;
padding: 1;
font-family: sans-serif; box-sizing: border-box;
}
```

v. index.html

```
<div id="root"></div>
```

w. index.js

```
import React from 'react';
import ReactDOM from 'react-dom'; import App from
'./App';
import './index.css';
ReactDOM.render(<App />, document.
getElementById("root"));
```

USING THE NAVIGATOR

React Navigation is one of the well-known React navigation frameworks. In this session, we will go over the principles of React Native navigation, show you how to get started with React Navigation in a React Native project, and walk through many React Native navigation examples.

React Navigation is developed in JavaScript and does not directly use iOS and Android's native navigation APIs. It instead recreates a subset of those APIs. This enables the integration of third-party JS plugins, maximum customization, and simpler debugging without the need to learn Objective-C, Swift, Java, Kotlin, and other programming languages.

React Navigation 5.0

So the time of writing, the most stable version of React Navigation is React Navigation 5.0, which was published in February 2020. The current update, according to the React Navigation blog, seeks to make the core React Navigation library and API more dynamic.

React Navigation 5.0 includes the following significant modifications and new features:

- Configuration is dynamic and component based.

- UseNavigation, useRoute, and useNavigationState are new hooks for typical use cases.

- A new setOptions method that simplifies specifying screen navigation options.

- Theme system has been redesigned to allow for greater personalization.

- TypeScript provides first-rate autocompletion and type-checking.

- Integration of Redux DevTools.

- Native stack navigator that navigates with react-native-screens by utilizing native navigation primitives.

- New Material top tab navigator backends based on react-native-viewpager and ScrollView.

Installing React Navigation

The first step is to build a React Native app, assuming you have Yarn installed. Expo tools are the easiest way to get started with React Native since they allow you to build a project without having to install and configure Xcode or Android Studio.

Install Expo by running this:

```
npm install -g expo-cli
```

If you receive an issue on your Mac, try executing it as follows:

```
sudo npm install --unsafe-perm -g expo-cli
```

Then, to start a new React Native project, use the following commands:

```
expo init ReactNavigationDemo
```

This will initiate some downloads and prompt you to provide certain configuration parameters. As seen below, select expo-template-blank and yarn for the dependency installation:

```
Emmanuels-MacBook-Pro:code emmyyusufu$ expo init ReactNavigationDemo
? Choose a template:
----- Managed workflow -----
> blank           minimal dependencies to run and an empty root component
  tabs            several example screens and tabs using react-navigation
----- Bare workflow -----
  bare-minimum    minimal setup for using unimodules

? Please enter a few initial configuration values.
  Read more: https://docs.expo.io/versions/latest/workflow/configuration/    50% completed
{
  "expo": {
    "name": "<The name of your app visible on the home screen>",
    "slug": "ReactNavigationDemo"
  }
}

Emmanuels-MacBook-Pro:code emmyyusufu$ expo init ReactNavigationDemo
? Choose a template: expo-template-blank
✓ Please enter a few initial configuration values.
  Read more: https://docs.expo.io/versions/latest/workflow/configuration/    100% completed
? Yarn v1.3.2 found. Use Yarn to install dependencies? (Y/n)
```

Next, cd into the project folder and launch your code editor:

```
cd ReactNavigationDemo
```

If you are using Visual Studio Code, you may access the current folder in the editor by typing:

Start the app with:

```
yarn start
```

The following step is to include the react-navigation library in your React Native project:

```
yarn add react-navigation
```

The React Native Stack Navigator

React Navigation is written in JavaScript and allows you to develop components and navigation patterns that look and feel like they are native to the platform.

React Navigation employs a stack navigator to handle a user's navigation history and the presentation of the relevant screen based on the route taken inside the app. At any one moment, a user is only shown one screen.

Consider a stack of paper; navigating to a new screen adds it to the stack, and navigating back removes it. The stack navigator also includes transitions and motions that are like those seen on native iOS and Android devices. It should note that an app can have many stack navigators.

React Native Navigation Examples

In this section, we'll look at several React Native navigation patterns and how to use the React Navigation module to implement them.

Using Stack Navigator to Navigate between the Screen Components

Let us begin by establishing /components folder in the project's root directory. Then we make two files, Homescreen.js and Aboutscreen.js.

```
// Homescreen.js
import React, { Component } from 'react';
import { Button, View, Text } from 'react-native';
import { createStackNavigator, createAppContainer }
from 'react-navigation';
export default class Homescreen extends Component {
 render() {
  return (
   <View style={{ flex: 1, alignItems: 'left',
justifyContent: 'center' }}>
    <Text>Home Screen</Text>
    <Button
    title="Go to About"
    onPress={() => this.props.navigation.navi
gate('About')}
    />
```

```
    </View>
   )
  }
}
```

Note onPress prop of the button above we will explain what it does later.

```
// Aboutscreen.js
import React, { Component } from 'react';
import { Button, View, Text } from 'react-native';
import { createStackNavigator, createAppContainer }
from 'react-navigation';
export default class Aboutscreen extends Component {
 render() {
  return (
   <View style={{ flex: 1, alignItems: 'left',
justifyContent: 'center' }}>
    <Text>About Screen</Text>
   </View>
  )
 }
}
```

Your project folder should look like what is shown in.

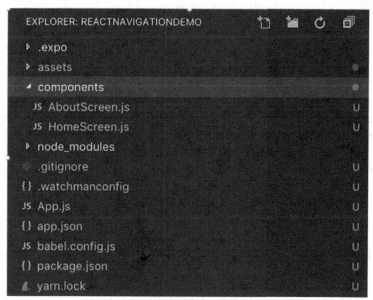

Look of the project folder.

Let us make some modifications to App.js as well. We will import everything we need from react-navigation and use that to construct our navigation.

We can create our navigation in the main App.js file since the component exported from Project.js is the entry point (or root component) for a React Native app and every other component is a child.

Every other component will be encapsulated within the navigation routines, as you will see.

```
// App.js
import React from 'react';
import { StyleSheet, Text, View } from
'react-native';
import { createStackNavigator, createAppContainer }
from "react-navigation";
import HomeScreen from './components/HomeScreen';
import AboutScreen from './components/AboutScreen';
export default class App extends React.Component {
  render() {
    return <AppContainer />;
  }
}
const AppNavigator = createStackNavigator({
  Home: {
    screen: HomeScreen
  },
  About: {
    screen: AboutScreen
  }
});
const AppContainer = createAppContainer(AppNaviga
tor);
const styles = StyleSheet.create({
  container: {
    flex: 1,
    backgroundColor: '#fff',
    alignItems: 'center',
    justifyContent: 'center',
  },
});
```

In the code above, createStackNavigator allows our program to transition between screens by stacking each new screen on top of the previous one. It is meant to resemble iOS and Android: on iOS, fresh displays glide in from the right, whereas on Android, they fade in from the bottom.

The createStackNavigator method is passed through a route configuration object. The Home route is equivalent to the HomeScreen, while the About route is equivalent to the AboutScreen.

The {screen: HomeScreen} configuration format is an optional, more succinct way of describing the route configuration.

In addition, as indicated by the API, we can optionally include another options object. We may add a separate object to specify which route is the initial one:

```
const AppNavigator = createStackNavigator({
  Home: {
    screen: HomeScreen
  },
  About: {
    screen: AboutScreen
  }
}, {
    initialRouteName: "Home"
});
```

It is worth noting that the Home and About route name-value pairs are surrounded by an overall route object. The choices object is not contained but exists as a distinct object.

Behind the scenes, the createStackNavigator method sends a navigation prop to the HomeScreen and AboutScreen components. You may use the navigate prop to go to a certain screen component. Therefore, we can use it on a button in HomeScreen.js that, when clicked, takes us to the AboutScreen page, as seen below.

```
<Button title="Go to About"
onPress={() => this.props.navigation.navi
gate('About')}
/>
```

We generated an app container in the App.js code by using const AppContainer = createAppContainer(AppNavigator);. This container oversees navigation state.

You must download the Expo client program before you can use the app. Versions for iOS and Android are available. While your command line is pointing to the project folder, type the following command.

```
npm start
```

On the terminal, you should see a QR code. Scan the QR code using the Expo app for Android, or the normal iPhone camera for iOS, which will provide you with a command to click to start the Expo app.

Using Tab Navigation

Most smartphone apps feature many screens. Tab-based navigation is a prevalent way of navigation in such mobile apps. In this section, we will look at how to use createBottomTabNavigator to construct tab navigation.

Create a ContactScreen.js file inside/components to add another screen to our project.

```
import React, { Component } from 'react'
export default class ContactScreen extends Component
{
 render() {
  return (
   <View style={{ flex: 2, alignItems: 'center',
justifyContent: 'center' }}>
    <Text>Contact Screen</Text>
   </View>
  )
 }
}
```

Let us add to the imports at the top of App.js file:

```
import ContactScreen from './components/ContactScreen';
```

Remember that we may create our navigation in the base App.js component. As a result, we will build our tab navigation in App.js by importing createBottomTabNavigator. Replace createStackNavigator with:

```
import { createBottomTabNavigator,
createAppContainer } from "react-navigation";
```

Also replace createStackNavigator with createBottomTabNavigator in the AppNavigator object:

```
const AppNavigator = createBottomTabNavigator({
 Home: {
  screen: HomeScreen
 },
 About: {
  screen: AboutScreen
 }
}, {
 initialRouteName: "Home"
});
```

Add new screen to the navigator object:

```
const AppNavigator = createBottomTabNavigator({
 Home: {
  screen: HomeScreen
 },
 About: {
  screen: AboutScreen
 },
 Contact: {
  screen: ContactScreen
 }
}, {
 initialRouteName: "Home"
});
```

You should see the bottom nav implemented if you run the project with npm start and open it in your Expo client.

Using Drawer Navigation

To begin building drawer navigation right away, replace createBottomTab-Navigator in the code with createDrawerNavigator.

Let's begin with the import statements:

```
import { createDrawerNavigator, createAppContainer }
from "react-navigation";
```

Let's also update the AppNavigator variable:

```
const AppNavigator = createDrawerNavigator({
 Home: {
  screen: HomeScreen
 },
 About: {
  screen: AboutScreen
 },
 Contact: {
  screen: ContactScreen
 }
}, {
  initialRouteName: "Home"
 });
```

You should be able to see the changes immediately away if you run npm start. To access the drawer navigation, swipe from the left.

You may personalize your drawer navigation by placing icons next to the route names.

We can customize by adding navigationOptions to the following screen component files:

```
// in HomeScreen.js
import React, { Component } from 'react';
import { Button, View, Text, Image, StyleSheet }
from 'react-native';
import { createStackNavigator, createAppContainer }
from 'react-navigation';
export default class HomeScreen extends Component {
 static navigationOptions = {
  drawerLabel: 'Home',
  drawerIcon: ({ tintColor }) => (
   <Image
    source={require('../assets/home-icon.png')}
    style={[styles.icon, { tintColor: tintColor }]}
   />
```

```
      ),
    };
    render() {
      return (
        <View style={{ flex: 1, alignItems: 'center',
justifyContent: 'center' }}>
          <Text>Home Screen</Text>
          <Button
            title="Go to About"
            onPress={() => this.props.navigation.navi
gate('About')}
          />
        </View>
      )
    }
}
const styles = StyleSheet.create({
  icon: {
    width: 24,
    height: 24,
  }
});
// in AboutScreen.js
import React, { Component } from 'react';
import { Button, View, Text, Image, StyleSheet }
from 'react-native';
import { createStackNavigator, createAppContainer }
from 'react-navigation';
export default class AboutScreen extends Component {
  static navigationOptions = {
    drawerLabel: 'About',
    drawerIcon: ({ tintColor }) => (
      ),
    };
    render() {
      return (
        About Screen
      )
    }
}
const styles = StyleSheet.create({
  icon: {
```

```
    width: 24,
    height: 24,
  }
});
// in ContactScreen.js
import React, { Component } from 'react';
import { Button, View, Text, Image, StyleSheet }
from 'react-native';
export default class ContactScreen extends Component
{
  static navigationOptions = {
    drawerLabel: 'Contact',
    drawerIcon: ({ tintColor }) => (
      ),
  };
  render() {
    return (
        Contact Screen
      )
  }
}
const styles = StyleSheet.create({
  icon: {
    width: 24,
    height: 24,
  }
});
```

You may use the tintColor prop to apply any color based on the active or inactive states of navigation tabs and labels. For example, we may alter the color of our nav drawer labels while they are in the active state. Add the following to the AppNavigator variable's options object:

```
const AppNavigator = createDrawerNavigator({
  Home: {
    screen: HomeScreen
  },
  About: {
    screen: AboutScreen
  },
  Contact: {
    screen: ContactScreen
```

```
      }
    }, {
      initialRouteName: "Home",
       contentOptions: {
        activeTintColor: '#e91e63'
       }
    });
```

Passing parameters to routes is as easy as two steps:

1. Add parameters to a route by passing them as a second argument to the navigation.navigate function:

   this.props.navigation.navigate('RouteName', { /* params go here */ })

2. Examine the parameters of your screen component:

   this.props.navigation.getParam(paramName, defaultValue)

CONCLUSION

In this chapter, we learned how to put it all together; in the following chapter, we will learn how to deploy it to the iOS app store.

Deploying to the iOS App Store

IN THIS CHAPTER

➤ Deploying to the iOS App Store

➤ Preparing your Xcode project

➤ Uploading your application

➤ Beta testing with TestFlight

➤ Submitting the application for review

We taught you how to put everything together in the previous chapter; in this chapter, we will learn how to dismantle it.

You'll want to get your excellent application into the hands of your customers now that you've made it. Depending on the platform, this procedure will be different. This chapter will cover the steps of presenting an app to the iOS App Store.

As web developers, we're accustomed to having more control over our deployment operations. You're probably used to sending code to production several times in a single day, and versions are typically unimportant. The iOS App Store makes deployment far more complicated, and new version releases frequently need 1–2 weeks of testing. As a result, it's vital to think about the App Store submission and approval process throughout the planning process.

DOI: 10.1201/9781003310440-10

iOS application development is a method of developing mobile applications for Apple devices such as the iPhone, iPad, and iPod Touch. The application is designed in Swift or Objective-C and then made accessible on the App Store for download.

You might be afraid of iOS development if you're a mobile app developer. Every developer, for example, requires a Mac computer, which is often more expensive than Windows-based competitors. Furthermore, once your product is complete, it must go through a stringent quality assurance process before it can be published on the App Store.

Regardless of whether your company's workers, clients, or partners are among the hundreds of millions of Apple iPhone and iPad users across the world, there are compelling reasons to engage in iOS app development. Furthermore, despite potentially high entry barriers, designing an iOS app may be just as simple (if not easier) as developing for Android. With proper preparation and materials, anyone may join the ranks of iOS app developers.

Are you ready to get started with iOS mobile app development? IBM provides step-by-step instructions for developing an iOS app with cloud-based push notifications and performance monitoring.

COMPLY WITH THE DEVELOPER'S SPECIFICATIONS

Before you create a single line of code in the iOS app development process, you must have the following:

- An Apple Mac machine running the most recent version of macOS, as well as Xcode, the integrated development environment (IDE) for macOS, which is accessible for free from the Mac App Store.

- An active Apple Developer account, which costs $99 per year.

These three requirements complement one another: Only active Apple Developer Program members can submit an app to the Apple App Store. Only apps signed and published by Xcode may be submitted to the App Store. Xcode is only available on macOS, which can only be found on Apple systems.

The good news is that Xcode provides far more than simply the ability to sign and publish your finished project. The IDE includes a user interface designer, code editor, testing engine, asset library, and other features that are essential for iOS app development.

CHOOSE AN IOS PROGRAMMING LANGUAGE

For the time being, there are two programming languages available for iOS app development.

1. **Objective-C**: Introduced in the early 1980s, Objective-C served as the dominant programming language for all Apple devices for decades. Objective-C, which is based on the C programming language, is an object-oriented programming language that focuses on sending messages to multiple processes (as opposed to invoking a process in traditional C programming). Many developers prefer to keep their traditional Objective-C programs rather than integrate them into the Swift framework, which was launched in 2014.

2. **Swift**: Swift is the new "official" programming language for iOS. While Swift and Objective-C have many similarities, Swift is intended to utilize a simpler syntax and is more security-focused than its predecessor. Because it shares a run time with Objective-C, legacy code may easily be merged into modern projects. Swift is straightforward to learn, especially for programmers who are new to the language. Swift is quicker, more secure, and easier to use than Objective-C, so unless you have a compelling reason to continue with Objective-C, you should intend to use it to create your iOS app.

TAP INTO APIS AND LIBRARIES

The wide array of developer materials available to you is one of the key benefits of iOS app development. Because of the standardization, functionality, and consistency of iOS app development, Apple is able to distribute reliable, feature-rich, and easy-to-use native APIs and libraries as kits. These iOS SDKs allow you to effortlessly link your app with Apple's current infrastructure.

If you're developing an app controller for a smart toaster oven, for example, you may utilize HomeKit to standardize communication between the toaster and the phone. Users will be able to communicate with their smart toaster oven and smart coffee maker simultaneously. There are developer kits for games, health applications, navigation, cameras, and Siri, Apple's virtual assistant.

These comprehensive kits let you easily make use of iOS capabilities and integrate third-party applications, allowing you to create apps that link to the social network, use the camera or native calendar app, or automatically capture replay footage of a particularly intense gaming moment.

EXPAND INTO THE CLOUD

iPhones are extremely powerful smartphones. However, when dealing with resource-intensive jobs, consider shifting the heavy lifting to the cloud. You may leverage the cloud for storage, database administration, and even app caching by connecting your app to cloud-based services via APIs. You may also add new next-generation services to your app.

IBM Cloud® enables server-side Swift frameworks, such as Kitura, for developing iOS back ends and web apps. REST APIs may be accessed from inside the iOS app. Kitura allows you to interact with a variety of IBM Cloud services, including push alerts and databases, as well as mobile analytics and machine learning.

TEST LOCALLY, TEST GLOBALLY

Even the finest coders don't always create ideal code the first time. After you finish developing your iOS app, you'll need to test it. Fortunately, unlike when building for Android, you will not need to test mobile devices from numerous manufacturers. iOS is Apple's exclusive mobile operating system, and it is only available on Apple iPhones. Even if you wish to test your iOS app on many versions of iPhones (with different operating systems), there are fewer devices to test on than with Android.

Your initial line of testing should be done in Xcode. Xcode has automated UI testing in addition to the typical unit tests you're familiar with. To find bugs, you may develop tests that traverse around your UI and interact with your app as if it were a user. The UI testing does not communicate with your code via APIs; instead, it simulates a genuine user's interaction with your app. As long as you build tests that cover every part of your app, you may achieve UI testing that is frequently more thorough than anything a human can do.

However, until your tests account for every conceivable interaction a user can have with your app, you should allow people to beta test it. While you may sideload programs to iOS devices without submitting them to the Tool Store, Apple's TestFlight app makes it simple for friends, family, or your user base to sample your app. Apple Developer Program participants can use TestFlight to conduct internal testing with up to 25 team members on up to 30 devices apiece. You may allow your iOS app development team to test your app in a limited group and prepare for the Apple Beta review before releasing your new iOS app to external testers.

Once the app has been approved by Apple according to its App Store review rules, you may invite up to 10,000 people to download a test version. These people install the TestFlight app and access your app through a unique URL. You may divide your external testers into bespoke groups and release different builds to each group, allowing you to do A/B testing and compare responses to features. In exchange, you will get use statistics immediately, and users will be able to readily provide feedback on any difficulties they encounter.

PUBLISH YOUR APP TO THE APP STORE

You'll need to submit your iOS app to the App Store once you've completed building and testing it. Xcode allows you to quickly publish and sign your software. Be patient: The app review process may be time consuming, often involving numerous cycles of rejection-revision-resubmission-rejection before receiving ultimate clearance.

Once you've received all necessary permissions, you may create your App Store page via a tool called App Store Connect and publish your app to the App Store. If you want to sell your program, keep in mind that Apple takes 30% of your sales in addition to the $99 yearly Developer Program cost.

Are you ready to dive into iOS app development? Want to see your iOS app on iPhones, iPads, and other Apple devices all around the world? IBM provides a step-by-step instruction for creating an iOS app with cloud-based push alerts and performance monitoring.

The Introduction to Mobile Foundation course, which is part of the IBM Cloud Professional Developer Program, educates you about the IBM Mobile Foundation's features and capabilities, as well as IBM Push Notifications.

Creating an Xcode Project for an App

Begin by establishing an Xcode project from a template for your app.

Overview

To start an Xcode project for your app, pick a template for the platform on which it will run and the sort of app you want to create, such as a single view, game, or document-based for iOS. Xcode templates offer necessary project information and files to enable you to get started on building your app as soon as possible.

Prepare Configuration Information
Gather the information that Xcode needs to identify your app and you as a developer before starting a project:

- **Product name**: The name of your app as it will appear in the App Store and when installed on a device. The product name must be at least two characters long and no more than 255 bytes in length, and it should be comparable to the app name you input later in App Store Connect.

- **Organization identifier**: A reverse DNS string that is unique to your business. Use com.example if you don't have a company identification. followed by the name of your organization, then replace it before distributing your app.

- **Organization name**: The name that displays across your project folder in boilerplate language. The organization name, for example, appears in the source and header file copyright strings. The organization name in your project differs from the organization name on the App Store.

Important
By default, the organization identification is included in the bundle ID (CFBundleIdentifier). When you first start your app on a device, Xcode utilizes the bundle ID to register an App ID. If you are not part of the Apple Developer Program, you are limited to a certain amount of App IDs, and you cannot change the App ID after submitting a build to App Store Connect, so choose your organization identification carefully.

Create a Project
Launch Xcode, then select File > New > Project or click "Create a new Xcode project" in the Welcome to Xcode window. Under Application, choose the target operating system or platform and a template from the sheet that displays. Fill out the forms and select choices on the following pages to configure your project.

You must include a product name and an organization identity since these are required to generate the bundle identification, which is used to identify your app throughout the system. Enter the name of your organization as well. Enter your name if you are not a member of an organization.

Choose SwiftUI as the user interface before clicking Next on this sheet to build for all platforms and receive an in

Manage Files in the Main Window

When you start a new project or access an existing one, the main window displays the files and resources required to construct your programe.

The navigation section in the main window allows you to reach various aspects of your project. Select files to edit in the editor area using the project navigator. When you choose a Swift file in the project navigator, for example, the file opens in the source editor, allowing you to alter the code and create breakpoints.

The inspector box on the right additionally displays information about the selected file. To update the properties of a file or user interface element, utilize the Attributes inspector in the inspector area. Click the "Conceal or reveal the Inspectors" button in the upper-right corner of the toolbar to hide the inspector to make more area for the editor.

The toolbar is used to design and launch your program on a simulated or real device. Choose the app target and a simulator or device from the run destination option in the toolbar for iOS apps, then click the Run button.

For macOS programs, just press the Run button. When you run your app, the debug section appears, allowing you to manage the execution of your program and analyze variables. When the program reaches the breakpoint, utilize the debug controls to walk through the code or resume execution. When you're through with the program, click the Stop button on the toolbar.

You may get an interactive preview of the user interface while creating your app if you utilize SwiftUI. The changes you make in the source file, the canvas on the right, and the inspector are all kept in sync by Xcode. You may also run the app with the debugger using the controls in the preview. See Creating Your App's Interface with SwiftUI for more information.

To alter the properties you specified when you created your project, click the project name in the project navigator at the top, and the project editor appears in the editing area. The majority of the properties you entered are displayed in the project editor's General pane.

BETA TESTING WITH TESTFLIGHT

Testflight Is Used for Beta Testing

It is general knowledge that beta testing is one of the acceptance testing procedures used by a client base. Its objective is to allow clients to assess their level of satisfaction with the project.

Customers, therefore, examine the product's usefulness, usability, quality, and interoperability with other apps. Beta testing is often carried out immediately following alpha testing.

We get prior experience working with the application and sending requests with its design, functionality, and interface during testing and based on its results.

Because beta testers evaluate the GM version of the app with all potential functionalities, these qualities provide for a qualitative evaluation of the final product.

There are two types of beta testing:

1. **Open:** When a large number of testers participate in the process it enables for a large number of recommendations and comments. Any interested party can participate in such testing and provide comments.

2. **Closed:** This testing may only be carried out by those who have been invited. Typically, this is done in small groups.

Advantages of Beta Testing

The key benefits of this type of testing should be highlighted:

1. Testers with access to the app and its functionality can assess the final product;

2. This sort of testing is performed by a wide number of people, each of whom brings a distinct viewpoint to the project and its qualities;

3. It's possible to cover a wide range of platforms, browsers, and operating systems;

4. The programe makes it easier to find and fix bugs in the app. After beta testing, regular usability issues (which clients confront and which were previously regarded as minor flaws) might turn into serious defects. Because of the problems, users are unable to fully utilize all of the product's capabilities.

Beta Testing by Using Testflight

You must use your own services if you want quick access to program data for beta testing. We'll look at one of the most commonly used applications for this type of testing. This product was released by Apple experts. It has to do with TestFlight.

Apple's official program for iOS devices, TestFlight, was designed with the goal of performing open beta testing of these devices. This solution helps to make the process of gathering code from devices that are being tested easier (UDID).

Customers can also use TestFlight to review new apps for iOS, watchOS, and tvOS that aren't yet available in the AppStore.

Because there are a few iOS devices with older versions than this one, this product only works with applications version 8.0 and up.

The fact that TestFlight is free is a significant benefit. Furthermore, the developers claim that the core functionality will remain free.

Main Functions of Testflight

- 1000 beta testers will have open access to the program via e-mail;

- Multiple devices will be tested simultaneously;

- Developers will be able to download, install, and update program testing builds;

- It is possible to download an official app from the App Store without providing the developer with a UDID code for testing purposes;

- Messaging on the release of a new software build (before e-mails);

- Beta testers can provide comments on this service to the customer or developer of the software;

- There are several test runs and software failures visible. There is also information about debugging.

TestFlight makes beta testing new products simple and straightforward.

Algorithm for Testing the Application's Beta Versions

1. Download TestFlight from the App Store. This procedure is identical to that of installing any other app on an iOS device.

2. After receiving a TestFlight invitation, you must download an official beta version of the program from the App Store (the link is in the TestFlight).

3. The service can activate from the home display once the installation is complete. Because of the orange dot before the program's name, you can tell this version is a demo.

4. In TestFlight, you can get more information about a product by clicking on its name. Developers occasionally provide information about topics that should be tested or new upgrades. It is possible to install the new application version from that screen. If you need to compare the functional capabilities of different versions, click to "Previous builds" and search for the ones you require.

5. The "Send Beta Feedback" tool allows you to send data regarding detected faults or write to the developers.

6. If you no longer want to test the software, simply click "Stop Testing" on the TestFlight window.

Not only may the TestFlight service be used to test the program's beta versions. It is also used to distribute program builds to testers.

Internal Testers

Up to 100 employees of your organization with the roles of Account Holder, Admin, App Manager, Developer, or Marketing can be designated as beta testers. You can even make numerous groups and assign different builds to each one, depending on the qualities each one should emphasize. While you iterate on your app, each user can test beta builds on up to 30 devices and have access to all of your beta builds.

External Testers and Groups

Invite up to 10,000 external testers by e-mail or by enabling and publishing a public link, which invites anyone to test your app. Create a group of testers and assign them to the builds you want them to test. You can even make numerous groups and assign different builds to each one based on the aspects you wish to emphasize. Before testing can begin, the initial build of your app must be authorized by TestFlight App Review. When you add a build to a group, it is automatically sent for review.

Using E-mail to Invite Testers

If you have a tester's e-mail address, you can send them an invitation along with a link to download and test your app. E-mail can be an excellent approach to distributing beta versions of your software with an existing group of external testers or specific persons you'd like to ask to test.

Using Public Links to Invite Testers

If you don't already have a network of testers, public links are a great way to connect with individuals who can test your app. It is not necessary to give any contact information. Simply go to your app's TestFlight page, choose an existing group, and then click Enable Public Link. After that, the URL may be copied and shared on social media, messaging platforms, e-mail campaigns, and other platforms. To promote your software, don't localize the TestFlight name or generate TestFlight badges.

You can also use the public link to limit the number of testers who can join. If the group limit is reached or your public link is disabled, anyone seeking to join your beta will receive a warning saying your beta is no longer accepting new testers. Consider where you distribute your public link and when it might be appropriate to remove it to provide a positive user experience.

Test Information

When sharing your app with external testers, you'll need to tell them what to test as well as any other pertinent information. These details should be entered on the Test Information tab of your app in App Store Connect. You should also include an e-mail address that you check regularly so that you can receive and respond to tester comments. When sending your software to internal testers, test information is optional.

Getting Feedback

Testers can give feedback immediately from your app using the TestFlight app for iOS, iPadOS, and macOS by taking a snapshot. They can also provide more information about an app crash right after it happens. Go to your app's TestFlight page in App Store Connect and click Crashes or Screenshots in the Feedback section to see this feedback. The e-mail address you give in Test Information will get feedback from testers on iOS 12 or earlier, tvOS, or watchOS.

SUBMITTING THE APPLICATION FOR REVIEW

You're publishing your first app, or you haven't done so in a long. To submit an app to App Store, it's not as simple as clicking a start button, but it's not as complicated as it may look.

This guide assumes you've already joined the Apple Developer Program, that your app complies with Apple's App Review and Human Interface Guidelines, and that you're ready to release. It's an updated version of Gustavo Ambrozio and Tony Dahbura's excellent guide, complete with information from the most recent version of Xcode, which streamlines some of the procedures and more context from Apple's own documentation. Here's how to get your app into the App Store for the beta testing or to go live in the App Store.

Code Signing: Create iOS Distribution Provisioning Profile and Distribution Certificate

You've been utilizing a development provisioning profile and a development certificate that are only for specified devices. To distribute your program to beta testers or consumers via the App Store, you'll need a separate distribution provisioning profile and distribution certificate.

The most straightforward method is to use Xcode. Xcode will build and manage certificates, signing IDs, and device registration for you if automatic signing is enabled. You can skip to step 2 if automatic signing is already activated or if you don't require assistance with signing.

(In some circumstances, manual signature may be preferable.) Here's a step-by-step guide to manually signing your app. Keep in mind that the signature mechanism for all targets in a bundle should be the same.

- First, if you haven't already, add your Developer Program account to Xcode. Select Xcode from the top menu, then Preferences.

- Go to Accounts and choose it. Press the + sign in the lower-left corner of the window, then Add Apple ID.

- Click Sign In after entering your Apple ID and password for the Apple Developer Program.

- After that, turn on automatic signing. Choose a target in the Project Editor and then General.

- To expand the settings, scroll down to the "Signing" section and click the triangle icon.

- Select the box that says "Automatically manage signatures." Choose your team.

When you attach a new device to your Mac, Xcode detects it and adds it to your team provisioning profile automatically. It's worth noting that in order for your app to run on a device, the device must register on your team provisioning profile.

Create App Store Connect Record for Your App

Get an App Store Connect account by:

- Being the team agent and creating your own App Store Connect organization.

- Being invited by existing organization as a user with Admin, Technical, or App Manager role.

- Signing in with the Apple ID you used to enroll in the Apple Developer Program. More information regarding App Store Connect user accounts may be found here.

For Paid Apps

If you're releasing a paid app, you'll need to sign a contract outlining payment arrangements.

- On the App Store Connect dashboard, choose Agreements, Tax, and Banking.

- Under "Request Contracts," select Request.

- Examine the agreement that displays, check the box indicating that you agree to the conditions, and then click "Submit."

- In the Contact Info column of "Contracts In Process," select Set Up.

- Click Add New Contact in the pop-up window and fill in your details.

- Click Set Up, then Add Bank Account in the "Bank Info" column of the "Contracts In Process" column to preserve your account information.

- Click Set Up in the "Tax Info" box. Because a U.S. Tax Form is required, click Set Up and fill out the necessary information. Set up any additional country tax forms that are required.

- The contract's status will now be "Processing" after you've performed the steps above. The contract will now display under "Contracts In Effect" after Apple has verified the information you submitted, which should take around one hour.

Add a New App

Select My Apps from App Store Connect panel and click the + sign in the upper left-hand corner, then New App.

To create a new App Store Connect record, you'll need the following information: platform, app name, default language, bundle ID, and SKU. You won't be able to change these details afterward, so proceed with caution.

- To make your app more discoverable, include keywords in the name.

- The bundle ID must match the bundle identification in your Xcode project Info.plist file (General > Identity section of the target).

- The SKU is hidden from users and must be specified by you. It could be a firm identity or something else that has personal importance for you. Letters, numerals, hyphens, periods, and underscores are all acceptable characters, and it must start with a letter or number.

At this point, you can also set user access if necessary.

Archive and Upload App Using Xcode

You must upload the build through Xcode before submitting your app for evaluation through App Store Connect.

- Select the Generic iOS Device as the deployment target in Xcode.

- From top menu, select Product and then Archive.

- The Xcode Organizer will open, revealing any previous archives you've generated.

- In the right-hand panel, make sure the current build is chosen and click Upload to App Store.

- Click Choose after selecting your credentials.

- Click Upload in the bottom right-hand corner of the next window that displays.

When the upload is complete, a success message will show. After that, click Done.

Configure App's Metadata and Further Details in its App Store Connect Record

Additional languages, categories, and your app's Privacy Policy URL can be added to the "App Information" page in the "App Store" tab of App Store Connect.

- On the "Pricing and Availability" page, make your app free or choose a price tier.

- You can configure any App Store technology in your app, such as Game Center and in-app purchases, under the "Features" page.

- In the left-hand panel under "App Store," your app is indicated with a yellow dot and the state "Prepare for Submission." Choose the build you want to customize. This is where you'll fill in the details for your App Store product page.

- Screenshots of your software should be uploaded (in JPEG or PNG format and without status bars). You can upload a group of screenshots for one device and then utilize them across all sizes.

- After your screenshots have finished uploading, click Save in the upper right-hand corner of the window.

  ○ Fill in your app's description, keywords, support URL, and marketing URL by scrolling down.

  ○ The description and keywords for your app are quite important. Make sure they're search engine friendly.

  ○ The support URL might be as simple as a contact form on a landing page.

  ○ The marketing URL is optional and can be your app's website.

- Upload your app's icon, version number, copyright, and contact information in the "General App Information" box below.

  ○ Your app's icon should be 1024px x 1024px, and the version number in Xcode should match exactly.

  ○ The copyright information is usually in the form of "Copyright (c) 2017, Instabug, Inc."

  ○ This is where users will see your contact information.

- Select the appropriate choices for your app by clicking Edit next to "Rating." Be truthful; if your app doesn't match its rating, it may be rejected during review.

- Enter your contact information, any notes you have for the reviewer, and the version release date in the "App Review Information" area.

  ○ The reviewer's contact information is listed here in case they need to contact you directly.

  ○ Details regarding specific hardware they might need or user account information they might need for access can be included in the reviewer's notes.

  ○ For first releases, the version release date should usually be set to automatic.

- Click Save in the upper right-hand corner. You're almost ready to hit the "Submit for Review" button.

Submit Your App for Review

- Scroll to the "Build" section in your app's App Store Connect record.

- Select "Select a build before submitting your app" from the drop-down menu.

- Select the Xcode build that you've uploaded. Then click Done in the bottom right corner, Save in the top right corner, and Submit for Review.

- Finally, click Submit after answering the questions about Export Compliance, Content Rights, and Advertising Identifier.

- The status of your app is currently "Waiting For Review."

Check on the Status of App

Select Activity from the top horizontal menu in App Store Connect, then App Store Versions from the left-hand panel.

How Long Does It Take to Get Approval from an App Store?

Approval usually takes one to three days, and it can take up to 24 hours for your app to show in the App Store once it has been approved. Here's a look at the current average app store review times.

At each level, you'll get an e-mail notification. Here is where you can find out more about each of the statuses.

You can request an accelerated review if you're on a tight deadline and need to time your release with a certain event or if you need to release a new version with an urgent bug patch.

If Your Application Has Been Rejected

Before you can resubmit your app for evaluation, you'll need to make the necessary changes. If you have any questions, use the Resolution Center in App Store Connect to contact Apple. If you think your app was wrongfully denied, you have the option to escalate the situation and file an appeal.

Performance is one of the most prevalent grounds for rejection from the Apple App Store. Make sure your program is finished, that you've thoroughly tested it, and that all bugs have been fixed. Using a bug reporting tool during beta testing will lessen the likelihood of your app being rejected due to performance issues.

If Your Application Has Been Approved

Congratulations! You've arrived at the App Store. App Store Connect allows you to see downloads, sales, ratings, and reviews immediately.

SUMMARY

Here's how to submit your app to the Apple App Store:

1. Create an iOS distribution provisioning profile and distribution certificate.

2. Create an App Store Connect record for your app.

3. Archive and upload your app using Xcode.

4. Configure your app's metadata and further details in its App Store Connect record.

5. Submit your app for review.

6. Check on the status of your app.

CONCLUSION

In this chapter we learned about deploying an app to IOS App Store, in the next chapter we will learn about deploying apps to the Android store.

Deploying Android Applications

IN THIS CHAPTER

> ➢ Deploying Android applications

> ➢ Setting application icon

> ➢ Building the APK for release

> ➢ Distributing via e-mail or other links

> ➢ Submitting your application to the play store

Here, you will learn how to install an application using Kubernetes WebUI and CLI. We will disclose the application through NodePort Service.

- Uninstall the app from the dashboard.

- Move the application from a YAML file using kubectl.

- Display the service using NodePort.

- Access the app without the Minikube collection.

We will start the minikube dashboard.

DOI: 10.1201/9781003310440-11

Launching this command will open a browser with Kubernetes Web UI. By default, the dashboard is connected to the defaultNamespace. All operations will be performed within the default name field.

In the event that the browser does not open a tab, try to access the dashboard in this URL:

http://127.0.0.1:377/api/v1/namespaces/kubernetes.dashboard/services/ https:kubernetes-dashboard:/proxy/.

Uninstall a web server using the Nginx image.

In the dashboard, we can access the creative interface, by clicking on the '+' icon. We will use the Create from the form tab to create our application.

Fill in the application name field, using the web dash. Dock image to use isnginx. We will set up 1 Pod, and define the Service field as external, the visible port is defined as 8080 and the target port as 80.

In advanced options, we can specify options such as labels, Namespace, etc. Just by clicking the Install button, we will activate the whole program. As expected, we see the post named web-dash in the default namespace. It will create ReplicaSet, which will eventually create an iPod with the default k8s: web-dashlabel.Applications is displayed The dashboard compares individual services displayed in CLI viakubectl.

We count the post.

```
$ kubectl get deploy
NAME     READY  UP-TO-DATE  AVAILABLE  AGE
web-dash  1/1    1           1          4m6s
We list the ReplicaSet
$ kubectl get rs
NAME           DESIRED  CURRENT  READY  AGE
web-dash-7797d85794  1    1        1      4m46s
```

And also list the Pods

```
$ kubectl get pods
NAME            .READY  STATUS   RESTARTS  AGE
web-dash-7797d85794-rrqt2  1/1   Running  0    5m34s
```

Let's also look at labels and selectors, which play a key role in equally collecting a subset of items for tasks.

See Pod Details, using the same word as kubectl find pods

```
$ kubectl describe pod
Name:     web-dash-7797d85794-rrqt2
Namespace: default
Priority:  1
Node:     minikube/191.168.237.232
Start Time: Tue, 15 Jan 2021 20:28:23 +0100
Labels:   k8s-app==web-dash
          pod-template-hash==7797d85794
Annotations: <none>
Status:    Running
IP:       172.17.0.5
IPs:
 IP:       172.17.0.5
Controlled By: ReplicaSet/web-dash-7797d85794
Containers:
 web-dash:
  Container ID:  docker://dfda29f03732b43da02904faab
a5a874f355d653e2eb35a976a5beb67344c7cb
  Image:     nginx
  Image ID:    docker-pullable://nginx@sha256:10b8
cc432d56da8b61b070f4c7d2543a9ed17c2b23010b43af434f
d40e2ca4aa
  Port:       <none>
  Host Port:   <none>
  State:      Running
   Started:   Tue, 14 Jan 2021 20:28:37 +0100
  Ready:      False
  Restart Count: 1
 . . .
```

We will only focus on the Labels field, then we have a set Label to k8s-app=web-dash, while the is more information about the Pod.

LIST THE PODS, WITH THEIR ATTACHED LABELS

With the L option we can add additional columns to the output to include Pods with their own labeled keys and their values.

```
$ kubectl get pods -L k8s-app, label2
NAME          READY STATUS RESTARTS AGE
K8S-APP LABEL2
web-dash-7797d85794-rrqt2 1/1  Running 0     12m
web-dash
```

SELECT PODS WITH THE LABEL PROVIDED

With the -l option we select all Pods with the Keyboard application for the k8s application set to create a web-dash

```
$ kubectl get pods -l k8s-app=web-dash
NAME              READY  STATUS  RESTARTS  AGE
web-dash-7797d85794-rrqt2 1/1   Running  0      15m
```

DEPLOY A WEBSERVER USING THE CLI

We will uninstall the application using CLI next, let's first uninstall the Post we created.

```
$ kubectl delete deploy web-dash
deployment.apps "web-dash" deleted
```

It will delete the ReplicaSet and Pods it created.

```
$ kubectl get rs
No resources found in default namespace.
$ kubectl get pods
No resources found in default namespace.
```

.

We will create a YAML configuration file with post details. We will name it webserver.yaml

```
apiVersion: applications / v1
type: Posting
metadata:
 Name: webserver
 labels:
  app: nginx
spec:
 templates: 3
 selector:
  matchL Labels:
   app: nginx
 template:
  metadata:
   labels:
    app: nginx
```

```
spec:
 containers:
 - name: nginx
   photo: nginx: alpine
   ports:
   - ContainerPort: 80
```

Next, we will create a post from this file. By using the -f option you can transfer the file as specified.

```
$ kubectl create -f webserver.YAML
deployment.apps/webserver created
```

LIST REPLICASETS AND PODS

```
$ kubectl get rs
NAME            DESIRED  CURRENT  READY  AGE
webserver-7fb7fd49b4  3      3      3    51s
$ kubectl get pods
NAME                 READY  STATUS   RESTARTS  AGE
webserver-7fb7fd49b4-5csv6  1/1   Running  0     64s
webserver-7fb7fd49b4-89d51  1/1   Running  0     65s
webserver-7fb7fd49b4-19ttt  1/1   Running  0     64s
```

EXPOSING AN APPLICATION

We have explored different ServiceTypes, with which we can define how to access the service. When we connect to that hole from anywhere, we are sent to ClusterIP Service. Let's create a NodePort ServiceType. We are building a webserver-svc.yaml.

```
apiVersion: v1
kind: Service
metadata:
 name: web-service
 labels:
  run: web-service
specfic:
 type: NodePort
 ports:
 - port: 8080
  protocol: TCP
```

```
selector:
 application: nginx
```

We will create a service object.

```
$ kubectl create -f webserver-svc.yaml
service / web service created
```

We are also provided with a direct way to create a Service by exposing Pre-built Submissions

```
$ kubectl expose deployment webserver --name = web-
service --type = NodePort
service / web service revealed
```

We can see its ClusterIP with a map of 80: 32255 in the port section, which means we have kept a 32255 vertical hole in place.

```
$ kubectl get svc
NAME       TYPE    CLUSTER-IP    EXTERNAL-IP   PORT(S)
AGE
kubernetes ClusterIP 10.96.0.1    <none>    443/
TCP    36m
web-service NodePort  10.100.112.57
<none>   80:32255/TCP  2m19s
```

To get more details about the Service, we are going to describe it.

```
$ kubectl get svc web-service
Name:          web-service
Namespace:      default
Labels:         run=web-service
Annotations:      <none>
Selector:        app=nginx
Type:          NodePort
IP Families:      <none>
IP:           10.100.112.57
IPs:          <none>
Port:          <unset> 80/TCP
TargetPort:      80/TCP
NodePort:        <unset> 32255/TCP/UDP
```

```
Endpoints:          272.17.0.5:80,172.17.0.0:80,172.
17.0.7:80
External Traffic Policy: Cluster
Events:             <none>
```

We can see that the service is using app=nginx as a Selector to logical group our three Pods, which are used as endpoints in the Endpoints section.

ACCESSING AN APPLICATION

First let us examine the IP of our minikube cluster

```
$ minikube IP
192.168.237.232
```

Now we should access our Nginx server via this IP and the hole in the list using kubectl get command.

LIFE AND READINESS TO TEST

In some cases, our requests may not be answered or may be delayed during the presentation. Lifetime Use and Readiness Testing allows Beletto to control app life in the Pod container and force re-responding of the unresponsive app container. It is to allow sufficient time for the Readiness Probe to fail a few times before passing, and only to check the Liveness Probe. Otherwise we may be caught in endless re-creation – loop failure, as the container may not reach the right situation. Liveness Probes can be set by specifying the Liveness command, Liveness HTTP request, or TCP Liveness probe.

Useful if the app crashes into a deadlock or crashes suddenly. In that case, the container will no longer work and may restart the container to make the request available again. For example, liveliveness command checks for file / tmp / health presence.

```
apiVersion: v1
kind: Pod
metadata:
 labels:
  test: liveness
 name: liveness-exec
spec:
```

```
containers:
- name: liveness
  image: k8s.gcr.io/busybox
  args:
  - /bin/sh
  - -c
  - touch /tmp/healthy; sleep 30; rm -rf /tmp/
healthy; sleep 600
  livenessProbe:
   exec:
    command:
    - cat
    - /tmp/healthy
   initialDelaySeconds: 3
   failureThreshold: 1
   periodSeconds: 5
```

File presence / tmp / health is scheduled to be checked every five seconds using the periodSeconds parameter. The first DelaySeconds parameter asks the kubelet to wait three seconds before the initial investigation. If you use a command-line argument on a container, we will first create a / tmp / healthy file, and then delete it after 30 seconds. File extraction will trigger probe failure, while the faillanceThreshold parameter set to 1 instructs kubelet to declare an unhealthy container after a single probe failure and trigger container reload as a result.

After 30 seconds we will explain the iPod, and look at its Events section.

```
$ kubectl describe pod liveness-exec
Events:
 Type    Reason    Age  from       Message
 ----    ------    ---- ----       -------
 Normal  Scheduled 63s  default-
scheduler Successfully assigned default/liveness-
exec to minikube
 Normal  Pulling   63s  kubelet    Pulling image
"k8s.gcr.io/busybox"
 Normal  Pulled    62s  kubelet    Successfully
pulled image "k8s.gcr.io/busybox" in 1.147125841s
 Normal  Created   62s  kubelet    Created container
liveness
 Normal  Started   61s  kubelet    Started container
liveness
```

```
Warning Unhealthy 28s  kubelet       Liveness probe
failed: cat: cannot open '/tmp/healthy': No such
file or directory
Normal  Killing  28s  kubelet      Container
liveness failed liveness probe, will be restarted
 Normal  Pulling  28s (x3 over 2m3 (about twice the
volume of a large
refrigerator)8s) kubelet        Pulling image "k8s.gcr
.io/busybox"
 Normal  Created  27s (x3 over 2m3 (about twice the
volume of a large
refrigerator)7s) kubelet        Created container
liveness
 Normal  Started  27s (x3 over 2m3 (about twice the
volume of a large
refrigerator)6s) kubelet        Started container
liveness
 Normal  Pulled   27s        kubelet       Successfully
pulled image "k8s.gcr.io/busybox" in 566.481414ms
(about half second)
```

We note that in some cases, the Liveness investigation failed when it was unable to resolve the cat command order in / tmp / healthyfile. After that failed test, the container will be created again.

In the following example kubelet sends an HTTP GET request to the application's location / health point. If it returns a failure, the kubelet will restart the affected container.

```
apiVersion: v1
kind: Pod
metadata:
 labels:
  test: liveness
 name: liveness-http
spec:
 containers:
 - name: liveness
   image: k8s.gcr.io/liveness
   args:
   - /server
   livenessProbe:
    httpGet:
```

```
path: /healthz
port: 8080
httpHeaders:
- name: Custom-Header
  value: Awesome
initialDelaySeconds: 3
periodSeconds: 3
```

With the TCP Liveness Probe, kubelet attempts to open the TCP Socket in a container, which uses the app, failing which the kubelet will mark it as unhealthy and restart the affected container.

```
apiVersion: v1
kind: Pod
metadata:
 name: goproxy
 labels:
  app: goproxy
spec:
 containers:
 - name: goproxy
   image: k8s.gcr.io/goproxy:0.1
   ports:
   - containerPort: 8080
   readinessProbe:
    tcpSocket:
     port: 8080
    initialDelaySeconds: 5
    periodSeconds: 10
   livenessProbe:
    tcpSocket:
     port: 8080
    initialDelaySeconds: 15
    periodSeconds: 20
```

After 15 seconds, view Pod events to verify that liveness probes.

BUILDING THE APK FOR RELEASE

React Native developers are often in a position to release their React Native apps in the Google Play Store for Android users to download. In this tutorial, we will learn how to create an APK for creating indigenous *Releases for Android*, using both ReactNative CLI and Studio IDE.

We have released all of our React Native to production templates (Google Play Store demos), so we are aware of the process and errors that may occur during the production of the React Native Release Android for APK. We write what we learn in this React Native tutorial to help mobile developers submit their Android apps for faster production.

There are two different ways to create a ready-to-produce Android app, so we present both below.

USING THE REACT NATIVE CLI

First of all, make sure the Android project is flawless. That is, it integrates and works successfully on an Android device or device. So, open an Android project using Android Studio or launch it in the command line. If everything is going as planned, you are ready to go.

STEP 1: Generate a Keystore

You will need the Java-generated signature key which is the store key file used to generate the usable React Native binary for Android. You can create one using keytool terminal with the following command

```
1. keytool -genkey -v -Keystore your_key_name.
Keystore your_key_alias -keyalg RSA -keysize 2048 -
validity 10000.
```

Once you have started the keytool service, you will be asked to type a password. Make sure you remember the password:

You can change your_your_word by any name you want, as well as your_your_ keywords. This key uses 2048 key size, instead of the default 1024 for security reasons.

Therefore, this command asks you to find the Keystore password, real key, and separate word fields for your key. Therefore, everything should be done manually and carefully.

- Enter your *Keystore* password: *password123*

- Re-enter new password: *password123*

- What is your first and last name? *ABC*

- What is the name of organizational unit? *Sample Company*

- What is the name of organization? *Sample*

- What is the Locality? *XYZ*

- What is the State or Province? *ABC*

- What is the country code for this unit? *XX*

Your terminal output will similar to this:

Press *Enter* when you are prompted to enter the password for <*my-key-alias*>. *Note*: If you have a new key password, then type it in.

As a result, it generates a store-key file in your project directory called my-release-key.keystore for 10,000 days (approximately 27.5 years). Most importantly, make a backup copy of this Keystore file and its details (store password, nickname, and password) that will be required later.

STEP 2: Adding Keystore to Your Project

First, you need to copy your_key_name.Keystore file and paste it under the Android/app directory in your React Native project folder.On Terminal.

```
mv my-release-key.Keystore /android/app
```

You need to open your file location such as *android\app\build.Gradle* file and add the Keystore configuration. There are two methods of configuring the project with keystore. First, the common and unsecured way:

```
1.  android {
2.  ....
3.  signingConfigs {
4.  release {
5.  storeFile file('your_key_name.keystore')
6.  storePassword 'your_key_store_password'
7.  keyAlias 'your_key_alias'
8.  keyPassword 'your_key_file_alias_password'
9.  }
10.  }
11.
12.  buildTypes {
13.
14.  release {
15.  ....
16.  signingConfig signingConfigs.release
17.
18.  }
```

```
19.  ^}
20.  ^}
```

This is not a good protection practice as you keep the password secret. Instead of storing your Keystore password in a .gradle file, you can set a build process to notify these passwords when you create a command line.

To request a password for the Gradle build file, change the configuration shown above to:

```
1.  ^signingConfigs {
2.  ^free {
3.  ^storeFile file ('your_key_name.keystore')
4.  ^storePassword System.console (). readLine ("\
    nShop password:")
5.  ^keyAlias System.console (). readLine ("\
    nAlias:")
6.  ^keyPassword System.console (). readLine ("\
    Alias password:")
7.  ^}
8.  ^}
```

Therefore, you should make sure that the *signing blockConfigs* appear before *the blockchain buildTypes* to avoid unnecessary errors. Additionally, before proceeding, make sure you have an asset folder under *android/app/ src/main/assets*. If not, create one. Then run the next command to build a pile.

1. React Native bundle – platform android – dev false index.js – bundle-output android / app / src / assets / index.android.bundle

2. --assets-dest android / app / src / main / res /

Note: If you have a filename installed, such as *index.android.js*, change it within the command.

STEP 3: Uninstall the APK Generation

Set your final guide on *android* using:

```
1.  cd android
```

Then run the next command.

For Windows,

1. Gradlew assembleReleased

With Linux and Mac OSX:

1. ./gradlew assembleRelease

As a result, *the APK process is done*. You can get the generated APK in *android/app/build/outputs/apk/app-release.apk*. This is a real app, which you can download to your phone or download to the Google Play Store. Congratulations, you have just released the React Native Release Build APK for Android.

There are some common errors that occur in this process sometimes, such as in the React Native app, when the React Native varies. We present here the most common Native building mistakes we have encountered in order to save time and headaches.

If your building fails by the following error:

1. : app: processReleaseResources FAILED

2. FAILURE: The structure failed without selection.

3. * What went wrong:

4. Failure at work ': app: processReleaseResources'.

5. > com.android.ide.common.process.ProcessException: Failed to use aapt

You can fix this React Native Android build error by getting started:

```
1. ^cd ..
2. ^
3. ^rm -rf android / app / src / res / drawable- *
4. ^
5. ^Lots of react-native --platform android --dev
   false \
6. ^--entry-file index.js \
7. ^
8. ^--bundle-output android / app / src / assets /
   index.android.bundle \
```

```
9.  ^
10.  ^--assets-dest android / app / build / res /
     merged / release /
11.  ^
12.  ^cd android && gradlew assembleRelease
```

These are the steps to create an APK Signed Out of React Native for Android apps, which can be published on the Google Play Console.

Generate React Native Release Build with Android Studio
As before, make sure your Android project is flawless.

Step 1: Set Your Android Product Location: To create an APK (app format you will download from the Google Store), you need to install Android Studio. Most importantly, make sure you have 27 versions of the SDK as React Native is used.

Step 2: Install JDK: You need to make sure you have the latest Java development kit installed (as in version 8). Installation varies depending on your location. As a result, you use Oracle's Java SDK or you can use SDKMAN to install other options, such as OpenJDK.

Step 3: Generate the released APK using Android Studio: Navigate to the app's side-release bar. Here, you can see a list of tracks for the various test categories. Click MANAGE on the production track. Then click CREATE RELEASE to create a Native Android build APK.

You will encounter a message about using Google Play Signing App. This is a new feature that puts key management in Google. This is an important feature because if you manage your keys and lose them, you will no longer be able to issue updates to your app.

In fact, you have to create a new one under a new name. For that, you need to generate an upload key.

1. Open that application in Editor by browsing the folder of your React Project.

2. Navigate to the *Build* tab, click on *Generate signed bundle / APK*

3. Select *APK* to generate release APK for React Android project., Click on *Next*.

4. Under *Key store path* click *Create new*.

5. Pick a path like */home/User/keystores/android.jks*.

6. Select passwords for the Keystore key and then enter the certificate information.

Thus, click on *OK*, then on *Next*. Select both the V1, and V2 signature version, then click *Finish*.

As a result, a build starts after which you can see both *app-x86-release .apk* & *app-armeabi-v7a-release.apk* inside of *android/app/release* in the project folder.

This way, you can generate an APK release version of your React Native Android project. This is the last step in producing the React Native Release Build for Android. You can now download your app to Google Play.

HOW TO SEND E-MAIL FROM REACT NATIVE APPLICATION

in fact, we will go to, cc, bcc, subject, body in function and open the Gmail name box. For this, we need to use the communication dependence i.e., React Native-communications. In the app, the client needs to send an e-mail to the support section or make a token. Today this is a common feature of the program so let us start with an example.

1. Create a new project.

In our case, we are using a previous expo project. You can create a new project using the following command:

```
>>> react-native init projectName
```

2. Add Dependence.

We need to use the communication dependence. use the following command to install it after successfully installing the next import command:

```
npm install react-native-communications --save
```

3. Import the following components.

Import the following components in JS file

```
        enter React, {Part} from "react";
enter {
Remember,
Style Sheet,
Text,
Text input,
Button,
Consolidation,
Court,
Warning
} from "react-native";
import Communication from "traditional-speaking";
```

4. Send an e-mail from the tradition.

al app

We use the following method to open the e-mail inbox. You can transfer to, cc, bcc, title, body text by parameters as below

```
/ * Email delivery function (to, cc, bcc, title,
body) * /
 openEmail = () => {
  Communications.email (
   ["techupcode@gmail.com", "contact@techup.co.in"],
<---- local emails
   null, <--- CC email
   null, <--- bcc
   "Enter Title", <--- Title
   "Enter body mail" <--- Body text
  );
 };
```

We need to call this function by clicking a button because I added one button so let's see the full point code for a better understanding.

5. App.js

Check this full score code from How to send e-mail from React Native application

```
import React, { Component } from "react";
import {
 View,
 StyleSheet,
 Text,
 TextInput,
 Button,
 Linking,
 Platform,
 Alert
} from "react-native";
import Communications from
"react-native-communications";
export default class App extends Component {
 constructor(props) {
  super(props);
  this.state = {
   bodayText: ""
  };
 }
 /*Function to send the mail function(to, cc, bcc,
subject, body)*/
 openEmail = () => {
  Communications.email(
   ["techupcode@gmail.com", "contact@techup.co.in"],
   null,
   null,
   "Enter Subject",
   "Enter body for the mail"
  );
 };
 render() {
  return (
   <View style={styles.container}>
    <Text
     style={{ textAlign: "center", fontSize: 20,
paddingVertical: 30 }}
    >
     Send Email from React-native App
```

```
    </Text>
    <TextInput
     value={this.state.bodayText}
     onChangeText={bodayText => this.setState({
bodayText })}
     placeholder={"Enter Body"}
     style={styles.input}
    />
    <View style={{ marginTop: 20 }}>
     <Button onPress={this.openEmail} title="Send
Email" />
    </View>
   </View>
  );
 }
}
const styles = StyleSheet.create({
 container: {
  flex: 1,
  alignItems: "center",
  padding: 30,
  backgroundColor: "#ffffff"
 },
 input: {
  width: 255,
  height: 44,
  padding: 10,
  margin: 10,
  backgroundColor: "#FFF",
  borderColor: "#000",
  borderRadius: 0.5,
  borderWidth: 0.5
 }
});
```

DISTRIBUTING THE REACT NATIVE APP
WITH MICROSOFT APP CENTER

After all the challenging work you have done in building the app, it is time to spread it out. There are many ways in which distribution can be done. Ad hoc distribution is done mainly using Diawi, upload to cloud storage, etc.

Here we will look at the App center. It is a Microsoft distribution tool. If you use App center, you can track download value, download region, and much more. It also tracks the built-in so you can track if something is wrong inside.

Getting Started

1. If you have already created your application in the portal, you can skip this step.

2. Go to app center.ms.

3. Register or log in ahead, click on Add new, then select Add an application from the drop-down menu.

4. Enter a word and a description of your choice.

5. Select the suitable OS (Android or iOS) and select React Native as the platform.

6. Click the bottom right button Add a new app.

7. Once you have created the app, you can see the Application Secret on the Settings page. It will be used later.

8. Insert SDK into your application:

9. NPM: npm install appcenter-analytics appcenter-crashes -save-exact.

    ART: thread add app center-analytics app center-crashs -exact

    Integrating SDKs: To compile SDKs you can find official documents here.

10. Create ad hoc layouts for consecutive locations with appropriate keys.

11. Go to the app page in the app center, click create new releases, and upload properties.

12. Create test groups to distribute properties to users.

13. Uninstall the app. Users will receive an e-mail from App center that the new system has been downloaded. Users can download the application using the link provided in the e-mail. You can see the statistics going to the statistics tab.

14. Three ways to send e-mails from your React Native app.

15. Let us explore three separate ways to share e-mails with users in your React Native app.

Three Ways to Send E-mails from React Native App

Let us explore three separate ways how to share e-mails with users from your React Native application.

Configuring Linking API

The way to make a request is to send electronic mail via React's Linking API. They can help not only by sending e-mails but also by inter-linking the application within the application, as well as pre-filling error reporting e-mails or submitting requests. To create and send an e-mail, let us use OpenURL (), a method used to open different links in the app. Before redirecting people to a client, the method will always ask to confirm their intent.

Suppose you need to send a quick customer satisfaction survey just after the first month to gather user information about your app. Since you will not be able to use the Linking API to post attachments, you will only need to enter the link. As well as the full version to encode:

```
// send-email.js
import qs from 'qs';
import { Linking } from 'react-native';
Export async sendEmail function (in, title, body,
options = {}) {
  const {cc, bcc} = options;
  let url = `mailto: $ {to}`;
  // Create an email link query
  const query = qs.stringify ({
    theme: theme,
    body: body,
    cc: cc,
    bcc: bc
  });
  if (question.t)) {
    url + = `? $ {query}`;
  }
  // check if we can use this link
  const canOpen = await Linking.canOpenURL (url);
```

```
if (! can unlock) {
  drop New Error ('provided URL cannot be
managed');
  }
  return Linking.openURL(url);
}
// example.js
import { sendEmail } from './send-email';
sendEmail(
  'user@domain.com',
    'We need your feedback',
    'UserName, we need 2 minutes of time to fill quick
survey [link]',
  { cc: 'user@domain.com; user2@domain.com; userx@
domain1.com' }
).then(() => {
  console.log('Your message was successfully
sent!');
});
```

The method is time effective, but again, you cannot send attachments.

Working with Your Own Server

For those who avoid working with third-party services providers, there is a single option to set up their server to enable outside system e-mail. One includes sending a message via Nodemailer. However, this method has its disadvantages; in order to use it, you will need to add details to your SMTP server, which may be a concern for security.

Another option is to set up a hosting server. While it allows sending e-mails away from the device, it also calls for additional upgrades and faster delivery. Usually, preparing your server for delivery takes a lot of time and effort, but this is an option if you do not want third parties to participate in this process.

Using Third-Party Tools

One of the strongest ways to send messages through the React Native app is to use third-party services. In order to share e-mails with others in the back of the app, you need to configure certain triggers example, clicking the "sign-in" button, etc. To do this, there are a number of third-party tools you can use.

First, you can combine Firebase with SendGrid and Zapier. After making an account with Firebase, the goal is to deliver the e-mails after a child's new record appears on the Firebase Website.

Since you can't send them directly, Zapier will activate the action in the tool you eventually select (for example, SendGrid), and add one "zaps" to the child's record.

Second, you have the option to integrate Firebase CloudBase, Gmail, and Nodemailer already known. As mentioned above, Firebase can quickly create multi-event number triggers based on user actions within the app and send redirecting people to their e-mail requests. Firebase CloudBase allows us to send such e-mails via Nodemailer. For this last one to work properly, you need to have an e-mail account that will handle the sending of letters. One of the tools you can use is Gmail, but you are free to choose SendGrid in any other way.

This method requires setting up and integrating a few tools, which may cause security concerns, but nevertheless, it is a very flexible way to get your React Native app to send e-mails.

Wrap Up

Making the app send e-mails by 2021 is worth trying to upgrade UX. Other than that, doing it in the React Native app is not a challenging task. You only need to choose the right path. If you just want to deliver simple e-mails with physical links, API Linking is your way of going. It is extremely easy and does not take much time to repair.

By sending several types of activated e-mails with custom HTML templates, you will need to integrate third-party tools. It takes time and money, though. For those on a less budget, setting up your proxy server would be a wonderful way to try, but you should spend time setting everything up properly.

Submit Your Request to the Google Play Store

Android requires that every application be signed with a certificate before it can be installed. In order to distribute your Android app with the Google Play Store, the store needs to be signed with the release key that needs to be used for all future updates. As of 2017 it is possible for Google Play to control the automatic sign-off release due to the Google Play functionality app signing. However, before your binary application can be uploaded to Google Play, it needs to be signed with a download key. Designing Your Applications page in Android Developer Documents explains the topic in detail. This guide summarizes the process and lists the steps needed to pack a lot of JavaScript.

Produces the Upload Key

You can create a private signing key using the key tool. In Windowskeytool, it should run in the C: \ Program Files \ Java \ jdkx.x.x_x \ bin.

```
keytool -genkeypair -v -storetype PKCS12 -.keystore
-alias my-key-alias -keyalg RSA -keysize 2048
-validity 10000
```

This command tells you to find the passwords in the key and key store and the Keyword fields for your key. It then generates a Keystore as a file called my-upload-key.keystore.

The key store contains a single key, which is valid for 10,000 days (about 27.5 years). A noun is a word you will use later when you sign up for your application, so remember to recognize the nickname.

On Mac, if you are not sure where your JDK bin folder is, do the following command to find it:

```
/usr/libexec/java_home
```

It will issue a JDK guide, which will look like this:

```
/Library/Java/JavaVirtualMachines/jdkX.X.X_XXX.JDK/
Contents/Home
```

Navigate to those texts using your commandcd / j /k / JDK / path and use the keytool command with sudo permission as shown below.

```
sudo keytool -genkey -v -Keystore my-upload-key.
-alias -keyalg RSA -keysize 2048 -validity 10000
```

Note: Keep the Keystore file private. In the event that you lose your loading key or are in danger, you must follow these instructions.

- Insert the the my file upload-key.Keystore under the Android/app directory in your project folder.

- Edit the file ~ / .gradle / gradle.propertiesorandroid / gradle.proper-ties, and add the following (exchange ***** enter the correct keystore password, nickname, and key password).

```
MYAPP_UPLOAD_STORE_FILE=my-upload-key.keystore
MYAPP_UPLOAD_KEY_ALIAS=my-key-alias
MYAPP_UPLOAD_STORE_PASSWORD=*****
MYAPP_UPLOAD_KEY_PASSWORD=*****
```

These will be the global Gradle variables, which we can use later in our Gradle configuration to sign our application.

Be careful with the git: Gradle's flexible storage above ~ / .gradle / gradle.properties instead ofandroid / gradle.properties prevents them from getting into the git. You may need to create ~ / .gradle / gradle.properties-file in your user's home directory before adding a separate one.

Security precautions: If you do not want to keep your passwords in plain text and use macOS, you can also store your personal information in the Keychain Access app. Then you can skip the last two lines of ~ / .gradle / Gradle.properties.

Add a Signing Setting to Gradle for Your App

The last step in the configuration that needs to be done is to set the output of the properties to be signed using the upload key. Edit the file android / app / build.gradlein folder for your project, then add the signature setting,

```
. . .
android {
  . . .
  defaultConfig { ... }
  signingConfigs {
    release {
      if (project.hasProperty('MYAPP_UPLOAD_STORE
_FILE')) {
        storeFile file(MYAPP_UPLOAD_STORE_FILE)
        storePassword MYAPP_UPLOAD_STORE_PASSWORD
        keyAlias MYAPP_UPLOAD_KEY_ALIAS
        keyPassword MYAPP_UPLOAD_KEY_PASSWORD
      }
    }
  }
}
```

```
buildTypes {
  release {
    . . .
    signingConfig signingConfigs.release
  }
}
}
```
. . .

Generating the Release AAB

Run the following in a terminal:

```
cd android
./gradlew bundleRelease
```

Gradle'sbundleRelease will integrate all the JavaScript required to launch your application in AAB (Android App Bundle). If you need to change the way JavaScript bulk and/or compile applications are collected (e.g., if you have changed the default file/folder names or standard project layouts), see the Android / app / build.gradleto to see how you can update them to reflect these changes.

Note: Make suregradle.properties does not includeorg.gradle.configureondemand = trueas which will override the overlay of JS and assets into the binary of the app.

Product AAB can be downloaded under android / app / build / outputs / bundle / release / app.aab, and is ready for download on Google Play.

For Google Play to accept the AAB format Signing the Google Play App requires your app configuration on the Google Play Console. If you are reviewing an existing application that does not use Google Play Signing App, please check our Transfer section to learn how to make such a configuration change.

Checking the release of your application release

Testing the Release Build of Your App

Before you upload a release layout to the Google Play Store, be sure to check it out properly. Start by uninstalling any previous version of the app that you have already installed. Install it on that same device using the following command at the root of the project:

```
npx react-native run-android --variant=release
```

Note that exception is only available if you have set the signature as described above. You can override any active batch situations, as your entire framework and JavaScript code are accumulated in the APK assets.

Publishing in Other Stores

By default, the generated APK contains your native code for both x86 and ARMv7a CPU architectures. This makes it easy to share APKs that work on almost all Android devices. However, this has the disadvantage that there will be unused native code on any device, leading to unnecessarily large APKs.

You can create an APK for each CPU by changing the following line in android / app / build.Gradle:

```
- ndk {
- abiFilters "armeabi-v7a", "x86"
-}
- def enableSeparateBuildPerCPUArchitecture = false
+ def enableSeparateBuildPerCPUArchitecture = true
```

Download both of these market files that support device identification, such as Google Play and Amazon AppStore, and users will automatically receive the appropriate APK. If you want to download to other markets, such as APKFiles, which does not support multiple APKs for a single application, change the next line again to create a default universal APK for both dual CPUs.

```
- universalApk lies // If true, and generate a
universal APK
+ universalApk true // If true, generate a universal
APK
```

Enables Proguard to Reduce APK Size (Optional)

Proguard is a tool that can reduce the size of the APK. It does this by removing parts of the React Native Java bypass (and its dependencies) that your app does not use. *Important*: Make sure you thoroughly check your application when you enable Proguard. Proguard usually requires a specific setup for each library you use. See app / proguard-rules.pro.

To enable Proguard, editandroid / app / build.gradle:

```
/**
 * To run the Proguard to shrink the bytecode in
release builds.
 */
def enableProguardInReleaseBuilds = true
```

Modify Old Android React Native Apps to Use Google Play Signing App

If you migrate to the previous version of React Native, chances are that your app does not use the Google Play app signing feature. We recommend that you allow that to take advantage of features such as the default app split. To get out of the old sign-up process, you need to start by generating a new download key and replacing it with the inandroid release / app / build.Gradle release to use the download key instead of the release (see the section on adding the slow signature setting). Once that is done, you must follow the instructions from the Google Play Help website to submit your actual release key to Google Play.

CONCLUSION

Here, we learned how to deploy apps in the Android play store.

Appraisal

I N THE PREVIOUS CHAPTER, we learned about deploying Android applications and a variety of associated topics; in this chapter, we will learn
about appraisal.

PERFORMANCE OVERVIEW

The ability to achieve 60 frames per second and a native appearance and
feel for your apps is a strong incentive to use React Native instead of
WebView-based solutions. We might want React Native to do the proper
thing and help you focus on your app rather than performance optimiza-
tion where possible, but there are some areas where we are not yet there,
and others where React Native (like writing native code directly) cannot
determine the best way to optimise for you and so manual intervention
will be required. We do our best to provide buttery-smooth UI performance by default, but this is not always possible.

This tutorial is meant to educate you on some fundamentals to assist
you in troubleshooting performance difficulties, as well as to explain typical sources of problems and proposed remedies.

What You Need to Know about Frames

For a reason, your grandparents' generation referred to movies as "moving
pictures": genuine motion in video is an illusion manufactured by rapidly
changing static images at a steady speed. Each of these photos is referred
to as a frame. The number of frames presented per second has a direct
influence on how smooth and lifelike a video appears to be. iOS devices
show 60 frames per second, giving you and the UI system about 16.67
ms to do all work required to build the static picture that the user will
view on the screen during that period. If you are unable to complete the
work required to create that frame within the permitted 16.67ms, you will
"drop a frame" and the UI will become unresponsive.

To further complicate matters, go to your app's developer menu and enable the Show Perf Monitor option. There are two distinct frame rates to observe.

JS Frame Rate (JavaScript Thread)
Your business logic will be executed on the JavaScript thread in most React Native applications. This is where your React application sits, where API calls are performed, touch events are handled, and so on. Unless you specify useNativeDriver: true, the Animated API presently calculates each keyframe on the JavaScript thread, whereas LayoutAnimation utilises Core Animation and is unaffected by JS thread and main thread frame drops. If the JavaScript thread is not responsive for a frame, the frame is deemed dropped. For example, if you used this.setState on the root component of a complicated application and it resulted in the re-rendering of computationally expensive component subtrees, it is possible that this might take 200 ms and result in the loss of 12 frames. During that period, any JavaScript-controlled animations would appear to freeze. The user will notice if anything takes more than 100 ms.

This frequently occurs during Navigator transitions: when you push a new route, the JavaScript thread must render all the scene's components to send the right commands to the native side to generate the supporting views. Because the JavaScript thread controls the transition, it is common for the process to take a few frames and generate junk. Components may sometimes perform additional work on componentDidMount, resulting in a second stall in transition.

Another instance is responding to touches: if you are working over many frames on the JavaScript thread, you may notice a delay in responding to TouchableOpacity, for example. This is due to the JavaScript thread being overloaded and unable to process the raw touch events sent across from the main thread. As a result, TouchableOpacity is unable to respond to touch events and instruct the native view to alter its opacity.

UI Frame Rate (Main Thread)
Many users have noted that NavigatorIOS performs better out of the box than Navigator. The reason for this is that the transition animations are entirely done on the main thread and so are not interrupted by frame drops on the JavaScript thread.

Similarly, even when the JavaScript thread is locked, you can merrily scroll up and down via a ScrollView since the ScrollView is on the main thread. The scroll events are sent to the JS thread, but they are not required for the scroll to happen.

Common Sources of Performance Problems

Running in Development Mode (dev=true)

When operating in dev mode, JavaScript thread performance falls. This is unavoidable: much more work must be done at runtime to give you useful warnings and error messages, such as verifying propTypes and numerous other assertions. Be careful to always test performance in release builds.

Using console.log Statements

These statements can cause a significant slowdown in the JavaScript thread while executing a packaged program. This includes debugging library calls like redux-logger, so be sure to remove them before bundling. You can also delete all console.* calls with this babel plugin. You must first install it using NPM I babel-plugin-transform-remove-console – save-dev before editing the .babelrc file in your project directory as follows:

```
{
  "env" : {
   "production" : {
    "plugins" : ["transform-remove-console"]
   }
  }
}
```

This will delete all console.* calls from your project's release (production) versions.

ListView Initial Rendering Is Slow or Scroll Performance Is Bad for Large Lsts

Instead, use the new FlatList or SectionList components. Aside from simplifying the API, the new list components feature considerable efficiency improvements, the most notable of which is near-constant memory use for whatever number of rows.

If your FlatList is taking too long to render, make sure you have used getItemLayout to minimize rendering speed by skipping the measurement of rendered items.

*JS FPS Plunges When Re-rendering View That Hardly
Changes ("Performance Overview React Native")*

If you use a ListView, you must provide a rowHasChanged method, which helps save time by immediately assessing whether a row must be re-rendered. If you are working with immutable data structures, all you would need is a reference equality check.

Similarly, you can use shouldComponentUpdate to specify the conditions under which you want the component to re-render. You may use PureComponent to perform this for you if you develop pure components (where the return result of the render method is fully based on props and state). Immutable data structures are important again to keep things fast – if you need to execute a thorough comparison of a huge list of objects, re-rendering your whole component may be faster, and it will surely need less code.

*Dropping the FPS of the JS Thread Since I'm Performing a
Lot of Work on the JavaScript Thread at the Same Time*

The most typical expression of this is "slow Navigator transitions," but it can occur at other times as well. InteractionManager can be a useful option, but if the cost of the user experience is too great to postpone work during an animation, you should choose LayoutAnimation.

The Animated API currently calculates each keyframe on the JavaScript thread unless you specify useNativeDriver: true, whereas LayoutAnimation uses Core Animation and is unaffected by JS thread and main thread frame drops.

One example is animating in a modal (sliding down from the top and fading in a translucent overlay) while initializing and getting responses for numerous network queries, displaying the contents of the modal, and updating the view from whence the modal was launched. For additional details on how to use LayoutAnimation, see the Animations documentation.

Caveats

- LayoutAnimation is only used for fire-and-forget animations (also known as "static" animations); if it has to be interrupted, use Animated.

*Moving View on the Screen (Scrolling, Rotating, or
Translating) Reduces the FPS of the UI Thread*

This is especially true when text with a transparent backdrop is placed on top of an image or in any other case where alpha compositing is necessary to redraw the view on each frame. Enabling shouldRasterizeIOS or renderToHardwareTextureAndroid can assist with this.

Be cautious not to overdo this, as your memory consumption will skyrocket. When utilizing these props, keep track of your performance and memory utilization. Turn this property off if you no longer intend to relocate a view.

Changing the Size of a Picture Reduces UI Thread FPS

When you modify the height or width of a Picture component on iOS, the picture is re-cropped and resized. This may be costly, especially for huge photos. To animate the size, use the transform: [{scale}] style attribute instead. When you tap a picture and zoom it in to full screen, here is an example of when you may do this.

My TouchableX View Is Not Very Responsive

If we perform an action while modifying the opacity or highlight of a component that is responsive to a touch, changing the size of a picture reduces UI thread FPS. You may not notice the effect until after the onPress method has returned. This might happen if onPress performs a setState that causes a lot of work and a few frames to be lost. A solution is to encapsulate any activity within your onPress handler with requestAnimationFrame:

```
handleOnPress() {
 requestAnimationFrame(() => {
  this.doExpensiveAction();
 });
}
```

Slow Navigator Transitions

The JavaScript thread, as previously stated, controls Navigator animations. Consider the "push from right" scene transition: each frame, the new scene is shifted from right to left, starting offscreen (say, at an x-offset of 320) and eventually settling at an x-offset of 0. The JavaScript thread must deliver a new x-offset to the main thread every frame throughout this transition. If the JavaScript thread is locked, it is unable to do so, resulting in no update on that frame and the animation stuttering.

Allowing JavaScript-based animations to be offloaded to the main thread is one way. If we used this strategy to accomplish the same thing as in the previous example, we could build a list of all x-offsets for the new scene when we start the transition and pass it to the main thread to execute in an optimal manner. Because the JavaScript thread is no longer responsible for this, it is not a huge concern if it skips a few frames while rendering the scene – you will not notice because you will be too distracted by the gorgeous transition.

One of the key purposes of the new React Navigation library is to solve this. React Navigation views employ native components and the animated package to provide 60 FPS animations that operate on the native thread.

Bibliography

adivinartec, by. (2021, January 7). *How to Publish Your App to the App Store in 2021*. Adivinar Tec. https://adivinartec.com/how-to-publish-your-app-to -the-app-store-in-2021/

Agarwal, H. (2020, July 31). *React Native Pros and Cons for Mobile App Development*. Techexactly. https://techexactly.com/blogs/advantages-and -disadvantages-of-using-react-native

ALGO, & View My Complete Profile. (2020, December 10). *My Collections: 2020*. https://sunzhen.blogspot.com/2020/

Anderson, W. (n.d.). *Cross-Platform App Development Benefits That Your Business Require*. Retrieved July 9, 2022, from https://morioh.com/p/258b3596afc3

Android Native Modules. (n.d.). React Native - W3cubDocs. Retrieved July 9, 2022, from https://docs.w3cub.com/react_native/native-modules-android .html

Android Native Modules. (2022, June 22). Android Native Modules - React Native. https://reactnative.dev/docs/native-modules-android

AsyncStorage. (n.d.). AsyncStorage -·React Native Archive. Retrieved July 9, 2022, from https://archive.reactnative.dev/docs/asyncstorage

Atluri, V., Cakmak, U., Lee, R., and Varanasi, S. (2012). Making smartphones brilliant: Ten trends. A publication of the Telecommunications, Media, and Technology Practice, McKinsey & Company. https://www.mckinsey. com/~/media/mckinsey/dotcom/client_service/high%20tech/pdfs/mak-ing_smartphones_brilliant_march_2012.pdf.

Best Apps for Studying. (2019, August 20). Swinburne Onlinehttps://www.swin-burneonline.edu.au/blog/best-apps-for-studying

Best Programming Language for Cross-Platform Mobile Development. (n.d.). Retrieved July 9, 2022, from https://distinguished.io/blog/best-cross-plat-form-programming-language

Building Your First Desktop Application. (n.d.). Cross-Platform Desktop Applications: Using Node, Electron, and NW.js. Retrieved July 9, 2022, from https://livebook.manning.com/book/cross-platform-desktop-applications/ chapter-3

Capacitor: Cross-Platform Native Runtime for Web Apps. (n.d.). Retrieved July 9, 2022, from https://capacitorjs.com/docs/apis/geolocation

CDK_Developer_Guide.pdf (jboss.org) (No proper page)

Debugging. (2020, October 29). React Native. https://reactnative.dev/docs/0.62/ debugging

Debugging Methods for React Native Applications. (2022, March 9). https:// www.topcoder.com/thrive/articles/debugging-methods-for-react-native-applications

Deploying a Stand-Alone Application - Chapter 11. (2021, January 24). Wahnsinn. https://blog.andreaskrahl.de/deploying-a-stand-alone-application-chapter-11/

Deshpande, V., & View My Complete Profile. (2019, February 11). *Debugging a Microsoft Teams Tab Built with SharePoint Framework.* https://www.vrdmn .com/2019/02/debugging-microsoft-teams-tab-built.html

Difference between Black Box Testing and White Box Testing. (2014, December 10). Software Testing Class. https://www.softwaretestingclass.com/difference-between-black-box-testing-and-white-box-testing/

Dikson. (2018, August 5). *How to Create Custom Component in React native?* Skcript. https://skcript.com/svr/how-to-create-custom-component-in-react -native/

Discord Hyperlinks: How to Make Links with Bot Embeds (2022 Guide). (2022, January 17). Shufflegazine. https://shufflegazine.com/make-discord-hyper-links-bot-embeds/

Dissanayake, R. (n.d.). *Mixing PHP and Java on Linux Systems.* Retrieved July 9, 2022, from https://www.raditha.com/php/java.php

Durgahee, CNN, B. A. (2012, March 20). *Goodbye Maps, Hello Apps: Planning Travel On the Go.* CNN. https://edition.cnn.com/2012/03/20/business/ travel-apps/index.html

Education, I. C. (2020, December 21). *iOS App Development.* IBM. https://www. ibm.com/cloud/learn/ios-app-development-explained

eHam.net. (n.d.). Retrieved July 9, 2022, from https://www.eham.net/reviews/ view-product?id=15324

Eisenman, B. (n.d.). *Learning React Native Building Native Mobile Apps with JavaScript 2nd Edition pdf.* Retrieved July 9, 2022, from https://123dok.com /document/zx9kjjdz-learning-react-native-building-native-mobile-javas-cript-edition.html

Evkoski, B. (2018, April 9). *React Native: What it is and How it Works.* Medium. https://medium.com/we-talk-it/react-native-what-it-is-and-how-it-works -e2182d008f5e

facebook. (n.d.). *react-native-website/flexbox.md at main · facebook/react-native-website.* GitHub; . github.com. Retrieved July 9, 2022, from https://github .com/facebook/react-native-website/blob/main/docs/flexbox.md

facebook. (2022, June 21). *react-native-website/signed-apk-android.md at main · facebook/react-native-website.* GitHub. https://github.com/facebook/react -native-website/blob/main/docs/signed-apk-android.md

Fullsour. (2017, August 6). *Style Inheritance of React Native.* Medium. https:// medium.com/@fullsour/style-inheritance-of-react-native-eca1c974f02b

Geolocation API. (n.d.). Retrieved July 9, 2022, from https://www.w3schools.com /js/js_api_geolocation.asp

Getting Started. (2020, October 29). React Native. https://reactnative.dev/docs/0 .60/enviroment-setup

Gite, S. (2020, August 30). *How to Send Email from React-Native Application.* Techup. www.techup.co.in. https://www.techup.co.in/how-to-send-email -from-react-native-application/

Goklani, B. (2018, September 7). *Important Tips to Follow for Improving the Performance of your React Native App.* www.mindinventory.com. https:// www.mindinventory.com/blog/optimizing-performance-of-react- native-app/

googlecreativelab. (2017, December 7). *GitHub - googlecreativelab/mystery-animal: A New Spin on the Classic 20-questions Game.* GitHub. https://github .com/googlecreativelab/mystery-animal

Hamedani, M. (2019, November 4). *JavaScript Console Debugging: Beyond The Basics.* Programming with Mosh. https://programmingwithmosh.com/ javascript/javascript-console-logging-beyond-the-basics/?shared=email &msg=fail

How to Generate a React Native Release Build APK for Android. (2022, March 27). Instamobile; instamobile.io. https://instamobile.io/android-development/ generate-react-native-release-build-android/

How Long Does it Take to Get Approval After Filing Form I-131? (2012, March 23). Immigration Direct. www.immigrationdirect.com. https://www.immi- grationdirect.com/immigration-articles/how-long-does-it-take-to-get -approval-after-filing-form-i-131/

How to Register Your App with Apple's App Store. (2022, April 24). The Tech Outlook. www.thetechoutlook.com. https://www.thetechoutlook.com/apps /how-to-register-your-app-with-apples-app-store/

How to Reserve an App Name on Windows Store and... Harry's Memo. harrys- memo.com

How to Send an Account Verification Email in React Native? (n.d.). Retrieved July 9, 2022, from https://www.devasking.com/issue/how-to-send-an-account -verification-email-in-react-native

How to Submit Your App to the App Store in 2022. (2022, May 25). Blog. https:// www.swing2app.com/blog/how-to-submit-your-app-to-the-app-store-in -2022/

How to Submit Your App to the App Store in 2022. (2022, January 5). Instabug Blog. https://blog.instabug.com/how-to-submit-app-to-app-store/

How to Use Doom 3 Map Editor. (n.d.). Deltapreview. Retrieved July 9, 2022, from https://deltapreview.weebly.com/how-to-use-doom-3-map-editor.html

HTML Geolocation API. (n.d.). Retrieved July 9, 2022, from https://www .w3schools.com/html/html5_geolocation.asp

An iDiot's Guide to Lilu and its Plug-ins. (2018, September 26). Tonymacx86. Com. https://www.tonymacx86.com/threads/an-idiots-guide-to-lilu-and- its-plug-ins.260063/

Inc., A. (n.d.). *TestFlight.* Apple Developer. Retrieved July 9, 2022, from https:// developer.apple.com/testflight/

intigriti. (2021, November 30). *Insecure Direct Object Reference (IDOR)*. Intigriti. https://blog.intigriti.com/hackademy/idor/

Introduction to React Native. (2017, June 7). GeeksforGeeks. https://www.geeksforgeeks.org/introduction-react-native/

iOS Native Modules. (2022, April 1). React Native. https://reactnative.dev/docs/0.65/native-modules-ios

Istio - Argo Rollouts - Kubernetes Progressive Delivery Controller. (n.d.). Retrieved July 9, 2022, from https://argoproj.github.io/argo-rollouts/features/traffic-management/istio/

Jackson, E. (n.d.). *Understanding Styling in React Native*. Retrieved July 9, 2022, from https://morioh.com/p/f38ebbe8f9fc

Jamil, M. S. (2021, October 20). *How to add Tab Navigation or Simple Navigation or Drawer Navigation in React Native*. Medium. https://medium.com/@fa18-bcs-062/how-to-add-tab-navigation-or-simple-navigation-or-drawer-navigation-in-react-native-a4374db12d23

javascript - Browser Crashes When Taking Picture with Camera. (2015, March 30). Stack Overflow. https://stackoverflow.com/questions/29352106/browser-crashes-when-taking-picture-with-camera

Krishnakumar. (2019, February 6). *Learn How to Build an Android App in React Native*. Eduonix Blog. https://blog.eduonix.com/android-tutorials/building-android-app-react-native/

Kumar, S. (2017, June 13). *How React Native Works?* GeeksforGeeks. https://www.geeksforgeeks.org/react-native-works/

Layout with Flexbox. (2022, March 30). React Native. https://reactnative.dev/docs/0.68/flexbox

Learn React Native Tutorial. (n.d.). Javatpoint. Retrieved July 9, 2022, from https://www.javatpoint.com/react-native-tutorial

Learning React Native. (n.d.). O'Reilly Online Learning. Retrieved July 9, 2022, from https://www.oreilly.com/library/view/learning-react-native/9781491929049/ch06.html

leejiwonn. (2021, December 6). *[RN] React Native Docs #10 0N] React Native*. Leejiwonn.Log. https://leejiwonn.tistory.com/67

Mobile Development. (n.d.). Mysol. Retrieved July 9, 2022, from https://mysol.tech/mobile-development

Must Declare the Scalar Varible "@Value1LastUpdatedDate." (2007, May 1). https://social.msdn.microsoft.com/Forums/en-US/45a0693a-47ab-4dea-ae24-7ce973ae1e65/must-declare-the-scalar-varible-quotvalue1lastupdateddatequot?forum=aspdatasourcecontrols

My Super Cat. (2022, June 18). https://fathimazainudheen.blogspot.com/2022/06/is-react-native-react-native-is-open.html

National Convention Continuing Education Saturday. (n.d.). American Massage Therapy Association. Retrieved July 9, 2022, from https://www.amtamassage.org/continuing-education/national-convention/continuing-education/continuing-education-saturday/

Nobrega, M. de. (2018, November 15). *Firebase Authentication with .NET Core (Including SignalR)*. Medium. https://medium.com/@matt.denobrega/firebase-authentication-with-net-core-including-signalr-b2c0034f0206

NVIDIA GPUs with Google Cloud's Anthos — NVIDIA Cloud Native Technologies Documentation. (2022, July 1). https://docs.nvidia.com/data-center/cloud-native/kubernetes/anthos-guide.html

Obtain Your Developer Token. (n.d.). Google Developers. Retrieved July 9, 2022, from https://developers.google.com/google-ads/api/docs/first-call/dev-token

Online Course: Node Package Manager Course: Build and Publish NPM Modules from Udemy. (2022, May 9). Class Central. www.classcentral.com. https://www.classcentral.com/course/udemy-node-package-manager-course-build-and-publi-24299

Orsmond, Q. (2021, July 17). *How to Position Things in React Native?* www.bitstoliveby.com. https://www.bitstoliveby.com/posts/how-to-position-things-in-react-native/

Performance – React Native | A Framework for Building Native Apps Using REACT. (n.d.). Retrieved July 9, 2022, from https://www.decoide.org/react-native/docs/performance.html

Performance Overview. (2022, April 21). React Native. https://reactnative.dev/docs/0.64/performance

Pickus, I. (2020, June 3). *Broadband Progress, Policy Varies by State.* WAMC. https://www.wamc.org/the-roundtable/2020-06-03/broadband-progress-policy-varies-by-state

Platform Specific Code. (n.d.). React Native. Retrieved July 9, 2022, from https://scarcoco.github.io/react-native/docs/0.10/platform-specific-code

Platform Specific Code. (2022, March 30). React Native. https://reactnative.dev/docs/0.68/platform-specific-code

Prince, S. (2022, May 18). *JAMB Result Checker: How to Check 2022 JAMB Result.* Nairablink. https://www.nairablink.com/jamb-result-checker-how-to-check-2022-jamb-result/

The Process of Beta Testing Using TestFlight. (2019, November 28). TestMatick. https://testmatick.com/the-process-of-beta-testing-using-testflight/

Progress KB - 4GL/ABL: Sample Code Using the IMPORT and EXPORT Statements with BLOB Fields. (n.d.). Progress Software Knowledgebase. Retrieved July 9, 2022, from https://knowledgebase.progress.com/articles/Article/P113369

Publishing to Google Play Store. (n.d.). React Native Archive. Retrieved July 9, 2022, from https://archive.reactnative.dev/docs/0.39/signed-apk-android

Publishing to Google Play Store. (2020, October 29). React Native. https://reactnative.dev/docs/0.61/signed-apk-android

React Native - AsyncStorage. (n.d.). Retrieved July 9, 2022, from https://www.tutorialspoint.com/react_native/react_native_asyncstorage.htm

React Native - Styling. (n.d.). Retrieved July 9, 2022, from https://www.tutorialspoint.com/react_native/react_native_styling.htm

React Native AsyncStorage Methods. (n.d.). Javatpoint. Retrieved July 9, 2022, from https://www.javatpoint.com/react-native-asyncstorage-methods

React-native Architecture - [Part One]. (2022, February 18). DEV Community. https://dev.to/salemabderaouf/react-native-architecture-part-one-26fg

Returns, P., & View My Complete Profile. (2013, July 17). *Tax Depreciation: July 2013.* Tax Depreciation. https://taxdepreciation12.blogspot.com/2013/07/

Riekert, M. (2022, March 22). *Risk Tolerance vs Your Investments Goals - A Personal Journey that Needs to be Explored.* https://www.fanews.co.za/article/investments/8/general/1133/risk-tolerance-vs-your-investments-goals-a-personal-journey-that-needs-to-be-explored/34138

Rogers, D. (2022, April 11). *Can I Inherit Styles When Using CreateStyles?* https://www.devasking.com/issue/can-i-inherit-styles-when-using-createstyles

Ryan, S. (2019, August 2). *What is an API Platform? | Discover the API Platform Definition.* Axway Blog. https://blog.axway.com/amplify-products/api-management/what-is-an-api-platform

Saha, R. (2020, October 23). *Random.* Random. https://arrayofrandommusings.blogspot.com/

SaidHayani@. (2020, November 13). *Styling in React Native. Explore the Best Ways to Style a React....* Medium. https://blog.bitsrc.io/styling-in-react-native-c48caddfbe47?gi=be1bb0742df4

SAP on Azure Implementation Guide. (n.d.). O'Reilly Online Learning. Retrieved July 9, 2022, from https://www.oreilly.com/library/view/sap-on-azure/9781838983987/Text/Chapter_2.xhtml

Schoeman, J., & Larsson, V. (2019, March 18). *React Native Styling: Structure for Style Organization.* Thoughtbot. https://thoughtbot.com/blog/structure-for-styling-in-react-native

Setting Up the Development Environment. (2021, July 22). React Native. https://reactnative.dev/docs/0.64/environment-setup

shanepeckham. (n.d.). *GitHub - shanepeckham/CADLab_Loyalty_Security: This Lab Demonstrates How to Secure the Loyalty Scenario Lab.* GitHub. Retrieved July 9, 2022, from https://github.com/shanepeckham/CADLab_Loyalty_Security

Smit, A., & Schlegel, R. (n.d.). *Chapter 11 Linear Mixed Models.* Basic Statistics. Retrieved July 9, 2022, from https://ajsmit.github.io/Basic_stats/linear-mixed-models.html

Style. (2022, March 30). React Native. https://reactnative.dev/docs/0.68/style

superkolos. (2021, January 1). *GitHub - superkolos/Audi-MIB2-Toolbox: Audi MIB Toolbox.* GitHub. https://github.com/superkolos/Audi-MIB2-Toolbox

TechnologyHQ. (2021, October 22). *Want to Try your Hand at iOS App Development? Here's How - TechnologyHQ.* TechnologyHQ - All about Technology, AI, Blockchain, Cybersecurity, Business. https://www.technologyhq.org/want-to-try-your-hand-at-ios-app-development-heres-how/

Top 10+ Hybrid Mobile App Development Companies. (n.d.). Firms Explorer. Retrieved July 9, 2022, from https://www.firmsexplorer.com/top-app-development-companies/hybrid/

Tsurbeliov, M. (2021, October 15). *How does React Native Works?* Medium. https://medium.com/akveo-engineering/how-does-react-native-works-3b7d5b4a007e

Tudip. (2021, October 5). *Distributing React Native App via Microsoft Appcenter.* Tudip. https://tudip.com/blog-post/distributing-react-native-app-via-microsoft-appcenter/

Ugorji, S. (2022, July 3). *How to Search Through a Table with JavaScript.* Medium. https://blog.devgenius.io/how-to-search-through-a-table-with-javascript -b8cbe5ec9757

"use strict" in Javascript. (2013, February 15). Stack Overflow. https://stackover-flow.com/questions/14889967/use-strict-in-javascript

Using Contingency Tables for Probability and Dependence. (2014, June 8). Learn Math and Stats with Dr. G. http://www.mathandstatistics.com/learn-stats /probability-and-percentage/using-contingency-tables-for-probability-and -dependence

Vajiram IAS App for UPSC Aspirants. (n.d.). WHO Considers Declaring Monkeypox a Global Health Emergency. Retrieved July 9, 2022, from https://vajiramias.com/article/who-considers-declaring-monkeypox-a -global-health-emergency/62b586e72acb75510dfa1ae2/

Walsh, D. (2015, April 30). *Mobilize Joins Microsoft on Windows 10 Tool.* Mobilize.Net. www.mobilize.net. https://www.mobilize.net/press/mobilize .net-accelerates-developer-adoption-of-windows-10

Webex Meetings: Adding Registration. https://www.in.gov/iot/files/WebEx -Registration-Guide.pdf

What is Components Inheritance in React ? (2021, July 12). GeeksforGeeks. www .geeksforgeeks.org. https://www.geeksforgeeks.org/what-is-components -inheritance-in-react/

What is React Native? (n.d.). Retrieved July 9, 2022, from https://www.tutorial-spoint.com/what-is-react-native

Yashpal. (n.d.). *How to Create Components in React Native?* Studytonight. Retrieved July 9, 2022, from https://www.studytonight.com/post/how-to -create-components-in-react-native

Yusufu, E. (2021, January 16). *React Native Navigation: React Navigation Examples and Tutorial.* LogRocket Blog. https://blog.logrocket.com/navi-gating-react-native-apps-using-react-navigation/

Index

Printed in the United States
by Baker & Taylor Publisher Services